Violence in America

Violence is a growing problem in American society, and hardly a day goes by that we don't hear about yet another heart-wrenching episode of mass violence. Such events, unfortunately, are only the most public manifestation of violence in America. The full nature and extent of daily violence, the various and pervasive forms it takes, and the enormous social, emotional, moral, and economic consequences that result, remain largely outside of our awareness. More importantly, our ability to identify the root causes and know how best to effectively intervene remains limited.

Most investigations in this field have focused on the individual psychodynamic characteristics of the perpetrators. The underlying group dynamic factors that include consideration of broader social, cultural, socioeconomic, and historical variables have received less attention. This volume brings together for the first time a collection of distinguished group psychotherapists, all of whom have been trained to recognize both individual psychodynamic characteristics and group dynamic factors, to apply the lessons learned through years of clinical practice to arrive at a deeper understanding of the etiology, treatment, and prevention of violence.

This book was originally published as a special issue of the *International Journal of Group Psychotherapy*.

Robert H. Klein is a clinical faculty member in the School of Medicine at Yale University, USA. He is a Fellow of the American Psychological Association and Diplomate in Group Psychology, as well as Past President and Distinguished Life Fellow of the American Group Psychotherapy Association. A recognized expert in the area of group psychotherapy and group dynamics, he lectures, consults, and supervises both nationally and internationally. He is editor/author of six books and maintains a private clinical practice with offices in Westport and Milford, CT.

Victor L. Schermer is a psychologist based in Philadelphia, PA, USA. He is a Life Fellow of the American Group Psychotherapy Association. He is author/editor of eight books and over 50 articles about psychotherapy and group dynamics, and is a frequent presenter of lectures and workshops internationally.

Violence in America
Group Therapists Reflect on Causes and Solutions

Edited by
**Robert H. Klein and
Victor L. Schermer**

LONDON AND NEW YORK

First published 2017
by Routledge
2 Park Square, Milton Park, Abingdon, Oxon, OX14 4RN, UK

and by Routledge
711 Third Avenue, New York, NY 10017, USA

Routledge is an imprint of the Taylor & Francis Group, an informa business

© 2017 American Group Psychotherapy Association

All rights reserved. No part of this book may be reprinted or reproduced or utilised in any form or by any electronic, mechanical, or other means, now known or hereafter invented, including photocopying and recording, or in any information storage or retrieval system, without permission in writing from the publishers.

Trademark notice: Product or corporate names may be trademarks or registered trademarks, and are used only for identification and explanation without intent to infringe.

British Library Cataloguing in Publication Data
A catalogue record for this book is available from the British Library

ISBN 13: 978-1-138-23123-8

Typeset in New Baskerville
by RefineCatch Limited, Bungay, Suffolk

Publisher's Note
The publisher accepts responsibility for any inconsistencies that may have arisen during the conversion of this book from journal articles to book chapters, namely the possible inclusion of journal terminology.

Disclaimer
Every effort has been made to contact copyright holders for their permission to reprint material in this book. The publishers would be grateful to hear from any copyright holder who is not here acknowledged and will undertake to rectify any errors or omissions in future editions of this book.

Contents

Citation Information   vii

1. Toward Understanding and Treating Violence in America: Some Contributions From Group Dynamic and Group Therapy Perspectives – Introduction to Part I   1
   Robert H. Klein and Victor L. Schermer

2. Violence, Threat, and Emotional "Malnourishment": An Interview With Dr. Dan Gottlieb   29
   Victor L. Schermer

3. A Group Therapist Reflects on Violence in America   38
   Cecil A. Rice

4. The Dangerous Role of Silence in the Relationship Between Trauma and Violence: A Group Response   60
   Suzanne B. Phillips

5. There's Always a Villain to Punish: Group Processes Contributing to Violence and Its Remediation   83
   Nina K. Thomas

6. Voices of Violence Video Series   102
   Bill Roller

7. Toward Understanding and Treating Violence in America: Some Contributions From Group Dynamic and Group Therapy Perspectives – Introduction to Part II   108
   Robert H. Klein and Victor L. Schermer

8. Group Process as a Mechanism of Change in the Group Treatment of Anger and Aggression   125
   James Gerhart, Krista Holman, Bailey Seymour, Brandy Dinges and George F. Ronan

CONTENTS

9. Multi-tiered Group Therapy Model to Identify and Treat the Root Causes of Domestic Violence: A Proposal Integrating Current Social Neuroscience Findings 153
Leslie M. Lothstein

10. Terrorism and Right-Wing Extremism: The Changing Face of Terrorism and Political Violence in the 21st Century: The Virtual Community of Hatred 183
Jerrold M. Post

11. Commentary on "Toward Understanding and Treating Violence in America: Some Contributions From Group Dynamic and Group Therapy Perspectives" 212
Bonnie J. Buchele

12. Commentary on "Toward Understanding and Treating Violence in America: Some Contributions From Group Dynamic and Group Therapy Perspectives" 223
Zachary Gabriel Green

Index 233

Citation Information

The following chapters were originally published in the *International Journal of Group Psychotherapy*, volume 65, issue 1 (January 2015). When citing this material, please use the original page numbering for each article, as follows:

Chapter 1
Toward Understanding and Treating Violence in America: Some Contributions From Group Dynamic and Group Therapy Perspectives – Introduction to Part I
Robert H. Klein and Victor L. Schermer
International Journal of Group Psychotherapy, volume 65, issue 1 (January 2015), pp. 1–28

Chapter 2
Violence, Threat, and Emotional "Malnourishment": An Interview With Dr. Dan Gottlieb
Victor L. Schermer
International Journal of Group Psychotherapy, volume 65, issue 1 (January 2015), pp. 31–39

Chapter 3
A Group Therapist Reflects on Violence in America
Cecil A. Rice
International Journal of Group Psychotherapy, volume 65, issue 1 (January 2015), pp. 41–62

CITATION INFORMATION

Chapter 4
The Dangerous Role of Silence in the Relationship Between Trauma and Violence: A Group Response
Suzanne B. Phillips
International Journal of Group Psychotherapy, volume 65, issue 1 (January 2015), pp. 65–87

Chapter 5
There's Always a Villain to Punish: Group Processes Contributing to Violence and Its Remediation
Nina K. Thomas
International Journal of Group Psychotherapy, volume 65, issue 1 (January 2015), pp. 89–107

Chapter 6
Voices of Violence Video Series
Bill Roller
International Journal of Group Psychotherapy, volume 65, issue 1 (January 2015), pp. 109–114

The following chapters were originally published in the *International Journal of Group Psychotherapy*, volume 65, issue 2 (April 2015). When citing this material, please use the original page numbering for each article, as follows:

Chapter 7
Toward Understanding and Treating Violence in America: Some Contributions From Group Dynamic and Group Therapy Perspectives – Introduction to Part II
Robert H. Klein and Victor L. Schermer
International Journal of Group Psychotherapy, volume 65, issue 2 (April 2015), pp. 163–179

Chapter 8
Group Process as a Mechanism of Change in the Group Treatment of Anger and Aggression
James Gerhart, Krista Holman, Bailey Seymour, Brandy Dinges and George F. Ronan
International Journal of Group Psychotherapy, volume 65, issue 2 (April 2015), pp. 181–208

CITATION INFORMATION

Chapter 9
Multi-tiered Group Therapy Model to Identify and Treat the Root Causes of Domestic Violence: A Proposal Integrating Current Social Neuroscience Findings
Leslie M. Lothstein
International Journal of Group Psychotherapy, volume 65, issue 2 (April 2015), pp. 211–240

Chapter 10
Terrorism and Right-Wing Extremism: The Changing Face of Terrorism and Political Violence in the 21st Century: The Virtual Community of Hatred
Jerrold M. Post
International Journal of Group Psychotherapy, volume 65, issue 2 (April 2015), pp. 243–271

Chapter 11
Commentary on "Toward Understanding and Treating Violence in America: Some Contributions From Group Dynamic and Group Therapy Perspectives"
Bonnie J. Buchele
International Journal of Group Psychotherapy, volume 65, issue 2 (April 2015), pp. 273–283

Chapter 12
Commentary on "Toward Understanding and Treating Violence in America: Some Contributions From Group Dynamic and Group Therapy Perspectives"
Zachary Gabriel Green
International Journal of Group Psychotherapy, volume 65, issue 2 (April 2015), pp. 285–294

For any permission-related enquiries please visit:
http://www.tandfonline.com/page/help/permissions

Toward Understanding and Treating Violence in America: Some Contributions From Group Dynamic and Group Therapy Perspectives

Introduction to Part I

ROBERT H. KLEIN, PH.D., ABPP, CGP, DLFAGPA
VICTOR L. SCHERMER, M.A., L.P.C., CAC, LFAGPA

ABSTRACT

The co-editors introduce a two-part Special Section of the Journal devoted to understanding and treating violence in America. They examine the relevance of clinical experience for contributions that can be made by group therapists and group dynamic thinkers to the growing national dialogue about this problem. The pervasive nature, causes, and different forms of violence in the United States are compared with those found in other countries. Underlying sociocultural values and myths, historical and current cultural contexts are considered breeding grounds for potential violence. How therapists can promote healthy change in their groups and in the broader society is explored. The articles contained in part one are reviewed against this backdrop.

There can be no doubt that violence in America is a major problem for our society. It is approaching a social pandemic. The nature and extent of such violence, the various forms it takes, and the enormous social, emotional, moral, and economic con-

---

Robert H. Klein is a Clinical Faculty member at the Yale School of Medicine and is in private practice in Westport and Milford, Connecticut. Victor L. Schermer is a psychologist in private practice in Philadelphia, Pennsylvania.

sequences that result, however, remain largely outside of our conscious awareness. Understanding and resolving the problem will certainly require collaborative, concerted, and comprehensive multidisciplinary scientific efforts, linked with widespread support from both the public and the government that endorse this as an important priority (Klein, Rice, & Schermer, 2009). This Special Issue of the *Journal*, consisting of two parts, is devoted to examining selected aspects of this vast and complex social issue from a group dynamics and group therapy perspective, one unique lens for understanding the problem, formulating interventions, and suggesting future pathways to explore. We remain grateful to our Editor, Dominick Grundy, for his willingness to permit us to tackle this important social problem.

This Special Issue began to take shape in the wake of the Newtown, Connecticut, school tragedy of December 14, 2012, that resulted in the deaths of 20 first-grade children and 6 adults. That event became a rallying point for renewed discussions about gun violence in America. Debate was stimulated, commissions were formed, legislation was brought forward, and our national leaders, including the President, took an active role in highlighting our collective pain and loss. Discussions ranged from placing armed guards in schools, to conducting more extensive background checks, to limiting gun sales and availability, to providing more and better mental health services (Diaz, 2013; Friedman, 2012; Sandy Hook school shootings, 2012). Older losses from past trauma such as 9/11, as well as our collective feelings of helplessness associated with other episodes of violence, were reawakened (Buchele & Spitz, 2004; Klein & Phillips, 2008; Klein & Schermer, 2000).

The Newtown shootings came to be viewed by many as the latest example of a far more widespread problem, the origins of which lay deeply embedded in our societal fabric. This disquieting recognition was accompanied by a growing realization that, worse yet, we prefer to not know about it. Sadly, the subject of violence in America generally receives increased attention only in the aftermath of trauma, when many innocent lives have been lost, usually at the hands of one or more individuals resorting to guns or bombs. After the fact, these "perpetrators," who often appear to be alienated, alone, and struggling with intense violent fantasies (like Adam Lanza who opened fire on the children and adults in Newtown), are frequently labeled as mentally ill. Retrospective accounts then document their disturbed personal and family histories, the accessibility of weapons, and the failure of mental health professionals to provide adequate and effective early detection and intervention. The endless barrage of news accounts that follow repeatedly highlight the horror of it all, provide information, and help to construct narrative but, in the process, often retraumatize those directly affected. Some constructive actions may be taken; for example, a school carefully examines the safety it provides for its students and personnel or panels appointed to investigate the problem make their recommendations. But, media coverage soon wanes, and many of us simply go on with our everyday lives. Whatever happened gradually recedes from our consciousness only to be reawakened following the next tragedy.

As the guest editors for this series, we were faced early on with the question of how to define violence. Should we select a more conventional narrow definition that focuses primarily on physical damage, injury, and/or death, or should we embrace a broader definition of violence that includes both immediate and longer-term psychological and emotional injury? A more narrow definition might well make for a neater, tidier, more concise presentation, but this could risk missing the less obvious, more disguised and subtle forms of violence, many of which are difficult to recognize. Further, focusing on mass shootings alone, which many of us are already thinking about, might fail to address the underlying causes of violence embedded in our societal context and the more widespread pattern that cannot be understood simply by investigating these as isolated incidents. We opted, therefore, for a more inclusive definition of violence because we believe that the forms of violence in this country go far beyond the highly publicized mass tragedies. While much violence in our society goes unreported, all violence is devastating in its implications.

Various forms of violence are part and parcel of our daily lives, ranging from violent crime, including robbery, rape, homicide, and suicide, to hate crime, to white collar crime, to bullying, to domestic violence. Perhaps we no longer even notice it, or have somehow become numb to it (Koop & Lundgren, 1992). As a country, we commit acts of violence on a daily basis during war, covert operations, drone strikes, secret prisons, and so forth. Often, we focus on our "chosen trauma" of 9/11 (Volkan, 1991, 1997) to justify violent government-sanctioned activities abroad, including our invasion of Iraq and the "war on terrorism." By so doing, we attempt to deny, split off, and projectively deposit many of our own aggressive and violent impulses into a small select subgroup of "others" whom we can then safely scrutinize at a distance, scapegoat, dehumanize, and demonize. Such responses should alert us to how much violence in ourselves and our culture as a whole tends to remain unacknowledged and poorly integrated into our collective psyche.

GROUPS AND THE PRINCIPLE OF ISOMORPHY

What, then, can group therapists and group dynamics thinkers add to the growing national dialogue about violence? As von Bertalanffy (1968) and Agazarian (1997) in her systems-centered approach have eloquently stated, isomorphy is a critically important concept in understanding how all living systems, including groups, function. This concept has great relevance in this context. Isomorphy holds that structures and functions that exist at one level of a complex system also exist at every other level within that system. Further, changing a system at one level has important implications at every other level. This can be thought of as a two-way street: One can gain understanding and promote change by working from lower to higher levels in any system, or the reverse. We suggest that we draw upon our own small groups as social microcosms (Yalom & Leszcz, 1995) of the larger society to understand precursors to violence at the small group and the higher, more complex societal level, how it is triggered, enacted, and may be modified and transformed. Each of us brings into our therapy groups the attitudes, beliefs systems, endorsed ways of thinking and acting, and cultural values developed within our society, along with our personal concerns. Our groups clearly reflect in microcosm the culture of which we are a part. In each of our therapy groups, through parallel process, we recreate and reenact the dilemmas that shape our lives and society.

VIOLENCE IN AMERICA

THE RELEVANCE OF OUR CLINICAL EXPERIENCE

Dealing with violence and threats of violence is a significant part of clinical practice in America. We and our patients are members of the broader community in which we practice. As mental health professionals, we are often asked to diagnostically evaluate marginalized, potentially violent people, many of whom may come to group voluntarily for treatment, while others come in response to the insistence of others. When treating problems of domestic violence, we work directly with people who are potentially violent or have already resorted to violence. Some of us treat prison inmates who have committed violent crimes throughout their lives. Following instances of mass tragedy, we may be called upon to provide direct clinical services and large-scale group interventions for individual survivors, families, and organizations. Others may be asked to design and implement programs for public education and for promoting early detection or to formulate prevention strategies, for example, to stem the flow of bullying in schools.

In the course of this work, we have had to learn how to deal with multiple forms of resistance to treatment, problems of denial, projection, and scapegoating, and with the inevitable feelings of loss, shame, helplessness, and social stigma that surround and permeate violence in our culture (Herman, 1997; Kohut, 1972, 1977; Stolorow, 2007). We have had to confront our own as well as our patients' powerful feelings and reactions to violence. We have come to understand the pain, loneliness, and anger suffered by those who feel socially isolated, marginalized, and devalued, and we have dealt firsthand with the destructive consequences of scapegoating and the use of the "other" as a projective receptacle. Through these efforts, we have begun to understand how we can help detoxify, recover, and reintegrate the disowned parts of ourselves, and thereby permit our group members to reestablish their connections with others.

Our work following mass violence has also taught us much about regrettable failures in communication and command structure in larger groups that are often retrospectively identified (Klein & Bernard, 2008). We know from our clinical experience that several important variables can impede better communication in systems, especially in the face of trauma and disaster:

1. Individuals within groups and systems often function as singletons and/or as members of smaller subgroups without maintaining any sense of themselves as part of a larger collective organization.
2. When difficulties arise within the larger group or system, the tendency is to withdraw and go it alone—"the American way" reflecting the icon of "rugged individualism" with distrust of authority—or to seek refuge and support within a smaller trusted subgroup.
3. In most groups and organizations in the United States, acknowledging individual distress or need for help is generally regarded as a bad idea or a "sign of weakness," and is frequently associated with fears of jeopardizing job or status within the larger organization.
4. During such events, trust in others plummets while suspicion rises, turf battles for control emerge, and victims feel frightened, helpless, and enraged; coordination, planning, and preparation are crucial in managing communication during disasters.
5. The more severe, overwhelming, and disorganizing the disaster and subsequent trauma, the more likely we are to see evidence of what Hopper (1997) has labeled "incohesion," a regressive state wherein individuals, fearful of annihilation, become increasingly disconnected from one another or fuse together to survive threats to identity.

As group therapists, then, we have learned that certain features of groups can help participants deal less destructively with violent urges and impulses:

- Talking helps; finding our voices; creating narrative; risking exposure of our inner lives; joining the group in whatever way we can.
- Putting things into words interposes delay of immediate gratification, substitutes dialogue for discharge/acting out, and provides an opportunity to establish a reflective space.
- Not permitting the group to scapegoat others or to use them as projective receptacles; encouraging participants to recover and to own all of their parts; encouraging respectful and thoughtful exploration of differences.
- Building constructive norms, particularly those of inclusion and empathic non-judgmental acceptance, developing

the group as a safe container and to humanize rather than demonize others.
- Becoming able to trust others—that we are all brothers and sisters who are much more alike than different and that no one is alone—sets the stage for exchange and interpersonal learning.
- Realizing that by working together we have the capacity to understand, learn from, forgive, and help ourselves and others.
- Recognizing and accepting that all that is expressed by any one of us is a part of all of us.
- Bearing witness and creating opportunities to heal the damaged sense of self following trauma.
- Learning that we and others are capable of change and growth, giving rise to hope and promoting courage to explore new pathways.

These are principles we rely on in effective therapy groups. In addition, we know that group members must be motivated to seek help to begin with, enter into a contract with an avowed purpose, and abide by a set of ground rules with a competent group leader who monitors the boundaries to insure safety, encourages participation, remains aware that isolates tend to feel devalued and become early dropouts, calls attention to enactments, and promotes optimal conditions within which change can occur.

Isomorphy suggests that we can apply these lessons beyond our own clinical practices. Namely, learning how to deal with problems of violence in our own groups should help us to formulate more effective strategies for detecting, understanding, and dealing with those same problems in larger groups within society. Such efforts on a smaller scale can themselves initiate important processes of change in the larger society within which we live and function.

As a prelude to thinking about the articles that follow in the two parts of the Special Issue, we think it is useful to provide: (1) a preliminary discussion of forms of violence in the United States, (2) comparative data from other countries, (3) a consideration of the alleged causes for violence, and (4) a brief historical perspective, along with a few thoughts about our current social climate identify underlying cultural factors that potentiate violence in our society.

FORMS OF VIOLENCE IN THE UNITED STATES

Mass Tragedies

Hardly a day goes by that we do not learn through newspapers and broadcasts of another act of mass violence. On April 9, 2014, as we were preparing this introduction, we learned of a 16-year-old youth who stabbed 21 people in a high school near Pittsburgh. This followed accounts from the previous week of a second violent incident at Fort Hood. April 15, 2014, will mark the first anniversary of the Boston Marathon bombing. Mass tragedies receive disproportionate coverage in the media but are only the tip of the iceberg. They are rare events that represent less than 1% of all homicides in the United States (Federal Bureau of Investigation [FBI], 2012). The prevalence of various other forms of violence, however, remains alarmingly high.

Violent Crime in the United States

Data has been assembled about violent crime and hate crime in the United States. The Annual Uniform Crime reports are provided by the FBI (2012) and by the National Crime Victimization Surveys from the Bureau of Justice Statistics (Smith & Cooper, 2013; Wilson, 2014).

Crime rates in the United States have varied over time. They rose after World War II, peaked between the 1970s and early 1990s, and have declined since then, with current rates approximately equal to those of the 1960s (FBI, 2012). Table 1 contains a list of violent crime rates in the United States for 2011 (FBI, 2011).

Among the violent crimes, gun-related deaths have captured most of our attention. In 2009 and 2010, nearly two-thirds of all homicides in the United States were perpetrated using a firearm (United Nations Office on Drugs and Crime [UNODC], 2013). In the 98 days following the horrendous shootings at Newtown, there were 2,243 gun homicides in the United States (FBI, 2012).

TABLE 1. U.S. Crime Rates for 2011

Crime Type	Rate (reported crimes per 100,000 population)
Homicide	4.7
Forcible Rape	26.8
Robbery	113.7
Aggravated Assault	241.1
Total Violent Crime	386.3 = 5.8 million violent victimizations (number of victims of a violent crime)

Note. These rates do not count Property Crime (burglary, larceny-theft, or motor vehicle theft). Source: FBI Crime in the United States (http://www.fbi.gov/about-uscjis/ucr/crime-in-the-u.s./2011crime-in-the-u.s.-2011).

For the past 30 years, there has been a steady rate of roughly 30,000 gun-related deaths in the United States per year, with approximately 10,000 gun homicides and 20,000 gun suicides (Diaz, 2013; FBI, 2012). The total deaths resulting from domestic terrorist attacks and related incidents from 1988–2013 is approximately 4,250 (www.johnstonsarchive.net, 2013). The total number of deaths from the wars in Iraq and Afghanistan is approximately 6,800 (antiwar.com, 2014; icasualties.org, 2013). Thus, we are killing our own people in our own country at a rate that is vastly greater per year than deaths caused by either domestic terrorists or wartime combatants.

Comparing the United States With Other Countries

The United States has far more gun-related killings than any other developed country in the world, but not the highest of any country in the world (Richardson & Hemenway, 2013; Rogers, 2012; UNODC, 2006). Gun-related death rates are estimated to be three to seven times higher in the United States than in countries that are considered economically and politically similar to it (Krug, Powell, & Dahlberg, 1998; Liem, Barber, Markwalder, Killias, & Nieuwbeerta, 2011). The highest rates are found in developing countries and countries with political instability, while developed countries with strict gun laws have essentially eliminated gun violence (Fisher, 2012), but not violence using other weapons.

The Congressional Research Service (Krause, 2012) estimated there were 310 million firearms in the United States in 2009 (not including weapons owned by the military), slightly exceeding the national census that year (U.S. Census Bureau, 2012). Phillip Gourevitch, a *New Yorker* correspondent who has visited many countries around the world, maintains that others see us as "crazy" when it comes to permitting access to and availability of automatic weapons, assault rifles, and the like, which are all much more tightly controlled almost everywhere else (Rogers, 2012).

Hate Crimes

With the recent Kansas City Jewish Center shootings, hate crimes are again in the news (Brunker, Alba, & Dedman, 2014). Brunker, Seveille, Alba, and Blankstein (2014) have called attention to the new dangers of "lone wolves." FBI statistics on hate crimes in 2012 documented 5,796 incidents, resulting in 7,164 victims (FBI, 2012). A separate survey by the Bureau of Justice reported a spike in hate crimes during 2011 and 2012 (Wilson, 2014), although the number of hate crimes documented by the FBI has fallen by about one-fourth over the years from 1995 through 2012.

Other Forms of Crime

When we consider all instances of what are officially regarded as violent crimes, plus hate crimes, physical and sexual abuse and neglect of children and the elderly, intimate partner violence, and more insidious forms of white collar crime, we begin to realize that violent crime alone is not the problem (Zimring & Hawkins, 1997), but that violence itself is vast, complex, and ever-present in our daily lives. The recent escalating tide of bullying and cyberbullying among our children is yet another disturbing variation on this theme (Litwiller & Brausch, 2013; Miller, 2014). This next generation of citizens is already learning how to use more sophisticated versions of interpersonal violence to deal destructively with differences and to assert power and domain. Further, they are using tools in our information age that permit the expression of violence on an anonymous, depersonalized level that renders it that much more insidious, harmful, and difficult to manage (Kim & Leventhal, 2008).

VIOLENCE IN AMERICA

THE BROADER SOCIOCULTURAL CONTEXT

The broader sociocultural context in which we live, as well as the language and metaphors we use, shape how we think about violence (Lakoff & Johnson, 1980), a subject that is explored more thoroughly by Nina Thomas in this issue. On an international level over the past 20 years, for example, our country has been involved in wartime activities in Iraq, Iran, Afghanistan, and, most recently, was on the verge of further activity in Syria. Our government also has engaged in a variety of domestic "wars" during this same period: the wars on terrorism, drugs, poverty, and illegal aliens. The war on terrorism, intended to protect our "national security," sanctioned both overt and covert actions by our government. Some covert actions have met with considerable opposition, for example, secret prisons, prolonged imprisonment for detainees without access to attorneys, use of "extreme" interrogation techniques including torture, drone strikes on civilian and military targets, use of various "black ops" to pursue our objectives, and surveillance of not only our "enemies," but also our friends, allies, and even our Congressional committees. But those who have raised serious questions about our policies and actions have run the risk of being labeled "soft on terrorism," accused of mistakenly placing civil liberties ahead of national security, or viewed as unpatriotic.

In addition, many acts of violence in the United States take the form of more sophisticated and polite violent crimes linked with broader issues of social and economic inequality. Discrimination in all its varied forms—economic and educational inequality, bullying, denial of basic rights, abuses of power by Wall Street and banks, the Ponzi schemes of Bernie Madoff and others—are examples of what we consider to be more "polite" violent crimes. But, these acts are just as damaging and lethal as those officially regarded as violent crimes. Each is enormously destructive, demoralizing, and dehumanizing, and collectively they pose a danger of eroding our sense of respect for the rights and needs of others, our basic human decency, and our morality.

To be sure, these are complex and difficult matters to address. Where does one draw the line about what constitutes violence?

Should more polite crimes be viewed as destructive but not violent? We, the guest editors, view all of these as interconnected examples of violence. All impact the social and moral contract we have with each other and shape the climate in which we live. Whether the violence is active and visibly destructive or passive and more disguised, from our point of view, makes little difference. More sophisticated and polite crimes count.

CAUSES OF VIOLENCE

While many acts of mass violence appear to be committed by people with mental illness, Friedman (2012) reported that only 4% of all gun deaths annually in the United States can be attributed to individuals with mental illness—far fewer than most people think. The vast majority of people with a diagnosable mental illness never commit a violent crime (Medscape, 2012; Sadock & Sadock, 2007). Of those who do commit a violent crime, suicide is far more likely than homicide, particularly by those diagnosed with either schizophrenia or depression (Hor & Taylor, 2010; Hunt et al., 2006; Toobin, 2013).

Multiple causes for violence have been identified (Albow & Winslow, 2013; Diaz, 2013; Fleegler, Lee, Monuteaux, Hemenway, & Mannix, 2013; Gun control offers no cure-all, 2012; Heroux, 2013; Mountjoy, 2013; Sandy Hook school shootings, 2012). At a broad societal level, many have pointed to increased tolerance for violence, easier weapon accessibility, increased stress, chronic poverty, downsizing and less control in the workplace, increased substance abuse, and inadequate mental health services. Consumerism and quick-fix solutions to every problem that provide shortcuts and escapes from relational dilemmas have also been implicated, as has an "each man for himself" attitude and a sense of self that is based on power and control over others in a culture that rewards and admires competition.

At an individual, personal level, other factors have received attention, including breakdown of family and community support systems, exposure to abuse, abandonment and neglect early in life, social isolation, alienation and marginalization, and repeated experiences involving shame, humiliation, and powerlessness (Kohut, 1972, 1977; Lothstein, 2014). At best, however, these can be considered "risk factors" implicated in violence. None of such variables, alone or in combination, permits us to accurately predict who will engage in violent activities. Ordinary citizens are perfectly capable of committing horrendous acts of violence (Casoni & Brunet, 2007). Roller, with respect to the prison population of violent offenders, states in this issue that, "the common experience for many of these men is sexual and physical abuse, emotional bullying, and parental neglect." Roller's observations strongly suggest that violent "types" share a common diagnosis of "complex PTSD" (Herman, 1997), an expansion of the PTSD diagnosis to include changes in interpersonal relations, self-concept, and life expectations. Several other authors imply that violence is an outcome of trauma. Yet, says Roller, within prison populations, the cognitive processes and personality styles of the perpetrators vary considerably.

ARE THERE DEVELOPMENTAL PATTERNS?

It is important to note that many perpetrators of violence were victims before becoming perpetrators, something often ignored. In fact, there appears to be a fourfold developmental pattern that characterizes many perpetrators of mass violence: 1) they are victims of abuse, traumatized, mentally ill, and/or disaffected with society; 2) they become loners, socially isolated, or conversely, merge their identity into social movements; 3) they undergo experiences that transform them from victim into perpetrator by justifying their feelings of persecution and giving them a distorted sense of empowerment; and 4) they become part of a system that supports their violent acting out. The system can be anything from a cult to a terrorist group to a set of "tools" they can use, such as availability of weapons, social disarray, ideology, and Internet resources).

To summarize then, not only is violence in America a complex problem that takes many forms, it largely passes unnoticed, unless there is some startling event covered in the media—then, there is a flurry of interest and attention that quickly fades. The language of violence is a routine part of our daily culture. While we can identify risk factors that may lead to or potentiate violence, our ability to predict who will actually become violent is quite limited. Further, certain forms of violence prevalent in our society, particularly domestic conflict, sexual abuse/rape, and various forms of child abuse, are "privatized." They are cloaked in silence and secrecy, and rendered inaccessible to proper intervention. Social stigma, shame, humiliation, and family and group pressure combine to conceal the true incidence and prevalence of these forms of violence in our society (Phillips, 2014). They tend to be under-reported and under-treated (Phillips, this issue). In fact, there remains widespread reluctance to publicly acknowledge their existence, much less to encourage people to voluntarily seek treatment for such problems. Treatment before tragedy remains a primary goal, not a reality.

A HISTORICAL PERSPECTIVE

We believe, however, that the roots of violence lie deeply embedded within our society and culture. Our history as a nation, briefly explored in what follows, has remained intertwined with violence. That history and culture, the warp and weft of our society, against which all else plays out (C. A. Rice, personal communication, 2014), has profoundly shaped us and its influence is often outside of our awareness. We all play a vital part in the continuing problem of violence in America. Like Lothstein (2014), who maintains that violence begins in the home, we view violence and our attitudes toward it as transmitted across generations through the family and the broader society's predispositions and accepted cultural mythology.

Let us start, as we would with any group large or small, by examining its history. What can be said more specifically about the American history of violence, viewed here as interpersonal acts, that might shed light on our current dilemma and help us to better understand some of our fundamental attitudes, beliefs, and expectations that sustain and underlie violence in this country? This examination is admittedly one-sided, but that is its purpose: to focus on the dark side, not to overlook, minimize, deny, or avoid it. Many more detailed comprehensive accounts of this history are available to the interested reader (e.g., Stannard, 1992; Zinn, 2008).

VIOLENCE IN AMERICA

Early History of Violence

Let us look first at Columbus and his treatment of the Native Americans/"Indians." Incentivized by the promise from Queen Isabella of Spain of a commission for his recovery of treasure, he overpowered and exploited the Native Americans he encountered. Subsequently, our first settlers put their families and all their worldly possessions on ships, preparing to travel for months across the ocean to a new unsettled wilderness. With them they brought a sense of desperation; a need to escape from deep feelings of disillusionment, oppression, and despair; a profound distrust of authority; a willingness to take major risks in the face of uncertainty; and self-reliance, curiosity, and a spirit of adventure (Philbrick, 2006). From the perspective of Bion (1961), the primary basic assumption, that is, the unconscious source of energy for these endeavors was fight/flight and, much more secondarily, pairing. Their wishes and hopes were certainly to get away and to create a new social order, one that was far better than the one they were leaving. It is precisely this fight/flight mentality, we believe, that paved the way for much that was to follow in our development as a country.

The American Revolution itself was fought against the British to establish our independence. Conquer, outwit, and dominate—not assimilate, learn from, and collaborate—became a primary theme in our early history. This theme pervades our dealings with the Native Americans. Our forebears generally waged war against and drove away the Native Americans, killed and slaughtered many, dealt dishonestly with those who remained, and bullied their way forward into the new land, driving the remaining Native Americans into progressively smaller and less desirable areas of land.

It was in this very cradle that the notion of "rugged individualism" took shape, neatly concealing and justifying all manner of what many now might label as unfair, selfish, and immoral actions. "Might makes right" and the "logic of force" prevailed as the country began to expand westward. In the "Wild West," the rule of law was often established by skill with firearms when "the end justifies the means" approach often triumphed.

VIOLENCE IN AMERICA

Retribution for perceived injustices, retaliation against wrongdoers, and revenge for past grievances are common themes in our history, literature, and folktales. It is not by accident that the strong, silent John Wayne persona, one that was tough, fearless, unencumbered by feelings, fiercely independent, and extremely capable at dealing with rustlers, gamblers, and gunslingers alike, became the iconic masculine figure in American mythology.

More Recent History of Violence

In a seemingly ironic twist of fate, our forebears who had fought for freedom against oppression made slavery an important part of our country's history. Dehumanization coupled with economic and social gains triumphed over human rights and morality until the Civil War pitted brother against brother in a prolonged and bloody battle. Nearly a century a passed until we began to see significant social change with the Civil Rights Movement, the contributions of Martin Luther King, Jr., and the Great Society legislation under President Lyndon Johnson.

Our historical treatment of women in this culture is little better. Again, many more detailed accounts are available elsewhere (e.g., Friedan, 1963), but it seems clear that women, too, were systematically deprived of education, opportunities, personal self-esteem, and identity. Only with the success of the Women's Movement did we begin to see some real changes in the ways women viewed themselves and how they were perceived and treated by the men around them.

Whether it be through the conduct of multiple wars with other countries or through more peaceful means, the theme of gaining power over others and exploiting them for individual personal gain remained an important thread in American culture as the country continued to expand and industrialize. Success became linked with the accumulation of wealth and power. The ways of achieving such success received relatively limited scrutiny, including the exploitation of successive waves of immigrant labor forces at home and the incursions of powerful American business interests abroad. The era of the "robber barons" during the nineteenth century who resorted to unethical practices, wielded widespread political influence, and accumulated enormous wealth, is eerily echoed by contemporary Wall Street and banking scandals.

Our more recent struggles to establish equal rights and equal treatment under the law for gays, lesbians, bisexuals, and transgender individuals, as well as our inconsistent immigration policies and our war against illegal aliens are yet other examples of the insidious forms of violence directed against minority groups within our own citizenry. The incidence of gay bashing and hate crimes further attests to the level of overt violence they face in our country. In addition, many believe that our war against drugs unfairly targets minority Latino and African-American citizens.

The role of our country on the international stage is also steeped in violence, projection, scapegoating, and attempts to avoid it. In the past seventy plus years, we have been involved in two World Wars, as well as wars in Korea, Vietnam, Somalia, Kuwait, Iraq, and Afghanistan. In each of these conflicts we managed to dehumanize and demonize our enemies and create a rationale for the conflict. Further, the Cold War flourished in our country for decades. We engaged in a variety of secret, covert, espionage activities with the avowed aim of "making the world safer for democracy." We also permitted the rise and fall of McCarthyism, an especially vicious and often insidious form of violence, borne out of our collective fears, our tolerance for demagoguery, and our desperate desire to locate and destroy our perceived enemies.

As a society that thinks of itself as peaceful and democratic, our fascination with and repulsion from split-off violence is mirrored too in our glorification of Special Ops activities, the exploits of Navy Seals and Army Rangers, drone strikes, and other sometimes questionable activities justified as needed to protect our country. A spate of recent books and movies document the successes of these modern cultural heroes (e.g., Blehm, 2012; Owen, 2013).

The Current Cultural Climate

Before leaving this area, we want to briefly call attention to two prominent examples of violence, in the form of entertainment, embedded in our current culture: football and video games.

VIOLENCE IN AMERICA

In the United States, the marketability and popularity of football, which is inherently violent, especially professional football, has skyrocketed over the past few decades. Football now appears to qualify at least on par with baseball as our national pastime, and the NFL may be seeking to expand its markets into Europe (NFL News/Fox Sports, 2013). The prospect of viewing "big hits" attracts customers. Both real and vicarious violence abounds in the safety of one's living room despite the likelihood that players will at some time experience traumatic brain injuries and longer-term chronic traumatic encephalitis (Lakis, Corona, Toshkezi, & Chin, 2013; Wortzel, Shura, & Brenner, 2013).

The growth of the video game market that features violent encounters is actually quite startling and disturbing (Huesmann, 2007). Murder and mayhem are a critical part of such games. These games seem to be aimed primarily at the fertile market of young children and teens. Some are even advertised with titillating comments about the thrill of unbridled killing but typically conclude by saying that "this game is rated M for Mature"—not M for murder, misanthropic, or misguided, as we might suggest. Whether exposure to these games encourages a callous and dehumanizing view of violence remains to be determined. But, millions of our young people are exposed to these video games every day.

We argue that, collectively, our history, culture, and language have paved the way for many of our current dilemmas in dealing with violence. They have shaped deeply embedded cultural attitudes and our sense of selfhood. Together, these provide a subtle feeding ground for violent behavior. The emphasis on strength and power as a basis for self-esteem, the "every man for himself" attitude, the prejudice against and hatred for the "out-group," and our ongoing participation in various foreign and domestic wars can all provide justifications for violence and render it almost commonplace.

HOW CAN THERAPISTS PROMOTE HEALTHY CHANGE?

Following the shootings in September 2013 at the Navy Yard in Washington, DC, Maureen Dowd (2013) quoted Dr. Janis Orlowski, chief operating officer of MedStar Washington Hospital Center, where the injured were being treated. She stated, "There's something evil in our society that we as Americans have to work to try and eradicate...There's something wrong and the only thing that I can say is we have to work together to get rid of it." Dr. Orlowski called it "a challenge to all of us," and concluded by saying, "This is not America.". Unfortunately, this is America, although not the America we want or how we want to be perceived by others.

Trauma theory distinguishes between three roles in response to trauma: victim, perpetrator, and responder vs. bystander. Most people in our society are either victims or bystanders, with some exceptions like 9/11 and the Boston Marathon bombing, where many people came to the aid of the victims. We need to find ways to help all of us not only to become responders, but also to be proactive in helping others before a crisis happens.

Several different pathways exist for us to become responders, rather than remain bystanders. All involve applications of what we have learned in working with our groups:

1. Draw attention to violence in our country as a necessary consciousness-raising. Promoting such awareness can begin on a daily level with others and can extend to our roles in our groups and our communities. The use of public educational forums and psychoeducational techniques lends itself to this.
2. Develop methods for more carefully assessing the potential for violence in the patients referred to us, and for detecting and preventing potential violence in those populations we know are likely to be at risk. Advocate for legislation that makes mental health care more available, especially to those we know are potentially violent populations, like PTSD veterans, gang members, and marginalized persons.
3. Help dispel the stigmatizing myths connecting mental illness with violence, challenge the reluctance of many to speak about violence or to seek professional help, and acknowledge our own inability to predict who may become violent.
4. Assist people to withstand the temptation to ascribe violence to various subgroups who can then be scapegoated. Scapegoating enables all of us to continue to avoid, deny, and projectively ascribe to others those parts of us, both conscious and unconscious, that are violent.

5. Pay more attention to how our patients affect those around them in their work and family lives. Had Adam Lanza's mother had been in treatment, for example, would her therapist have been concerned about how she was affecting her son? Schermer (personal communication, 2014) recently formulated a concept called the "penumbra group" to designate all the people whose lives mutually interact with and affect the group members. If we thought seriously about this larger group and our impact on them, we might develop a very different picture of our work as therapists.
6. Extend the work we do into the community by first taking a leadership role in developing group models for communities to dialogue and process issues of violence in their neighborhoods, and then exploring the possibilities for developing "violence prevention" group models for containing and holding potentially violent members of the community.
7. Assist in developing non-violent ways for members of our groups, organizations, and communities to express their emotions, establish a code of "do no harm," and lead more productive lives. Such models might then be used by police, teachers, and clergy in their work with communities.
8. Help develop better communication within school systems and other larger groups to avert mass disasters in the future. Determine what factors inhibit, restrain, or block such communication and what can be done to overcome or change them.
9. Finally, at a deeper cultural level, we need to help tackle the underlying lack of a sense of collective in this country. While we know that cohesion is essential for groups to function effectively, we in the United States rarely think of ourselves as a group or community, except in the aftermath of tragedy. When faced with a common enemy, we are able to rally together and tolerate, subordinate, or overlook our differences. More typically, we tend to view ourselves as individuals first and foremost. Secondarily, we see ourselves as members of various small groups, including families, religious organizations, and work groups. The lack of an overall "we" is most apparent at the level of national government, which operates as competing subgroups and individuals and often seems incapable of concerted action. How we can highlight this and move toward an increased sense of national community remains a complex problem that requires urgent attention. Convincing people that we share collective needs and interests has always been a hard sell in this country and is often linked with being anti-American.

Most importantly, if we cannot help to build a sense of "we," then a safe container that serves as a reflective space with constructive norms at broader community and national levels cannot be established. To reduce scapegoating, we must own our violent impulses and culture as a nation. Dialogue must involve a sense of the group as a whole in which we encounter the "other" in ourselves. We are all in this together. And, we must accept the idea that any changes in our culture will come about slowly.

THE CONTENT OF THESE TWO ISSUES

In this two-part Special Issue on Violence in America, we have asked a distinguished panel of experts in group psychotherapy and group dynamics to join in the search for underlying causes of violence in our society and what can be done to effectively address this problem. Each will focus on a particular aspect of a vitally important social issue. Because our subject matter is so complex, we have had to make difficult decisions about what to include here due to space limitations. Some notable omissions include articles about cult and gang violence, where the influence of the group to which one belongs can be extremely powerful. (Jerrold Post, one of our contributors, does however highlight the power of the group in shaping political terrorist initiatives and actions.) Another important area that is not systematically explored here is that of countertransference, although several authors discuss its relevance during the treatment process.

Our intention here is to heighten awareness of violence in our country, to promote a deeper understanding of these issues from a group dynamics perspective, and to determine how we as group psychotherapists and group dynamics thinkers can promote healthier diagnostic, treatment, and prevention approaches, not just in our own groups but for the larger society in which we live.

This issue begins with an interview with Dr. Dan Gottlieb, psychologist and host of the NPR program, "Voices in the Family." Gottlieb has gained perspective on community issues from his work as a prominent broadcaster and lecturer. He sees violence as a consequence of interpersonal "malnourishment," a lack of empathy, trust, and connectedness in our society. He believes that the therapist's stance of openness and non-judgmental reflection is helpful in establishing connections and diminishing anger and violence, and that such empathy can be used outside the consulting room. He advocates that therapists engage in social action by facilitating community meetings to bring people together to discuss their conflicts

Cecil Rice draws on his extensive experience as a group therapist and consultant to hospitals and other mental health facilities, as well as efforts to resolve inter-group conflicts, notably in Northern Ireland. He explores the ways in which the dynamics of therapy groups shed light on the large group context of violence in American society. He emphasizes the difference between experiencing feelings and the desire to act on them, the latter often eventuating in scapegoating, an ever-present concern for both therapy groups and society. Rice holds that social violence and unrest emerge out of threats to individual or group identities often embedded in unfinished crises and "chosen trauma" from the past that become rationalizations for "justice" and revenge. He points to the role of reparation and forgiveness in de-escalating the potential for future violence.

Suzanne Phillips calls attention to the critical role that silence plays in the space between violence and trauma. She holds that silence invites and intensifies trauma and that "unspoken, unwitnessed and unclaimed trauma" paves the way for more violence and the maintenance of a tragic vicious cycle. She reviews the empirical evidence that links violence with trauma and explores the mediating role of silence as an important intervening variable in this. She then draws on her considerable experience with suicide survivors and military women to illustrate how group process can be effectively used to overcome silence, to establish new and healthier interpersonal connections, and to help uncover and confront the hidden scars borne from violence. Phillips concludes by underscoring how powerful groups can be in both treatment and non-treatment formats in furnishing a safe holding environment that promotes the reintegration of self and replaces the silence of violence with a healing narrative.

Nina Thomas examines in depth our efforts to collectively disown our own aggression, to identify suitable targets as villains, and to projectively encapsulate the widespread forms of violence in the United States in the familiar drama of victim and persecutor. She draws a link between being shunned to the margins of society, shame and humiliation, and narcissistic rage as precursors to violence. She suggests that how we as a society use language to encode and remember profoundly affects and shapes our culture and experience, and she argues that our linguistic metaphors conceal as much as they convey. The language that is used in connection with our "chosen trauma" of 9/11, Thomas believes, serves as a justification for more widespread culturally sanctioned forms of aggression and violence. In our efforts to deal with violence, she draws an important set of distinctions between "restorative" and "retributive" justice, which characterizes much of our own more traditional justice system. She concludes by exploring what might happen here in the United States were we to try to adopt a model that more closely resembled restorative justice, an idea reinforced by Bill Roller's video review of two prison populations with a history of violent crime and homicide. Roller compares his own clinical experience with an educational video that depicts the history and nature of treatment within a prison setting of individuals with a violent history. Instead of the stereotyped view of these criminals as genetically or otherwise flawed, Roller contends that, "the common experience for many of these men is sexual and physical abuse, emotional bullying, and parental neglect. Of particular import is the insecure attachment and the chaotic emotional climate that exist in violent families." Thus, he brings humane interpersonal and developmental understanding to work that has long emphasized social control. This is a difficult road to traverse, but it holds out great promise. As mentioned earlier, balancing and integrating boundaries, rules, and social control with empathic understanding is one of the fundamental problems of working with violence, whether in therapy groups, structured social interventions, or social policy and change.

Our hope is that these articles, and those to follow in the next part of this series, will stimulate you, the reader, to join us in this important discussion.

REFERENCES

Agazarian, Y. M. (1997). *Systems-centered therapy for groups.* New York: Guilford.

Albow, K., & Winslow, D. (2013). A realistic, workable plan to reduce violence in America. Retreived from http://www.foxnews.com/opinion/2013/04/15/can-reduce-violence-in-America-if-fix-our-mental-health-system

Antiwar.com. (2014). Casualties in Iraq. Retrieved from http://antiwar.com/casualties/

Bertalanffy, L. von (1968). *General systems theory.* New York: Braziller.

Bion, W. R. (1961). *Experiences in groups.* London: Tavistock.

Blehm, E. (2012). *Fearless: The undaunted courage and ultimate sacrifice of Navy SEAL Team Six operator Adam Brown.* Colorado Springs, CO: Waterbook.

Brunker, M., Alba, M., & Dedman, B. (2014). Snapshot: Hate crime in America, by the numbers. Retrieved from http://www.nbcnews.com/storyline/jewish-center-shootings/snapshot-hate-crime-america-numbers-n81521

Brunker, M., Seveille, L.R., Alba, M., & Blankstein, A. (2014). Kansas Jewish Center shootings reveal new dangers of "lone wolves." Retrieved from http://www.nbcnews.com/storyline/jewish-center-shootings/kansas-jewish-center-shootings-reveal-new-dangers-lone-wolves-n81331

Buchele, B., & Spitz, H. (2004). *Group interventions for treatment of psychological trauma.* New York: American Group Psychotherapy Association.

Casoni, D., & Brunet, L. (2007). The psychodynamics that lead to violence, Part 2: The case of "ordinary" people involved in mass violence. *Canadian Journal of Psychoanalysis, 15,* 261-280.

Diaz, T. (2013). *The last gun: How changes in the gun industry are killing Americans and what it will take to stop it.* New York: New Free Press.

Dowd, M. (2013, September 18). Losing the room. *New York Times.*

Federal Bureau of Investigation. (2011). *Crime in the United States.* Retrived from http://www.fbi.gov/about-uscjis/ucr/crime-in-the-u.s./2011crime-in-the-u.s.-2011

Federal Bureau of Investigation. (2012). *Uniform Crime Report: Crime in the United States, 2012.* Retrieved from http://www.fbi.gov/about-uscjis/ucr.

Fisher, M. (2012, July 23). A land without guns: How Japan has virtually eliminated shooting deaths. *Atlantic.*

Fleegler, E. W., Lee, L. K., Monuteaux, M. C., Hemenway, D., & Mannix, R. (2013). Firearm legislation and firearm-related fatalities in the United States. *JAMA Internal Medicine, 173*(9), 732-740.

Friedan, B. (1963). *The feminine mystique.* New York: Vanguard.

Friedman, R. A. (2012, December 17). In gun debate, a misguided focus on mental illness. *New York Times.*

Gun control offers no cure-all in America. (2012). Retrieved from http://nbcpolitics.nbcnews.com/_2012/12/18/15977143-gun-cntrol-offers-no-cure-all-in-america?lite

Herman, J. (1997). *Trauma and recovery: The aftermath of violence from domestic violence to political terror.* New York: Basic Books.

Heroux, P. (2013). America's violence problem (and it's not just with guns). Retrieved from http://www.huffingtonpost.com/paul-heroux/America-violence_b_28614445.html

Hopper, E. (1997). Traumatic experience in the unconscious life of groups: A fourth Basic Assumption. *Group Analysis, 34*(1), 439-470.

Hor, K., & Taylor, M. (2010). Suicide and schizophrenia: A systematic review of rates and risk factors. *Journal of Psychopharmacology, 24*(Suppl. 4), 81-90.

Huesmann, L. R. (2007). The impact of electronic media violence: Scientific theory and research. *Journal of Adolescent Health, 41*(6 Suppl 1), S6–S13.

Hunt, I. M., Kapur, N., Windfuhr, K., Robinson, J., Bickley, H., Flynn, S., et al. (2006). National confidential inquiry into suicide and homicide by people with mental illness, suicide in schizophrenia: Findings from a national clinical survey. *Journal of Psychiatric Practice, 12*(3), 139-147.

icasualties. (2014). Operation Iraqi Freedom; Operation Enduring Freedom. Retrieved from icasualties.org.

Johnston's Archive. (2013). Terrorist attacks and related incidents in the United States. Retrieved from http://www.johnstonsarchive.net/terrorism/wrjp255a.html

Kim, Y., & Leventhal, B. (2008). Bullying and suicide: A review. *International Journal of Adolescent Medical Health, 20*(2), 133-154.

Klein, R. H., & Bernard, H. S. (2008). The role of the philanthropic community in disaster response. In R. H. Klein & S. B. Phillips (Eds.), *Public mental health service delivery protocols: Group interventions for disaster preparedness and response* (pp. 201–210). New York: American Group Psychotherapy Association.

Klein, R. H., & Phillips, S. B. (Eds.) (2008). *Public mental health service delivery protocols: Group interventions for disaster preparedness and response.* New York: American Group Psychotherapy Association.

Klein, R. H., Rice, C. A., & Schermer, V. L. (Eds.). (2009). *Leadership in a changing world*. New York: Lexington Books.

Klein, R. H., & Schermer, V. L. (Eds.). (2000). *Group psychotherapy for psychological trauma*. New York: Guilford.

Kohut, H. (1972). Thoughts on narcissism and narcissistic rage. *Psychoanalytic Study of the Child, 27*, 360-400.

Kohut, H. (1977). *The restoration of self*. New York: International Universities Press.

Koop, C. E., & Lundgren, G. D. (1992). Violence in America: A public health emergency. *Journal of the American Medical Association, 267*(22), 3075–3076.

Krause, W. J. (2012). *Gun control legislation*. Washington, DC: Congressional Research Service.

Krug, E. G., Powell, K. E., & Dahlberg, L. L. (1998). Firearm-related deaths in the United States and 35 other high- and upper-middle income countries. *International Journal of Epidemiology, 27*(2), 214-221.

Lakis, N., Corona, R. J., Toshkezi, G., & Chin, L. S. (2013). Chronic traumatic encephalopathy—neuropathology in athletes and war veterans. *Neurological Research, 35*(3), 290-299.

Lakoff, G., & Johnson, M. (1980). *Metaphors we live by*. Chicago: University of Chicago Press.

Liem, M., Barber, C., Markwalder, N., Killias, M., & Nieuwbeerta, P. (2011). Homicide-suicide and other violent deaths: An international comparison. *Forensic Science International, 207*(1–3), 70-76.

Litwiller, B. J., & Brausch, A. M. (2013). Cyber bullying and physical bullying: The role of violent behavior and substance abuse. *Journal of Youth and Adolescence, 42*, 675-684.

Lothstein, L. (2014, March). *Understanding and treating sexual violence in personality disordered men: Group therapy in the age of the social neurosciences*. Paper presented at the 23rd Annual Conference International Association of Forensic Psychotherapy. University of Utrecht, Zeist, The Netherlands.

Medscape. (2012). Epidemiology of depression and suicide. Retrieved from http://emedicine.medscape.com/article/805459-overview3a-w2aab6b4

Miller, A. (2014). Threat assessment in action. *Monitor on Psychology, 45*(2), 37-42.

Mountjoy, P. (2013). Violence in America: The workplace is a breeding ground. Retrieved from http://communities.washingtontimes.com/neighborhood/steps-authentic...psychology/2013/apr/19/violence-america-workplace-breeding-ground..

NFL News/Fox Sports. (2013). Goodell: London, LA could get teams.

Owen, M. (2013). *No easy day*. New York: Penguin.

Philbrick, N. (2006). *Mayflower: A story of courage, community and war.* New York: Viking.

Phillips, S. (2014). No innocent bystanders: The role we play in reducing violence. *Psych Central.* Retrieved February 10, 2014, from http://blogs.psychcentral.com/healing-together/2014/01/no-innocent-bystandersthe-role-we-play-in-reducing-violence/

Richardson, E. G., & Hemenway, D. (2011). Homicide, suicide, and unintentional firearm fatality: Comparing the United States with other high-income countries, *Journal of Trauma, 70*(1), 238-243.

Rogers, H. (2012). *Gun control: An international comparison.* Retrieved from http://ivn.us.2012/07/25/gun-control-an-international-comparison

Sadock, B. J., & Sadock, V. A. (Eds.). (2007). *Kaplan & Sadock's synopsis of psychiatry: Behavioral sciences/clinical psychiatry* (10th ed.). Philadelphia, PA: Lippincott, Williams, & Williams.

Sandy Hook school shootings. (2012). Retrieved from http://www.cnn.com/SPECIALS/us/connecticut-school-shooting

Smith, E. L., & Cooper, A. (2013). *Homicide in the U.S. known to law enforcement, 2011.* Washington, DC: Bureau of Justice Statistics. Retrieved from http://www.bjs.gov/content/pub/pdf/hus11.pdf

Stannard, D. E. (1992). *American Holocaust: A conquest of the New World.* New York: Oxford University Press.

Stolorow, R. (2007). *Trauma and human existence: Autobiographical, psychoanalytic, and philosophical reflections.* New York: Analytic Press.

Toobin, A. (2013). Panel refutes link between mental illness and gun violence. Retrieved from http://www.browndailyherald.com/2013/04/10/panel-refutes-link-between-mental-illness-and-gun-violence/

United Nations Office on Drugs and Crime. (2006). *The seventh United Nations survey on crime trends and the operations of criminal justice systems (1998-2000).* Retrieved from http://www.unodc.org/unodc/en/data-and-analysis/homicide.html

United Nations Office on Drugs and Crime. (2013). *Homicide statistics.* Retrieved from http://www.unodc.org/unodc/en/data-and-analysis/homicide.html

U.S. Census Bureau. (2012). Census Bureau Projects U.S. population of 305.5 million on New Year's Day. Retrieved from https://www.census.gov/newsroom/releases/archives/population/cb12-255.html

Volkan, V. D. (1997). *Blood lines: From ethnic pride to ethnic terrorism.* New York: Farrar, Straus & Giroux.

Volkan, V. D. (1991). On chosen trauma. *Mind and Human Interaction, 3*, 13-38.

Wilson, M. M. (2014). *Hate crime victimization, 2004–2012–Statistical tables*. Washington, DC: Bureau of Justice Statistics. Retrieved from http://www.bjs.gov/index.cfm?tv=pbdetail&lid-4883

Wortzel, H. S., Shura, R. D., & Brenner, L. A. (2013). Chronic traumatic encephalopathy and suicide: A systematic review. *BioMed Research International, 2013*, Article ID 424280. doi:10.1155/2013/424280

Yalom, I. B., & Leszcz, M. (1995). *The theory and practice of group psychotherapy*. New York: Basic Books.

Zimring, F., & Hawkins, G. (1997). *Crime is not the problem: Lethal violence in America*. New York: Oxford University Press.

Zinn, H. (2008). *A people's history of the United States: 1492–present*. New York: HarperCollins.

Violence, Threat, and Emotional "Malnourishment": An Interview With Dr. Dan Gottlieb

VICTOR L. SCHERMER, M.A., L.P.C., CAC, FAGPA

ABSTRACT

Daniel Gottlieb, Ph.D., is a psychologist and host of the National Public Radio (NPR) program Voices in the Family. He is interviewed here by Victor Schermer about his views on the increase in violence in American society. He sees violence to be partly a consequence of interpersonal "malnourishment," a lack of empathy, trust, and connectedness in our communities. Thus, the therapist's openness and non-judgmental reflection is helpful in establishing social connectedness and diminishing anger and violence. He advocates that therapists engage in social action by facilitating community meetings to bring people together to discuss their conflicts and find commonalities among them.

Psychologist Daniel Gottlieb, Ph.D., is a noted author and the long-time host of the award-winning NPR radio program *Voices in the Family*, in which he interviews professionals, authors, and members of the community about key psychological issues of our time, engaging the larger community of call-in listeners in the dialogue. Beyond his practice of psychotherapy, he has thus become keenly aware of the broader needs of individuals, families, and the society at large. Like his listeners, he is deeply concerned about the problem of violence in America today.

Victor L. Schermer is a psychologist in private practice in Philadelphia, Pennsylvania.

Dr. Gottlieb suffered his own trauma, and in order to help others, he frequently gives presentations to both practitioners and the general public about what he has learned from his personal experience. Several decades ago, Gottlieb was injured in a catastrophic car accident and as a result is quadriplegic. Gradually accepting the physical limitations of his impairment, he made a remarkable emotional recovery, resuming his private practice, media involvement, family life, spirituality, and wide network of friends and colleagues. He frequently uses his personal experience in his lectures and books about mental health and psychological trauma. Gottlieb's grandson Sam is diagnosed with an autistic spectrum disorder. The best-selling book, *Letters to Sam* (Gottlieb, 2008), is a classic in the field of child development.

The guest editors of the *International Journal of Group Psychotherapy* wanted to bring a voice from the community into our Special Issue. They felt that Gottlieb would be an ideal representative and asked him to reflect on the causes of violence in our communities and what can be done to help alleviate the problems. For this purpose, he was interviewed by me as co–guest editor.

Gottlieb began by quoting one of his favorite poems:

> *Who Are My People?*
> —Rosa Zagnoni Marinoni
>
> My People? Who are they?
> . . .
>
> I went into the land where I was born,
> Where men spoke my language.
> I was a stranger there.
> "My people," my soul cried. "Who are my people?"
>
> Last night in the rain I met an old man
> Who spoke a language I do not speak...
> [H]e offered me
> The shelter of his patched umbrella.
> I met his eyes . . . And then I knew.

VIOLENCE IN AMERICA

SCHERMER: How does this beautiful poem relate to the violence in our culture today?

GOTTLIEB: I see the underpinning of the anger as fear, anxiety, and insecurity. Also, I think there's a quality of malnourishment in our culture. Many of us are malnourished spiritually, emotionally, and physically. Just look at the weight problem in our culture— between obesity and, if not anorexia, then our obsession with weight. We're malnourished at both ends of the continuum. We live in a starvation mentality.

SCHERMER: We live in a consumer culture. We eat, take in, buy, devour.

GOTTLIEB: And yet we're still not satisfied.

SCHERMER: So there is an element of insatiability.

GOTTLIEB: No, it's not insatiability. It's because we remain malnourished. If you give someone who's malnourished a room full of candy bars, they're still going to be malnourished.

SCHERMER: Are you saying that when Americans are not getting nourished by emotional contact and empathy, they become angry and take it out on others?

GOTTLIEB: It's not that direct. I think it's more about anxiety. So, here's how I think it manifests itself. We're more likely to see others as a threat to ourselves. Whenever we suffer, we become self-absorbed. The lens of our world becomes narrower. We focus on self, or self and family. Whenever we suffer, that happens. And you know that's adaptive. But if it goes on and on, and the more narrow our lens gets, the more threatened we feel by the "other." So that, for example, when someone cuts us off on the street, we react as though someone is trying to take our meat! It's as if the other person, so to speak, is a mountain lion or a mastodon.

SCHERMER: So we live under a lot of threat from one another.

GOTTLIEB: *Perceived* threat.

SCHERMER: There's a trust issue. How does that relate to not being nourished?

GOTTLIEB: We suffer because we don't have the nutrients we need. So what are the nutrients we need? We need love, we need well-being, we need compassion, we need faith. And I don't necessarily mean faith in God. You can't have well-being without faith— and maybe they're both the same (Gottlieb, 2014).

SCHERMER: By faith, do you perhaps mean faith in ourselves, in the future, in life? However, there are cultures that are under duress like we are, and yet people respond in a more caring, communal way.

GOTTLIEB: We do that here! Like after 9/11 or after Hurricane Sandy—we all came together to help and support.

SCHERMER: There are many opposites and contradictions in American culture. People in our society are so loving and caring in some contexts, while in other situations they become defensive, isolated, violent, abusive, and carry grudges.

GOTTLIEB: Well, that's what happens when you have a mind! We embrace hypocrisy. It's the only way we can survive. But I want to talk about, "What is our responsibility now as therapists, as humans on this planet?" And the way violence is experienced. Early on, after my accident, if I went into a restaurant, the hostess wouldn't talk to me and instead would talk to the person I was with. "Where would he like to sit; would he be staying in his wheelchair?" I experienced that as violent, and I reacted to that with violence. Social violence. I reacted violently, internally, I didn't *do* anything. But I felt fury.

SCHERMER: Part of that violent feeling comes from being unacknowledged, ignored, negated.

GOTTLIEB: Right. That's why I brought up that poem." I looked him in the eye, and then I knew." In Judaism, it's sometimes said that the Messiah will come to us as a homeless person so we should look every homeless person in the eye as if he is the Messiah. That changes the world.

SCHERMER: That's acknowledgment, and that's empathy. And that's part of what we try to do as therapists: To connect on that level.

GOTTLIEB: Think of Zimmerman [the neighborhood watch volunteer who fatally shot Trayvon Martin]. Is he evil? It's irrelevant. Look him in the eye and find his humanity. If you look someone in the eye long enough, you'll see their soul. And I believe that's the only way you can find your own. Our brains are social organs. When we isolate, we die. Getting back to what I said earlier, we become malnourished. The starvation feeds on itself.

SCHERMER: You're talking about the importance of Buber's I–Thou relationship. So, how do you relate this to the problem of violence?

VIOLENCE IN AMERICA

GOTTLIEB: You uncross your arms.

SCHERMER: So how do we therapists help people to do that, both as part of our work, and as members of society? How can we help people to connect on such a level that it would diminish the tendencies toward violence?

GOTTLIEB: It can't be done in our office as such. I believe that the path to mental health is through the pursuit of social health. So part of psychotherapy has to be the pursuit of social health. For example, I see some patients who cannot afford my fee. For every hour of therapy, they spend two hours doing volunteer work and make the world a better place. It was started by psychiatrist Dori Middleman. I do it routinely with my patients. I had a woman years ago who was terribly depressed. Her medication wasn't working, and she had to leave work, but it's dangerous to take away their structure if they're depressed. So I told her I'd write the letter excusing her from work, but she would have to volunteer ten hours a week, it would have to be direct work with "sentient beings," and she would have to make eye contact with them. It could be animals, people, the homeless or the elderly— that didn't matter, but she'd have to make contact. So she did that, and after a couple of weeks, her depression began to lift. She was socializing, she was meeting people, she was feeling more valuable in the world. And slowly her arms began to open, and then her eyes did, and then her heart did.

I talk about open arms a lot. Imagine if someone was coming towards you with a threatening look. Imagine how you would disarm them by smiling and opening your arms to them.

SCHERMER: The word "dis-*arm*" is interesting. We call weapons "*arms*."

GOTTLIEB: Dis-armed. Don't respond. Don't respond to the hostility. Respond only to the humanity.

SCHERMER: OK. So let's say we therapists encounter someone in our practice who is a "real" perpetrator. Maybe he's a husband. Maybe he came back from the Iraq war, has a lot of pent-up rage, and abuses his spouse. Or may it's one of the young people—the young man who massacred the children and staff at Sandy Hook, or the one who shot the people in the movie theater in Aurora, Colorado. Suppose we encounter one of these individuals in our practice, perhaps before the violent episode has occurred, but the person is on the brink. How do we offer help to this individual that might change his direction and prevent violence?

VIOLENCE IN AMERICA

GOTTLIEB: First of all, in order for a person to be compassionate or loving, they first have to be accountable for their behavior. To begin with, the task of dealing with the potential violent behavior may be so difficult that we as therapists have to decide if we need external help and supervision. It's hard, because we're in a difficult position, because it's our job not to be judgmental, but in a way we have to be. So if I had a patient who was potentially violent, I would engage him at that level. And I would talk about my own fears and anxieties. What happens to me when I experience violence? What can we do to keep you and your loved ones safe? I don't think anybody really wants to hurt someone, really destroy their lives.

SCHERMER: We relate to the humanity and not to the violence.

GOTTLIEB: Exactly. You relate to the humanity and not to the violence. I learned a lesson from my [autistic] grandson, Sam. Because of his history, he doesn't have the receptor site in his brain for violence. Like, he doesn't get it when someone acts mean to him. So a kid comes up to him in the hall at school. A bully. He says to Sam, "You know I could knock you on your ass if I wanted." And Sam just simply hears this as data and opinion. So he says, "I don't know. I don't think you can. But maybe you can." And he walks away! And the bully is probably thinking, "What the hell just happened here?"

SCHERMER: He's scratching his head [laughter]. That's a beautiful story. It's interesting that we call autism a "deficit," but it's also a gift! And maybe part of the helping process with violence is getting people to see their strengths. One of the reasons people get violent is to assert their power. If they saw their own gifts, perhaps they wouldn't be so violent.

GOTTLIEB: If anyone has to assert their power, the only reason they do that is because they feel powerless. Any power struggle, say in the office, is between two people who feel powerless.

SCHERMER: I think people do feel powerless in our society in general, and that may be a source of some of the violence we see. There are two kinds of powerlessness. One is simply that the world is bigger than we are. The other occurs when our justifiable empowerment is taken away from us.

GOTTLIEB: Through poverty, discrimination, disability.

SCHERMER: It's likely that most of the perpetrators of violent incidents like Columbine, Virginia Tech, the movie theater in Aurora, the massacre of children in Sandy Hook, and so on, felt marginalized and powerless, and this potentiated their violent ideas and actions. And that also speaks to group therapists, because a lot of the work of group therapy consists of helping the members feel they belong in the group and are empowered to make positive changes.

GOTTLIEB: Yes, that's what makes groups so powerful. More than anything. More than words. It's being with kindred spirits.

SCHERMER: And how does one get to feel that way? That poem says something about it.

GOTTLIEB: It does. I have many of my patients—and I do this exercise myself—make eye contact with themselves, literally. I have them look at themselves in the mirror, look deeply into their own eyes, see the boy or girl they were when they were little, how they experienced life back then, as an adolescent, as a young person. And just look deeply into their own eyes—it's a powerful exercise.

SCHERMER: So in group, there's face-to-face contact, mirrors of each other. Like the woman for whom you prescribed face-to-face contact.

GOTTLIEB: Yes, that's how we know each other.

SCHERMER: And groups have that built in. The members look at and face one another. I'm very affected, Dan, by the way you communicate. It gets me to listen. And you come at the issues very clearly.

GOTTLIEB: Thank you.

SCHERMER: On the other side of the equation, what does the culture of violence do to us; how does violence affect us at that deeper level you just mentioned?

GOTTLIEB: If we're not being mindful. If we're surrounded by people who experience themselves and their lives as if they're impoverished, and there's anxiety, and if you have mirror neurons, you're going to absorb it, and you're going to feel the same way. As therapists, we're very dexterous with our defenses. We can pretend we're OK.

SCHERMER: In most of the literature on mirror neurons, they don't mention the mirroring of aggression. You're bringing up something really powerful, that violence perpetuates violence by activating that mirroring response.

GOTTLIEB: Sure, how can it not? If you feel everyone around you wants to pick up a gun, wants to grab your food, of course you'll want to pick up the gun and respond in kind.

SCHERMER: And that's what's happening in our society. People want their guns more than ever!

GOTTLIEB: Because they're scared.

SCHERMER: In that connection, it might be interesting to consider how trauma affects mirror neurons. Psychological trauma is very pervasive in our society. People are walking around traumatized. And part of the traumatic response is rage.

To change the topic a bit, I'm concerned that we therapists tend to stay aloof from political and social issues. How can we get therapists to be more socially conscious and be change agents in our society?

GOTTLIEB: We have to do what we ask our patients to do. We need to get out there and start talking about it. And we've also got to help people in our society. We've got to make eye contact with homeless people.

SCHERMER: So we need to do community service.

GOTTLIEB: Of course we do.

SCHERMER: Should we do that community service simply as citizens and human beings, or should we do that specifically from our positions as therapists?

GOTTLIEB: Is there a difference?

SCHERMER: As a person, I can do volunteer work, and I can try to connect more with people in my daily life. As a therapist, I can go to Congress and advocate for gun control from a mental health standpoint.

GOTTLIEB: I couldn't agree more. I had an experience a few years ago on my radio show. I interviewed the Nobel Peace Prize winner from Northern Ireland, Betty Williams, about how she got mobilized and did all she did to promote the peace process. Toward the end of the show, I said, OK, you've got all our listeners motivated to help make the world a better place. So tell us what to do. Give us our marching orders right now. And she says, "If you're asking me for marching orders, you're not ready. When you're ready, open your door and go do it." She shamed me! I thought she was great!

SCHERMER: Northern Ireland has been flooded with violence at various times in its history. We could learn a lot from each other's experience. And I understand that now that there's peace between the conflicting groups there, people are unfortunately turning against themselves and their own cohorts, with an increase in suicide and general hostility. They're still angry even though they're not taking sides. So how do we therapists change in such a way that we go beyond being passive listeners and become social activists?

GOTTLIEB: I've got a pillow on my couch that quotes Gandhi: "We must be the change we wish to see in the world." I just want to change pronouns here. Instead of the generic, "What can we do," let's ask "What can I do tomorrow" to start this process?" And If I'm ready, I'll have answers—I'll know what I can do. If I want to mobilize, I'll send out emails to everyone I know. I'll set up a meeting. We know how to do it—we just have to be ready to do it.

SCHERMER: Finally, do you see any changes in the mental health system itself that might help resolve these problems?

GOTTLIEB: We have to believe that social health is the path to mental health. We have to take a look at the mental health of the world—there isn't anybody else to do it.

(Interview conducted July 23, 2013 in Philadelphia, Pennsylvania)

REFERENCES

Gottlieb, D. (2008). *Letters to Sam.* New York: Sterling.
Gottlieb, D. (2014). *The wisdom we're born with: Restoring our faith in ourselves.* New York: Sterling Ethos.

A Group Therapist Reflects on Violence in America

CECIL A. RICE, PH.D., CGP, DFAGPA

ABSTRACT

In this paper, the author draws on his experience as a group therapist, noting parallels between the often intense but well contained dynamics of therapy groups and what they can tell us about violence in America. He examines the tension between bearing and understanding feelings and the desire to act on them, sometimes destructively in therapy groups and in society. He notes the omnipresent desire to find scapegoats rather than bear our own discomforts and notes the same in the abuse through which those in power scapegoat those under their control. Using the ideas of Roche, Volkan, and others, he also notes that current violence emerges from threats to individual or group identities often embedded in unfinished crises in the past, whether in a therapy group or in American society. Unresolved racial tensions reaching into the past is one outstanding example. He concludes noting the important role of reparation and forgiveness in therapy groups and society to slow the forward movement of violence.

    Fellow-citizens, we cannot escape history.
       –Abraham Lincoln, Annual Message to Congress, 1862

    The group must have the capacity to face discontent within the group and must have the means to cope with discontent.
       —Wilfred Bion, *Experiences in Groups*

Cecil Rice is affiliated with the Boston Institute for Psychotherapy and is in private practice.

VIOLENCE IN AMERICA

Group therapists and consultants are well aware of the role of aggression in their patients and groups but often do not address the parallels and causes related to hostility and violence in society at large. Recent events of mass destructiveness, such as the elementary school massacre in Connecticut, the movie theater shooting in Colorado, and the Boston Marathon terrorist bombing, have drawn increased attention to the level of violence in the United States. It has generated shock and cries for solutions, such as placing police in schools, increasing gun control, and arming ourselves for protection, some of which may paradoxically threaten greater violence. Understandably, we seemed to be running scared. These events have triggered angry reactions and verbal violence among special interest groups, such as gun lobbies, irate citizens, and political parties (Cillizza, 2012; Patterson, 2012).

The striking statistics cited by Klein and Schermer (2015) in their introduction support the impression of the pervasive impact of hostility and violence in America. Why would a nation that prides itself on the domesticity of family life, searches for peace in the world, and seems otherwise to have so much going for it be so dangerous and rife with so many forms of violence? Can lessons learned from group psychotherapy and group dynamics shed light on this?

Violence is multifaceted, such that various violent events require different understanding and different responses. This paper treats violence in broad terms. It reflects on historical and current contexts in which violence is set and by which some of it is triggered. Therapy groups and the understanding of small, median, and large group dynamics provide potential means to address the problem on a societal level.

VIOLENCE AS A SURVIVAL MECHANISM AND AS A DEFENSE OF A VULNERABLE SELF

It is natural to see violence as an unvarnished evil. Yet if we think about it, violence is a key element in all of creation, as seen in the Big Bang theory, volcanoes, earthquakes, and tectonic shifts. Even the birth process is violent, though nature's violence may be less willful and vengeful than human violence, making it easier to tolerate though nonetheless exposing our vulnerability. However, violence is also embedded in the limbic brain as part of a triangle of survival defenses of fight, flight, and freeze. It sometimes finds expression in violent acts to protect ourselves and our loved ones from threats of others (Allan, McKenna, & Hind, 2012). In brief, violence is a capacity we all share and which, on occasion, is necessary. Although it can be an important defense when assaulted by another, some outstanding world leaders, such as Mahatma Gandhi and Martin Luther King, Jr., forswore violence for moral and ethical reasons and brought about major social changes through civil disobedience. One can of course choose to flee or freeze in order to avoid violence, as happened in Newtown, Connecticut, where some quickly got out of the way, while others hid in a closet and "froze" until the danger had passed.

However, violence is not simply a defense against assaults from others; it can also be used to protect a vulnerable self. Meloy (1998/2004), in his study of criminals and psychopaths, described them as men who lay on the narcissistic continuum and had a vulnerable sense of self. Often this vulnerability led them to present a façade of strength and certainty. If that façade was challenged, it could lead to violence to protect that vulnerable self, a last ditch defense against primitive anxieties that lurk beneath the surface of the individual and the group. Members' anger and vulnerability are frequently encountered and addressed in psychotherapy groups. What can group therapy practitioners and researchers tell us about violence in America and how we might address it?

REFLECTIONS ON VIOLENCE FROM WORKING WITH GROUPS

Psychotherapy groups are a valuable resource for addressing our topic. Group and social dynamics are in the forefront as well as the interpersonal dynamics of individual therapy. In a group, those interpersonal dynamics are more diverse and include others besides the therapist. Groups can vacillate from being stable and secure to being unstable and insecure; they can provide support, or be riven by conflict. Paradoxically, the more effectively the group members manage the instability and conflict, the safer the group becomes. Although therapy groups are much less com-

VIOLENCE IN AMERICA

plex than a large society like the United States, they share common features that may make for an effective conversation.

The work in the field of median (up to 20 members) and large groups (as many as 100 members) usually focuses more on group-as-a-whole dynamics and less on the individuals and their relationships. In so doing, they highlight the instability of groups and the ease with which paranoid and other fantasies can take over the group and threaten its life (DeMare, 1972; Foulkes, 1948, 1977; Hopper, 2003). The ideas of Hopper (2012), Rouchy (2002), Tuckman and Jensen (1997), Volkan (1998, 2006), and other clinicians and researchers link the therapy group with larger societal groups such as the United States.

GROUP DYNAMICS: REFLECTING ON FEELINGS VERSUS ACTING OUT FEELINGS

The behavior of psychotherapy groups and of their members is usually lawful and non-violent because group therapists adhere to boundary conditions and agreements that limit or avoid violence in their groups, even when emotions are at a fever pitch. One key agreement in therapy groups is that, "Members agree to put feelings into words and not actions" (Rutan, Stone, & Shay, 2007). We will use the following example to demonstrate that lawfulness and how it can work to members' advantage, enabling them to reflect on their experiences and understand rather than act in ways that may be harmful. This also provides a working model that could be employed in diverse ways in institutions in the larger society.

One evening, the therapy group in my practice was restive after having continued smoothly. Robert was especially angry at other members and bitching about women in particular, both at work and in the group. Soon, this expanded and became anger toward the group in general, including the leader.

The leader noted that this was a striking change in the group's behavior and invited the members to be curious about the fight. In that and in succeeding sessions, members tried to make sense of their and Robert's behavior. The leader was also puzzled, but noted silently that we were getting close to the summer break. Finally, he wondered aloud whether the members were angry about his upcoming vacation. Triggered by this, Robert remembered that this was the time of year some two years earlier when Suzie left the group to begin a new career. She was the first woman he had ever loved and around whom he felt safe. In his mid-sixties, Robert had never had a relationship, far less an intimate one with a woman, an after-effect of a relentlessly abusing mother and a timid father. That he felt safe with this woman was an important breakthrough; however, the pain of this loss was added to by Robert's belief that Suzie loved another man in the group, who had since left, more than she loved him. The other group members did not see it that way, but it was difficult for Robert to believe that he was especially desired.

Why did it take so long before the group became able to address Robert's loss and move toward a resolution of his jealousy and grief? The members wondered also. With prompting from the therapist, they recalled Steve, a quiet man who had joined the group more than four years earlier. Later, he became seriously ill but remained in the group until shortly before he died. The members visited him when he was in hospice, saw him die, and took part in his memorial service. The group members' mourning lasted, on and off, for some time. Following a successful course of therapy, Suzie then left after Steve's death, which added to the group's grief. But Steve's loss dominated the group's life, with just occasional mention of Suzie. Thus, the members and Robert had to recover from the trauma of Steve's illness and death and mourn their loss before they could help Robert with his unfinished business with Suzie. When the group addressed it, the anger in the group reduced and Robert's jealousy and anger also reduced, and he felt at ease. He also recalled that he and the group had talked about Suzie earlier, but not as fully and forcefully as this time.

Robert demonstrated the agreement to put feelings into words and not actions. He was very angry and confused, but kept talking and reflecting, and the members joined him in that process. He did not storm out or threaten anyone; rather, his anger was expressed in words. Through his and the other members' associations, and through the free flow of conversation and interactions that was democratic rather than authoritarian, the group gradually got to the bottom of his frustration, and he was able to grieve his loss.

This process can be very difficult for some group members. For instance, in another therapy group, Dave often became overwhelmed by anger and found it very difficult to put his feelings into words. Rather, he was more prone to storm out of the group. On one occasion, he pulled the door behind him so hard that the glass fell out and broke. In the next session, he returned and talked about his outburst. It was difficult for Dave to talk about what happened without blaming other members. He had been severely abused as a child. He had not seen anger contained or spoken about, but had seen it in action often and felt its sting. The above agreement gave him a framework in which to talk about his impulsivity when he became angry. It also gave him an opportunity to talk about the door, which he agreed to pay for—a reparative gesture following discussion. Reflection continued to be difficult for Dave as he struggled with the impulse to act violently. Last, the above agreement also gave members a framework within which they could confront him without becoming violent themselves.

Violence and the Failure of Reflection in the United States

The United States, which has had and continues to have many troubling events individually and collectively, also has laws and spoken and unspoken agreements of respect. Within that framework, many people reflect on their behavior publicly and privately. But others, like Dave, driven by their unaddressed psychic pain or lack of safety, act instead. Unfortunately, many of those acts are violent while their pain and fears remain uncontained.

For instance, in October 7, 1998, two young men attacked and brutally assaulted 21-year-old Matthew Shepard in Casper, Wyoming, because he was gay. After the beating, he was left tied to a fence to die several hours later (Hudson, 2013). Why were they unable to contain their disdain and murderous rage? These men were trying to destroy in Shepard what they feared in themselves (Johnson, 1997)—vulnerable male identities that were threatened by someone who was gay and had a less stereotypical male identity. Sadly, like Dave, they chose action over containment and reflection, devastating at least one family and shocking many others. Unfortunately, in the large group of which they were a part, the United States, many others shared and acted on similar fears. This made it easier for them to act on those fears rather than contain them (Hudson, 2013). In other words, among certain groups in society, there was no agreement to reflect and understand their fears, to talk rather than act out. For instance, during the trial of these murderers, members and supporters of the Westboro Baptist Church of Topeka, Kansas, under the direction of Pastor Fred Phelps staged a protest outside the court saying that Matthew Shepard was now living in hell for his sin of being gay. Ideology and action overrode reflection. By contrast, Matthew's parents pleaded with the court on behalf of the perpetrators, and the court reduced their punishment from execution to life imprisonment: reflection and thoughtful action (Roy, 2002, pp. 148-149).

What this also illustrates is the importance of having a containing community with agreements, as in a therapy group, that helps support members' capacity to reflect on and contain impulses and intrapsychic conflicts. Sadly, the above-mentioned church encouraged the projection of the members' intrapsychic conflicts and fears onto outside targets. Acting out rather than thoughtful reflection takes various forms. In the next two illustrations, we describe two common actions that take place in treatment groups as well as in society at large: scapegoating and leadership abuse of power.

GROUP DYNAMICS: CREATING A GROUP SCAPEGOAT VERSUS TAKING OWNERSHIP

A common concern in group therapy practice is the role of the scapegoat. As the author wrote elsewhere:

> In ancient Israel, the role of the scapegoat during a religious rite symbolically carried the sins of the group (tribe) into the wilderness, allowing the group to atone for its sins and protect itself from the wrath of God and the punishment that would follow (Leviticus 16, 21f)... In group therapy the scapegoat carries less grand functions, but it is often one way in which a chosen member is invited to bear the discomforts, fears or other feelings that the rest

of the group wishes to avoid. In a therapy group, the scapegoat is usually a co-conspirator in this process, sometimes because being a scapegoat was a common role in his or her family of origin or elsewhere, where it served a similar purpose as it now does in the group. Rarely in this situation does actual physical torture occur, but the scapegoat may nevertheless feel tortured. Commonly, resolution takes place when the whole group can articulate and share such unpleasant emotions as fears and angers rather than have the scapegoat carry the burden of those feelings alone. The scapegoat must also reflect on her/his contribution. (Rice, 2011, pp. 73–74)

In a community meeting at a psychiatric hospital where the author was chief psychologist and head of the group therapy program, Marcia and Betsy were patients and friends. As sometimes happens in psychiatric hospitals, couples become intensely bonded. Once bonded, they permit nothing and no one to come between them, but after the intense bonding establishes itself, the couple usually breaks apart in great animosity. This situation was a little different. Marcia and Betsy found Ted, a vulnerable patient who was a shy loner. They befriended him briefly on the floors then slowly spread rumors about him throughout the hospital. Others joined this couple, formed a tightly knit group, and joined in the animosity toward Ted. Even those who thought favorably of Ted, or had no strong feelings about him, began to distrust him. Those who overtly supported Ted found themselves tarred with the same brush as Ted and became a group that one could not trust. Rumors were also spread among the staff. The most troubling part of this conflict was that it was unclear what the actual charges were. The attacks directed toward Ted and his supporters were primarily innuendos, but given his withdrawn nature, there was little to contradict those innuendos. Clearly, this behavior could destroy Ted and take down several others with him. An additional risk in this scenario was that the staff might also begin to distrust Ted.

The community meeting also became contaminated by these rumors, but fortunately it provided an opportunity as well. The co-leaders spoke about the conflict and strain they saw in the hospital community and now sensed in the community meeting. They did not name any names, since naming Ted in particular would have been to join in the conspiracy and expose him. A distraught young man named Peter stood in the back and yelled, "Jesus saves," and then reentered his private space. The leaders agreed to do some saving. A difficult silence followed. After some encouragement from the leaders, the members began to talk.

Unsurprisingly, Marcia and Betsy in unison blamed Ted for the stress because of his secretive behavior. More silence followed. Then slowly one person took a risky step by saying he did not think Ted was the problem and tentatively pointed the finger at Marcia and Betsy. A complex, angry dialogue followed, but soon a shift took place and the conflict between opposing groups reduced significantly. The leaders gave Marcia and Betsy a chance to speak; earlier, they would have spoken readily in unison, but not this time. They were awkward, each asking the other to speak, and then by degrees each denying they were part of the conspiracy. Soon, the meeting ended. In the next few days, the relationship between Marcia and Betsy fell apart, and by the next community meeting the conspiracy was gone. Marcia and Betsy had needed it to hold their relationship together and could not allow differences to enter it. They had masked their differences by projecting them outward. They garnered some support for this by adding co-conspirators, "true believers," to help sustain them so they could continue the bullying of Ted and others. That group also fell apart, which made continued treatment possible for all parties that the scapegoating temporarily had prevented.

Hopper (2012), addressing this phenomenon in groups, added to Bion's three basic assumption groups—Dependency, Fight/Flight, and Pairing—a fourth basic assumption group he called Incohesion: Aggregation/Massification. This essentially describes what happens when dependency fails and the group experiences a loss of cohesion. It becomes a group of disconnected parts and members are mere aggregates. The other pole, Massification, is a mass with no disparate parts, a whole without connection, a guard against annihilation. An example of this is soccer hooliganism, in which a mass (Massification) of fans races onto a field doing damage to whomever or whatever, after which the group breaks up—disintegrates (Aggregation)—until some future event inspires it into another unified assault. It is also seen in gang violence where often the gang replaces and compensates for the family. It is sustained by Massification bolstered by projecting differences onto outside gangs, with no differences allowed within the gang: To differ risks bodily harm or one's life, a form of aggregation (Thornberry, Krohn, Lizotte, & Smith, 2003). Marcia and Betsy and their group were in a state of Massification, and finding a scapegoat was essential to sustaining it. When Marcia and Betsy and their tight subgroup fell apart, they went from Massification to Aggregation. Scapegoating is a primary mechanism for violence that the basic assumption of Incohesion facilitates.

Role of Scapegoating in the United States

Scapegoating is a common feature of our national life. Here are several examples. The Ku Klux Klan (KKK) has been a presence in American culture for many years, having gone through several iterations (Ku Klux Klan, n.d.). The impact of a mass of people all wearing the same white-hooded uniform that hides distinguishing features struck terror into African Americans, as was intended. Those being terrified had no way of knowing who was assaulting them. Afterwards, the uniforms came off and the guilty faded into the general population: Massification to Aggregation. In this action, the KKK also conveyed to African Americans how they were hated, seen as the carriers of evil and a threat to the white man's way of life. By wiping out an enemy, they hoped their projected fears and inadequacies would be quelled.

Volkan (2006) argues that such early assaults, traumas, and fears are transgenerational and travel down the generations on both sides of the divide. Although the KKK is now a shadow of its former self, the long-term effects of such behavior are seen in the profiling of various non-white groups, including Native Americans and others by police and other citizens (American Civil Liberties Union, 2005; Sentencing Project, 2004). Due to uneven application of the law, those profiled lead more guarded lives. They are among our current scapegoats in the sense that they become containers for the anxieties of the profilers. They are also potential sources of violence today.

Another example of scapegoating is bullying in our schools. The same mechanisms are in operation. A particular kid, or set of kids, is chosen for attack, often indirectly and with the bullies' identities well hidden. This is especially true in cyber-attacks. The victims do not know whom to trust or fear, their grades plummet, their parents are often unaware, and teachers are not trusted. Belle Hankey, 18, put it this way. "I hated walking in the halls, thinking that you could be walking by the person that [sic] hates you... It's terrifying. You think that it could be your friends, a stranger, anyone. The person sitting next to you in math class" (Allen, 2013). Earlier, Phoebe Prince killed herself in response to bullying (Giacobbe, 2010).

As elsewhere, the bullies project their fears onto the victims in the unconscious belief that through the scapegoats the perpetrators' intrapsychic "sins" will be removed. More specifically, scapegoats are chosen to cover the perpetrators' own vulnerabilities. Sadly, this bullying may lead to a violent and deadly response by those bullied. A year after Columbine, "an analysis by officials at the US Secret Service of 37 premeditated school shootings found that bullying, which some of the shooters described 'in terms that approached torment,' played the major role in more than two-thirds of the attacks" (Adams & Roussakoff, 1999).

The same process is often in operation in violence among intimates: A perception of betrayal by a spouse, lover or family member often leads to outbursts of rage, bodily harm, and even death. Someone must bear the "sin" and pay the price to ease the injury and shame of betrayal by assaulting the betrayer(s). In many of these situations, easy access to guns makes a fatal outcome even more likely.

GROUP DYNAMICS: ABUSE OF POWER BY THE GROUP LEADER

In therapy groups large and small the leader is a key figure, and though often quiet, the leader is very involved emotionally. This is especially true when there is high tension and matching feelings in the group. As the author often says, the feelings in the group pass through his body, enabling him to share in the group experience and giving him another way to understand the group struggle. Sometimes the leader is unable to bear the tension and acts to protect her/himself from that discomfort, but doing this often harms the group. Some of the harm is modest and easily corrected, but sometimes it is more serious. Sometimes, it can become an abuse of the leader's role and have characteristics similar to scapegoating in that the leader is asking the group to bear the leader's discomfort.

For example, in one psychiatric hospital, a successful community meeting leader was replaced by a young psychiatrist named Ted, a seemingly pleasant man, though he had an edge. Stressed by the complexity and intensity of a 50+ person group and staff, his edge became sharpened. Community meetings can easily regress into disorder if not managed in a firm but understanding manner. This additional stress led Ted to enforce his authority and respond in a non-empathic manner, sometimes making snide and injurious responses. The rage from these injuries spilled into all hospital activities. Patients arrived at their group therapy sessions belligerent and in pain and often raged at the group therapists. It spread to occupational therapy, individual therapy sessions, and onto the floors. Unwittingly, the community leader had abused his power and caused considerable injury.

The community meeting was what Rouchy (2002) called a secondary group of belonging, whose task was to be a container for the patients and staff and the other subgroups of the hospital. When it failed in its containing function, the other subgroups became ineffective and some patients became violent. The management of the second group of belonging resolved this by replacing Ted with a leader who addressed the injuries and significantly reduced their occurrence. For Rouchy (2002), primary groups of belonging are the extended family in which one is imbedded and "includes cousins, close friends, domestic help, pets etc." (p. 211). Depending on the culture, they can also include "religious affiliation, class, ethnic group" (p. 211). This primary group of belonging forms one's cultural identity. The secondary groups of belonging are social institutions for certain purposes outside the primary ones, such as businesses and governmental bodies that can protect the primary groups of belonging (p. 213). Therapy groups would fall into the second category, as would community meetings and a management group.

VIOLENCE IN AMERICA

Role of the Abuse of Power in the United States

Stressful issues at the United States level are much more intense and complex than those of the therapy group or the community meeting and its hospital-wide effects, but the dynamics are similar. As with the community meeting, abuse of power humiliates those subject to that power, and such humiliation generates rage and the risk of counterviolence, as had happened throughout the hospital. Humiliation by the powerful has been a theme throughout U.S. history since the time of Columbus, which Stannard (1992, Prologue) argues led to "the most massive act of genocide in the history of the world" of Native Americans in the Americas. That initial demeaning, cruelty, and violence inflicted on Native Americans repeated itself with other groups, the most notable being African Americans and slavery (Zinn, 2009). Many other well-known internal conflicts and abuses of power have raged over the years in the United States and elsewhere. Important as those abuses of power may be, I will focus on a few examples of abuse involving African Americans and outline what knowledge of therapy groups and community meetings can bring to that table.

For instance, on March 3, 1991, police officers stopped Rodney King following a high-speed car chase, brutally kicked and beat him while other officers stood by and watched. Later, the officers involved were cleared of all charges (Rodney King, n.d.). The rioting that ensued was an understandable response to injustice and abuse of power, but it is much more complex than that. As Rouchy (2002) argues, when a dominant race treats another race as inferior, it cuts to the core of the identity of that group and its members. It threatens their primary groups of belonging.

Observing an intercultural conference using large group and small group settings, Rouchy noted their dynamics. The participants met in small groups where the members spoke in their own language and in a large multilingual group—without translation. The members represented four national groups. Each had activities and groups in which their own language was spoken, except for one whose language was not used. This was protested and resulted in negation of feelings of belonging and a fragmentation of identity. In brief, the group whose language was not included felt demeaned, whether the abuse was intended or not. Rouchy (2002) noted that those whose language was not included suffered an assault on their primary group of belonging that language represents, threatening a core aspect of their identity.

Using somewhat different language, Volkan (1998), a psychoanalyst and group therapist, described the same phenomena in large nation-size or subnation-size groups. He noted how lost battles in the sometime distant past, which were often brutal and humiliating, could generate a victim identity in that nation and with it a desire for revenge to correct that. He calls such events "chosen traumas," in which, though the large group makes the choice out of awareness, the chosen trauma encapsulates the group's experience, giving it meaning and a new group identity. Further, as noted elsewhere, he argues that such injuries and humiliations are transgenerational and are carried in the psyches of future generations, nurturing future conflict (Volkan, 2006). Rice and Benson (2005) applied the same framework to understanding the relationship between the humiliation of the Irish Famine through British neglect and the subsequent civil war in Northern Ireland. One could view this as the final battle in a series that began in the 12th century and followed a transgenerational path, passed down through stories, myths, and projective identification from parents to children, making the pain ever present. This long-term transgenerational humiliation—and its threat to the African Americans' primary groups of belonging in Los Angeles—was part of the dynamic in the outburst around Rodney King, noted above, whose wistful comment, "Can we all get along" will be addressed later. The same history was carried within the police force leading to the assault. More recently, the Trayvon Martin case in Florida resurrected the issue again (Shooting of Trayvon Martin, n.d.). The abuse had traveled down the generations, leading to potential retaliation. Other authors suggest similar unfinished business that has traveled through the generations with Native Americans (Poupart, 2002; Stannard, 1992; Zinn, 2009).

Is there any solution? Must we just go on killing each other? Sometimes it seems that is how it will be. Positions among different groups in the United States seem entrenched, angry, and fearful. However, some group therapy research and a case example suggest a more hopeful direction.

GROUP DYNAMICS: REPARATION IN THERAPY GROUPS AS A WAY TO CONTAIN CONFLICT AND MANAGE IT IN THE FUTURE

A therapy group can be a vehicle for healing and also a source of conflict and injury. Addressing those injuries effectively generates more healing, though it is not always easy. Tuckman and Jensen (1977) reviewed research on the developmental phases of time-limited groups, including the original work of Tuckman himself (1965). They found the results had much in common and confirmed the observation of Tuckman's original work. From this study, the authors revised Tuckman's original observation of four developmental stages to five. The original four stages were described alliteratively as Forming, Storming, Norming, and Performing, to which they now added Adjourning, addressing the ending of the group. In brief, the groups perform a series of tasks to enable the collective to function. One learns that this is a place to speak about concerns and differences with relative safety. When the group cannot do this, it becomes difficult to do its task, and the group's safety and effectiveness become compromised. Elsewhere, the author likened this stage and its processes to what Klein called movement from the paranoid-schizoid position to the depressive position, from seeing others as "its" to persons like oneself. The depressive position refers to the loss of the isolation and narcissism of the paranoid-schizoid position and to the inclusion and valuing of the other that allows reparation (Rice, 1992). DeMare (1972) speaks similarly about the tension in any group between movement from "oneness to multiplicity" in groups, where one can be a whole unit and also recognize its multiplicity at the same time and allow a place for it.

An example of storming in a group led by the author occurred one evening when Mary got into a head-to-head battle with Bob. She stormed out of the group, as she had often done in the past, sometimes for several weeks. This time, she sat in her car and returned in about 15 minutes. While she was gone, members disagreed about what had happened between Mary and Bob. When she returned, the group welcomed her back and she spoke openly about how Bob had minimized her pain at the upcoming loss to cancer of a recent friend to whom she had become strongly attached. He even seemed to mock her, she added. Mary often fled as her first choice when addressing the demeaning behavior of her mother. In situations like this, she was returning to behavior that had served her in the past, but usually with limited returns. The group pressed Bob to look at his part in the process. He was quiet for some time, then broke the silence by telling how he had been with his family over the weekend and had watched his father, who has Parkinson's disease, struggle to eat his food. Frequently, when trying to get food into his mouth, his face fell onto his plate, and his mother had to help him lift it off. Bob knew his father was going to die from Parkinson's, but not when. He could not bear to watch his father's deterioration.

When Bob told his story, the group shifted because members understood what had happened. Mary felt much less injured and understood how her story had affected Bob. Bob apologized for his treatment of Mary, saying her concern brought his painful weekend back to him. It was as though attacking Mary would take away his pain. Without this careful reflection by the group members, this event could have turned into scapegoating. Had the rest of the group joined Bob in his criticism of Mary, they might well have driven her out of the group or placed her in unnecessary pain by allowing her to bear the group's discomfort and take it with her or within her—at least for now.

Reparation in the United States

Rodney King's plaintive cry, "Can we all get along," needs a response. A first step in this direction may be found in the Indian poet White Wolf's complaint (White Wolf, 2013) and Hitchens's commentary (Hitchens, 2000). White Wolf complained that even after all the Native American genocide, there had never been an apology from the U.S. government, and Hitchens noted the same for both Native and African Americans. By contrast, Germany, through Chancellor Willy Brandt, acknowledged its complicity in the Holocaust (Fastenberg, 2010), and Prime Minister Tony Blair publicly apologized to Ireland for Britain's responsibility for its genocide-like behavior toward Ireland and the Irish during the famine (Marks, 1997).

In fact, despite White Wolf's complaint, the U.S. government, through President Obama, did issue an apology to Native Americans for its genocidal behavior (H.R. 3326, 2010). That apology, however, is a long legal document. This is an important start, but it still needs to become public and enter the marketplace of day-to-day life and conversation, so the entire United States can have its Norming phase or Reparation process.

This is not to suggest that marketplace conversations about and apologies for injuries that have lasted for hundreds of years inflicted by the dominant parts of society on less powerful parts will prevent future violence. Nor will they remove the wish for acts of revenge by those abused. However, some such processes may make the need for violence and revenge less likely because it makes the individual and collective unconscious conscious, gives it a voice, and reduces the need for violent action. This gets us a little closer to Rodney King's wish.

Ironically, as the author was writing this, President Obama had just responded to the outcome of the Trayvon Martin/George Zimmerman trial in Florida. Zimmerman was declared not guilty, leading to large protests throughout the country and a potential for violence. The President accepted the verdict as within the letter of the law. However, speaking as an African American, he told the nation that because of a long violent history African Americans, himself included, view the world differently from white people. He said they were used to being followed by store owners when intending to purchase something, which does not happen to white people (Obama, 2013). And this suggests spontaneous profiling: A black man cannot be trusted. This began a reparative conversation, letting other members of a very large group, the United States, know what it was like to be different and to have a different and violent history. The question is, will others join in the conversation.

A government cannot mandate such a conversation, though it may model it as in this instance and support the process. Other secondary groups of belonging within a society can begin such conversations. Although it may not have seemed so at the time, Martin Luther King, Jr., triggered conversations about race relations that have continued right up to the recent movie, *Lee Daniel's The Butler* (Daniels, 2013).

GROUP DYNAMICS: REPARATION AND MOURNING

Although reparation provides an opportunity to acknowledge collective and inflicted hurts on others and be forgiven and forgive, it also prepares the way for personal and collective mourning. It is a way of finding a place in the collective psyche where the mourning maintains consciously and subconsciously the reality of our history and owns it. Robert, the group member discussed earlier, was unable to move forward in the group until he mourned his loss of Suzie and found a place for her in his memory and his group experience. For Jews, memorials such as the Holocaust Memorial Museum in Washington, DC, help facilitate their mourning process. Being able to own and mourn both the injuries we and our progenitors inflicted on others and those inflicted on us, we continue the conversation and may reduce repeating the violence in our history. Better to build memorials than continue our wars.

CONCLUSION

In this paper, I as a group therapist reflected on violence in the United States on the broad canvas upon which all other violent acts are set. Using examples from therapy groups large and small, I discussed the role of impulsive actions over actions informed by reflection in the generating of violence. I examined the roles of scapegoating and abuse of power as particular cases in point. I also noted how such potentially violent processes, if left unaddressed, will move forward often out of awareness and hamper the work of the group.

There are parallels between these group processes and sources of violence in the United States: for example, the effects of the slaughter of Native Americans beginning with Columbus and the slavery of African Americans that followed. Unfinished business, including desires for revenge on both sides of a divide, is carried forward over the generations through stories, myths, and projective identification from parents to children. Reparation has an important role in healing old injuries in psychotherapy groups and also in the injuries that we as a society carry into the present. This is not to suggest that the violent context triggers all acts of violence, but as in all types of psychotherapy groups, the context is crucial to the resolution of conflict. If the group-as-a-whole is unsafe, it becomes difficult to resolve interpersonal conflicts within the group.

Just as there are some people who do not respond well to group therapy, so there are some people who are more prone to violence than others whatever the context, such as psychopaths, whose violence occurs within intimate relations and is often considered the result of early failed attachments (Meloy, 1992) or of unusual brain functioning (Dutton, 2012, p. 6). To understand who is more prone to such violence requires ongoing careful research and astute clinical observation. Meanwhile, we cannot neglect the context and the transgenerational memories in which all such violence and conflicts are set. A sound secondary group of belonging can help contain such events, though some suggest that society—a large secondary group of belonging—may be becoming more psychopathic (Dutton, 2012, p. 131). If true, this makes understanding the context of violence even more important.

REFERENCES

Adams, L., & Russakoff, D. (1999, June 12). Dissecting Columbine's cult of the athlete. *Washington Post*. Retrieved July 25, 2013, from http://www.washingtonpost.com/wp-srv/national/daily/june99/columbine12.htm

Allan, J. F., McKenna, J., & Hind, K. (2012). Brain resilience: Shedding light into the black box of adventure processes. *Australian Journal of Outdoor Education, 16*(1), 3-14.

Allen, E. (2013, August 7). A happy school life lost to unseen tormentors. *Boston Globe*. Retrieved September 12, 2013, from http://www.bostonglobe.com/metro/2013/08/06/former-concord-carlisle-high-school-student-recounts-terrifying-incidents-bullying/LtYtan0u4y7bsvGOgAgbwL/story.html

American Civil Liberties Union (ACLU). (2005). Racial profiling: Definition. Retrieved September 15, 2013, from https://www.aclu.org/racial-justice/racial-profiling-definition

Cillizza, C. (December 16, 2012). The gun debate: Are the. Newtown, Conn., killings a tipping point? *Washington Post*. Retrieved November 27, from http://articles.washingtonpost.com/2012-12-16/politics/35864130_1_gun-control-gun-ownership-stricter-gun-laws

Daniels, L. (Director). (2013). *Lee Daniels' The Butler* [Motion picture]. US: Laura Ziskind Productions.

DeMare, P. B. (1972). *Perspectives in group psychotherapy: A theoretical background*. New York: Science House.

Dutton, K. (2012). *The wisdom of psychopaths: What saints, spies and serial killers can teach us about success*. New York: Scientific American, Farrar, Straus and Giroux.

Fastenberg, D. (2010. June 17). The Holocaust. Retrieved July 30, 2013, from http://www.time.com/time/specials/packages/article/0,28804,1997272_1997273_1997275,00.html

Foulkes, S. H. (1948). *Introduction to group-analytic psychotherapy: Studies in the social integration of individuals and groups*. Exeter, England: Wheaton, Ltd.

Foulkes, S. H. (1977). *Therapeutic group analysis*. New York: International Universities Press.

Giacobbe, A. (2010, June). Who failed Phoebe Prince? *Boson Magazine*. Retrieved September 12, 2013, from http://www.bostonmagazine.com/2010/05/phoebe-prince/

Hitchens, C. (2000, May 29). Who's sorry now? *The Nation*, p. 9.

Hopper, E. (2012). Introduction: Aggregation/massification as the fourth basic assumption in the unconscious life of groups and group-like social systems. In *Trauma and organizations: The theory of incohesion* (pp. xxxi-li). London: Karnac.

Hopper, E. (2003). *The social unconscious*. London: Jessica Kingsley.

H.R. 3326, 111th Cong. (2010).

Hudson, W. (2013, November 7). Remembering Matthew Shepard: 13 years later. Retrieved October 10, 2013, from http://www.huffingtonpost.com/waymon-hudson/matthew-shepard_b_1006878.html

Johnson, R. (1997). Contested borders, contingent lives: An introduction. In D. L. Steinberg, D. Epstein, & R. Johnson (Eds.), *Border patrols: Policing the boundaries of heterosexuality* (pp. 1-31). London: Cassell.

Klein, R. H., & Schermer, V. L. (2015). Toward understanding and treating violence in america: Some contributions from group dynamic and group therapy perspectives. *International Journal of Group Psychotherapy, 65*(1), 1-28.

Ku Klux Klan. (n.d.). In *Wikipedia*. Retrieved September 12, 2013, from http://en.wikipedia.org/wiki/Ku_Klux_Klan

Marks, K. (1997, June 2). Blair issues apology for Irish Potato Famine. Retrieved September, 25, 2013, from http://www.independent.co.uk/news/blair-issues-apology-for-irish-potato-famine-1253790.html

Meloy, J. R. (2004). *The psychopathic mind: Origins, dynamics and treatment*. Lanham, MD: Rowman & Littlefield (Original work published 1998).

Meloy, J. R. (1992). *Violent attachments*. Northvale, NJ: Jason Aronson.

Obama, B. (2013). Transcript: President Obama addresses race, profiling and Florida law. Retrieved October 13, 2013, from http://www.cnn.com/2013/07/19/politics/obama-zimmerman-verdict/index.html

Patterson, T. (2012, December 18). Will Newtown change America's attitudes toward guns? Retrieved November 27, 2013, from http://www.cnn.com/2012/12/17/us/newtown-gun-control

Poupart, L. M. (2002). Crime and justice in American Indian communities. *Social Justice, 29*(1–2), 144.

Rice, C. A. (1992). Contributions from object relations. In R. H. Klein, H. S. Bernard, & D. L. Singer (Eds.), *Handbook of contemporary group psychotherapy: Contributions from object relations, self psychology, and social systems theories* (pp. 27-54). Madison, CT: International Universities Press.

Rice, C. A. (2011). Three perspectives on the treatment of political prisoners and trauma victims: A commentary. *International Journal of Group Psychotherapy, 61*(1), 73-83.

Rice, C. A., & Benson, J. (2005). Hungering for revenge: The Irish famine, the Troubles and shame-rage cycles, and their role in group therapy in Northern Ireland. *Group Analysis, 38*(2), 219-235.

Rodney King. (n.d.). In *Wikipedia*. Retrieved August 12, 2013, from http://en.wikipedia.org/wiki/Rodney_King

Rouchy, J. C. (2002). Cultural identity and groups of belonging. *Group, 26*(3), 205-217.

Roy, J. M. (2002). *Love to hate: America's obsession with hatred and violence*. New York: Columbia University Press.

Rutan, J. S., Stone, W., & Shea, J. J. (2007). *Psychodynamic group psychotherapy*. New York: Guilford.

Sentencing Project. (2004). *Reducing racial disparity in the criminal justice system: A manual for practitioners and policymakers*. Washington, DC: The Sentencing Project: Research and Advocacy for Reform. Retrieved September 15, 2013, from http://www.sentencingproject.org/doc/publications/rd_reducingracialdisparity.pdf

Shooting of Trayvon Martin. (n.d.). In *Wikipedia*. Retrived August 30, 2013, from http://en.wikipedia.org/wiki/Shooting_of_Trayvon_Martin

Stannard, D. E. (1992). *American holocaust: A conquest of the New World.* New York: Oxford University Press.

Thornberry, T. P., Krohn, M. D., Lizotte, A. J., & Smith, C. A. (2003). *Gangs and delinquency in developmental perspective.* New York: Cambridge University Press.

Tuckman, B. W. (1965). Developmental sequence in small groups. *Psychological Bulletin, 63,* 384-399.

Tuckman, B. W., & Jensen, M. A. C. (1977). Stages of small group development revisited. *Group & Organization Studies, 2*(4), 419-427.

Volkan, V. (1998). *Blood lines: From ethnic pride to ethnic terrorism.* Boulder, CO: Westview.

Volkan, V. (2006). *Killing in the name of identity: A study of bloody conflicts.* Charlottesville, VA: Pitchstone.

White wolf. (2013). *the indigenous* [Video file]. Retrieved August 15, 2013, from http://www.youtube.com/watch?v=YR0FAfVban4

Zinn, H. (2009). *A people's history of the United States: 1492–present.* New York: Harper Collins.

The Dangerous Role of Silence in the Relationship Between Trauma and Violence: A Group Response

SUZANNE B. PHILLIPS, PSY.D., ABPP, CGP, FAGPA

ABSTRACT

This article considers that somewhere in the space between violence and trauma is dangerous silence. Silence intensifies the impact of trauma, and trauma that goes unspoken, un-witnessed, and unclaimed too often "outs itself" as more violence to self or others. Relevant empirical evidence on the impact of civilian interpersonal violence, combat trauma, school shootings, bullying, and domestic violence confirms this tragic cycle. Crucial to addressing the danger of silence in this cycle, the article examines the centrality of silence existentially, neuropsychologically, psychologically, developmentally, interpersonally, and culturally in relation to violence. The bridge to voicing and assimilating the unspeakable is empathic connection with others. Drawing upon two different types of group programs, the article demonstrates that group can serve as that bridge. Group process has the potential to undo the dangerous role of silence in the relationship of trauma and violence.

What makes silence dangerous in the aftermath of violence is that it invites and intensifies trauma. It precludes the safety, remembering, grieving and connection necessary to heal from traumatic events. According to van der Merwe & Gobodo-Madikizela (2008) "trauma will out" in one way or another, even if

---

Suzanne B. Phillips is Adjunct Full Professor at Long Island University Post.

it is silenced or denied (p. 33). Cathy Caruth (1996) tells us that trauma haunts the survivor. It "imposes itself" repeatedly, be it in nightmare, bodily experience, or behavior (p. 4). Trauma is "always a story of a wound that cries out" to be heard and to be assimilated (p. 4). As such, I suggest that unspoken, unwitnessed and unclaimed trauma from violence "outs itself" as violence to self or others, a vicious cycle that is tragic.

The goal of this article is to make this reality clear and to consider the potential of group experience to disrupt this cycle by making room for trauma to be held, witnessed, understood, enacted, voiced, and shared on many levels and in many ways. I begin with a brief look at the empirical evidence that underscores the role of violence in causing trauma and the nature of unvoiced and unassimilated trauma in manifesting as more violence. From there, I will consider the centrality and complexity of silence in the interconnection of violence and trauma. To consider the varying ways that group process addresses the silent scars of violence, I will draw upon my own experience with varied group experiences, including a program for suicide survivors and an informal group with military women.

There have been theoretical considerations that confirm the relevance, stages, and efficacy of group in the aftermath of trauma (Herman, 2007; Klein & Phillips, 2008; Klein & Schermer, 2000) as well as descriptions of evidenced-based group interventions (Buchele & Spitz, 2004; Lubin & Johnson, 2008; Mendelsohn et al., 2011). What I propose here is that varied types of group experience, even if not specifically designed as trauma treatment, serve to break the silence imposed by violent trauma and facilitate healing that reduces the potential for trauma to escalate more violence. "The self is both autonomous and socially dependent, vulnerable enough to be undone by violence and yet resilient enough to be reconstructed with the help of empathic others" (Brison, 2002, p. 38).

THE ROLE OF VIOLENCE IN CAUSING TRAUMA

Violence is defined as "the intentional use of physical force or power, threatened or actual, against oneself, another person, or against a group or community, which either results in, or has a high likelihood of resulting in injury, death, psychological harm, mal-development, or deprivation" (World Health Organization, 2003). It is estimated that violence takes the lives of more than 1.5 million people annually, with just over 50% due to suicide, 35% due to homicide, and just over 12% as a direct result of war or some other form of conflict (World Health Organization, 2008).

Recent research on the effects of interpersonal violence on psychological outcomes in men and women corroborate earlier studies and underscore the impact. Using data drawn from the National Comorbidity Survey Replication Study involving 5,692 women and men, Iverson and colleagues (2012) found that approximately 46% of the women and 42% of the men reported one or more types of interpersonal violence in their lifetime. Women were more likely to experience kidnapping, physical assault by an intimate partner, rape, sexual assault, and stalking, whereas men were more likely to experience mugging or physical assault by someone other than parents or an intimate partner. The results revealed that interpersonal violence is associated with risk for many mental disorders and attempted suicide.

Further evidence of the impact of violence are the latest studies reported by the National Center for Post Traumatic Stress that suggest that 10–18% of combat troops serving in Operation Iraqi Freedom (OIF) and Operation Enduring Freedom (OEF) have probable post traumatic stress disorder (PTSD) following deployment, with continued prevalence over time. Adding to this, for both female and male veterans, the risk of developing PTSD from sexual assault in the military is similar in magnitude to the risk of substantial combat trauma (Kang, Dalager, Mahan, & Ishii, 2005), and female and male veterans with a history of military sexual trauma (MST) are more likely to meet criteria for depression (Kimerling et al., 2010).

TRAUMA RESULTING IN VIOLENCE TO SELF

Given the degree of trauma suffered in combat and from MST, there is evidence that such trauma often results in violence to self. Statistics indicate that nationally, one in every five suicides is a veteran (Hargarten, Burnson, Campo, & Cook, 2014). Weiner, Richmond, Conigliaro, and Wiebe (2011) found that 25% of all female deaths in the military are attributed to suicide. Suicide is the leading cause of death among military women.

Echoing the danger of silence, one veteran who lost his friend to suicide shares, "The bad part about it is that he didn't give us a chance to talk. I mean, if he had just said, 'Hey, Clint, I'm thinking about doing this.' I could have said, 'Hey man, I'm thinking about doing it too. You got to have that conversation. You have to tell somebody, as embarrassing as it is,'" he said. "All I ever considered when I thought about [suicide] was the guilt I was feeling and just wanting a way out, wanting to not have those memories anymore" (Hargarten et al., 2013).

VIOLENCE AND TRAUMA RESULTING IN VIOLENCE TOWARD OTHERS

In addition to self-directed violence, aggression perpetrated by veterans has become a concern in the media, the judicial system, and clinical settings (Alvarez & Sontag, 2008; Taft et al., 2009). Killgore and colleagues (2008) in surveying over 1,000 Operation Iraqi Freedom veterans found that exposure to violent combat, killing another person, and contact with high levels of human trauma were predictive of greater risk-taking, including greater alcohol use and physical and verbal aggression to others, even before returning home.

Recent research finds that PTSD symptom severity adds to and is a much stronger predictor of aggressive behavior than the impact of combat alone (Hoge, Auchterlonie, & Milliken, 2006). Given the military code of silence, the expectation that civilians will not understand, and the anger and avoidance associated with PTSD, the finding that PTSD exacerbates the impact of combat exposure becomes understandable.

A 2006 study in the *Journal of Marital and Family Therapy* looked at veterans who sought marital counseling at a Veterans Affairs medical center in the Midwest between 1997 and 2003. Those given a diagnosis of PTSD were "significantly more likely to perpetrate violence toward their partners," with more than 80 percent committing at least one act of violence in the previous year and almost half committing at least one severe act (Alvarez & Sontag, 2008).

A 2004 study by the United States Department of Justice of the U.S. veteran prison population found that U.S. veterans were less likely than the general population to offend, but if they were in prison, it was for violent and sexual offenses. As such, it is important to recognize that such violence often results in a legacy of domestic violence that adds to the evidence of violence suffered and repeated. Michael Paymar (2000), author of *Violent No More*, reports that, "Children are present during 80% of the assaults against their mothers" (p. 1). The most recent research on domestic violence suggests that exposure to interparental violence (IPV) leaves one at risk of both later perpetration and victimization, with the exposure history of one's partner adding to the risk (Fritz, Slep, & O'Leary, 2012).

The cycle of violence and unspoken trauma resulting in more violence is also found in the civilian population. Two studies on threat assessment co-directed by Robert Fein and conducted by the U.S. Secret Service were reported in the February 2014 *Monitor on Psychology;* the studies consider those people who have already been violent in attacks on public figures and school shooting cases (Fein & Vossekuil, 1999; Vossekuil et al., 2002). Fein indicates that "targeted violence is the end result of an understandable and often discernible process of thinking and behavior—people just don't snap" (p. 38). What is of great concern is that a common theme reported by attackers includes an experience of loss, failure, or public humiliation in the days or weeks before the attack. Often the attackers felt that they had been bullied or persecuted by others. Commenting on this in terms of threat assessment, Robert Fein suggests that when normal ways of coping with stress don't work and life feels unbearably stressful, some resort to violence (Miller, 2014).

Bullying-related suicides in the United States and other countries add to this picture. Yale University research, considering 37 studies from different countries, suggests that bully victims are between two to nine times more likely to consider suicide than non-victims (Kim & Leventhal, 2008). Underscoring the role of silence in the trauma to violence connection is a study of more than 3,000 high school students, which reports that even when students were personally threatened, they remained silent. Of the

12% who actually reported being threatened at school, only 26% told a teacher or school official (Miller, 2014).

The recent film *Strain* (Chang, Havener, & Armstrong, 2012)), captures this dangerous silence. It is an 11-minute anti-bullying film that tells the story of two friends. One is bullied while the other (one of the filmmakers) watches but remains silent. The bullied friend dies by suicide (Breschisci, 2013). The film is the silent friend's attempt to bear witness and send a message to avert such tragedy. In a unique example of the medium being the message, this film uses silence in a poignant way. Only background sounds and noises are heard—there are no voices.

THE CENTRALITY OF SILENCE IN THE IMPACT OF VIOLENT TRAUMA

Existentially, neuropsychologically, psychologically, developmentally, interpersonally, and culturally, violent traumatic events silence us and those around us. Unclaimed and unvoiced, such violence often "outs" as more violence.

Existentially

Existentially, violent trauma is one that cannot be comprehended. Trauma feels unspeakable because of the inadequacy of language to convey the experience. Philosopher and survivor of rape and attempted murder, Susan Brison (2002) suggests that trauma introduces a "surd"—a nonsensical entry into the series of events of our life, making it difficult to carry on with the series. In Latin, "surd" comes from "surdus" meaning deaf, silent, stupid. Linguistically, a surd is a voiceless sound. In math, it is an irrational number. For Brison, the violent rape that was intended to kill her was an event that fit no predictable pattern and "more importantly it was a loss of sound—silence." She asks, "How do we speak the unspeakable?" (p. 103).

Neuropsychologically

Faced with a life-threatening event, our human neuropsychology takes over. Most people do not have a coherent story of what has happened because they have been busy surviving. The right hemisphere of the brain associated with survival behaviors and emotional expression is activated and the left verbal-linguistic part of our brain is suppressed. The body prepares to respond with the survival reflexes of fight, flight, and freeze.

Given the nature of this response, it is likely that most people who have experienced traumatic events will have lingering traces manifested in symptoms of hyperarousal, intrusion, numbing, avoidance, and negative thoughts and moods. Rape survivor Nancy Raine (1999) describes the experience as follows: "The instant I was free the seed of terror that had been planted in those hours burst open spitting out an uncharted island where I was now stranded.... Terror overwhelmed me" (p. 15). Because violent events are encoded under fight/flight/freeze conditions, the memory of the traumatic event is not like the memory for ordinary events that can be told as narrative with a beginning, middle, and end. Memories are experienced as fragments of highly charged visual images, bodily feelings, tactile sensations, or sensory reactivity to reminders of the event. Traumatic memories are the imprints of trauma without words. "Words had no referents and no beauty of their own. Memories were drained of meaning because the person who had them no longer existed" (Raine, 1999, p. 14).

Psychologically—The Loss of the Core Self

Adult onset trauma is what Gloria Boulanger (2007) refers to as being "wounded by reality," and which she describes as a dismantling of the known self—one's physical capacities, cognitive ability, time, and verbal and emotional connections to others. Boulanger describes victims as suffering a "loss of the sense of agency," that is, the ability to think, problem solve, make things happen. In work with rape victims, I have come to know that the sounds, smells, and sights that serve as trauma triggers bring back not only terror but a sense of shame and self-blame for not fighting, for being victims. So many ask, "How can I be a victim?"

Adding to this is a loss of time continuity, of feeling frozen in the traumatic moment without a sense of the past, an interest in the present, or access to the future. Both the self-blame and the feeling of being lost in time become barriers to thinking, much less talking, about the horror endured. "Survivors instinctively understand that what they experience is different in kind from all other experience. This difference seems to destroy the threads of narrative the moment one tries to weave them" (Raine, 1999, p. 112).

Developmentally—The Unclaimed Self

Compared to adult onset trauma, relational or developmental trauma is the wordless horror of child abuse, the assault on the body and mind of a child that necessitates dissociation as defense because the chaotic, convulsive flooding of unregulated affect is beyond what can be endured or represented (Bromberg, 2011). Early on, it must be split off into a self-state that cannot coexist in a single state of consciousness without destabilizing self-continuity. From there, it stays split off as a dissociated mental structure that vigilantly anticipates the "shadow" of trauma before it can arrive unexpectedly. Dissociation turns the mind into a smoke detector and life into an unlived waiting period. Silence is intrinsic to the legacy because experiences have been invalidated by significant others and language has been used to translate them out of experience.

Interpersonally

Relevant to the centrality of silence in the aftermath of violent trauma is the loss of community and connectedness. Trauma isolates us from our familiar self as well as from others. Stolorow (2007) describes emotional trauma with the accompanying feelings of "singularity, estrangement, and solitude" (p. 49). Reflecting the sense of losing touch on many levels, rape survivor Brison (2002) describes, "The trauma has changed me forever, and if I insist too often that my friends and family acknowledge it, that's because I'm afraid they don't know who I am" (p. 21).

Often the link between violence, trauma, and more violence is a function of the fact that "Trauma won't be heard." Drawing on the research of Harber and Pennebaker (1992), Bloom and Reichert (1998) state,

> Bearers of disturbing information and negative emotions are suppressed in various ways. Listeners switch the topic away from trauma. They attempt to press their own less upsetting perspective of the trauma upon the victim. Listeners tend to exaggerate the victim's personal responsibility in the traumatic situation. If these strategies do not work to get the victim to stop talking, then the listener will avoid contact with the victim altogether. (p. 89)

Included in this social response is that of "the bystanders." Violence is not just a function of the dyad of perpetrator and victim (Bloom & Reichert, 1998). It includes the bystander whose reaction bears on the degree of violence. If we consider that unspoken and unheard trauma potentiates more violence because silence implies compliance, then there are no innocent bystanders (Phillips, 2014).

A painful example is the devastation and danger of being silenced as a survivor of suicide. In the aftermath of losing their son to suicide, Bill and Beverly Feigelman (Feigelman, Jordan, McIntosh, & Feigelman, 2012) describe a bereavement group at which a parent is told that the group is only for those whose children have died by natural means. They report the case of a neighbor who crosses the street in order not to speak to a parent suicide survivor. They describe the silence borne of assumed judgment, self-stigmatization, and the social ambiguity that leaves some bystanders not knowing what to say.

Culturally

Be it the culture of an organized religion, a military setting, or an extended family, dangerous silence often reflects a code embraced by victim and perpetrator. In what has been termed the "sacred silence" of the church scandals, the perpetrators exploited the confused and frightened silence of children and the idealization of congregations to cover atrocity (Cozzens, 2002). There were no words or signs of the "soul murder" (Shengold, 1989).

The military code of silence takes a toll on those who carry home from war the memories, moral wounds, and imprints of the horror they dare not share. Be it out of shame, guilt, or fear of contaminating those they love, silencing "the things that they carried" too often unfolds as violence to self or others (O'Brien,

2009). From another perspective, this code of silence has been misused by perpetrators of military sexual trauma. Perpetrators have exploited rank and characterized silence as strength to violate others and then have disavowed their crimes. As described in the 2013 documentary film, *The Invisible War,* seeking help by victims is physically, culturally, and emotionally dangerous (Ziering, Barklow, & Kirby, 2012).

In the silence of generations who have known atrocity, like survivors of the Holocaust, there is the mix of needing to remember, wishing to forget, and protecting future generations. The result is a haunting legacy. As Gabrille Schwab (2010) says of her childhood in postwar Germany, "Words could be split into what they said and what they did not say...I had a vague sense of something deadly, of words filled with skeletons" (p. 43).

GROUP RESPONSES TO SILENCE

Violence traumatizes people and destroys language. The silence that often results compromises healing, assaults connection, and perpetuates more violence. As such, the group modality, in many configurations, becomes an invaluable resource and response. (In the examples that follow, information has been deleted or altered to protect confidentiality.)

In *Narrating Our Healing,* Chris N. van de Merwe and Pumla Gobodo-Madikizela (2008) draw on their experiences with the Truth and Reconciliation Commission (TRC) in South Africa. They remind us that telling the story of trauma is difficult, and that it is not in the simple sharing that healing begins but in being listened to with empathic concern. Stolorow (2007) refers to the need for an intersubjective context, a relational home to come into the language of emotional experience.

UNDOING THE SILENCE OF DEVASTATING LOSS

The loss of a loved one by suicide is devastating. It not only reflects the victim's violence to self from unbearable psychic pain, it unfolds into considerable trauma for the loved ones. Complicating and exacerbating the traumatic loss is silence.

Included in a research survey of 575 cases of parents who lost children from traumatic and non-traumatic causes, 462 were parents of children who died by suicide (Feigelman et al., 2012). Their responses to open-ended survey questions revealed experiences of stigma and stigmatization often expressed in subtle and non-obtrusive ways like silence and dismissal. As one father reports,

> People never said anything really bad to me [after Bobby hung himself]. It was not what they said; it was what they didn't say. Some people who I thought would offer solace remained quiet. And most people just said nothing [after my son's death] and seemed to try to avoid any discussion. It was as if my son never existed. (p. 39)

Most survivors are plagued by the question of why and feel shame, anger, guilt, and fear of judgment, both of self and loved one. Edwin Shneidman (1972) suggests that it is as if the person who commits suicide leaves his psychological skeleton in the survivor's emotional closet. The pain of this situation is often heightened by the ambiguous or withheld responses of others. As such, too many suicides remain hidden and silenced by family members. Because the suicide of a family member is a significant suicide risk factor for surviving family members, it is crucial we help survivors find a voice that can be heard by others.

INTERNATIONAL SUICIDE SURVIVOR DAY

> "If someone speaks, it gets lighter." (Freud, 1916–1917/1958, p. 407)

One of most valuable and utilized recommendations for suicide survivors has been suicide-survivor groups. Whether they are peer or professionally run, or even virtual groups, they have proven to be valuable for healing (Cerel, Padgett, & Reed, 2009; Feigelman et al., 2012; Garvin, 1997).

My own group experience with suicide survivors has been as a volunteer group leader on International Survivors of Suicide

Day. Leaders are a mix of professionals and those who themselves have suffered a loss. This annual event is held in cities and countries throughout the world on the Saturday before Thanksgiving, the start of the holiday season. On that day, 50 to 100 people gather to share an informal lunch with other survivors; view a film of a "leader-led survivor group"; listen to questions asked and answered by a trauma expert on the film; and in the afternoon, participate in homogeneous (loss of child, spouse, sibling, etc.) leader-led breakout groups (Feigelman et al., 2012).

For me, this is an example of how different configurations of group experience address multiple and complex needs. The survivors experience a large group event, an informal table group of mixed survivors, a psychoeducational group experience, the shared experience of viewing a survivor group on film, and the experience of being in small homogeneous groups. As such, this full-day group program offers many transformative aspects of trauma group intervention: safety, bearing witness, psychoeducation, validation and containment of feelings, finding a voice, altruism, and hope. Inherent in these aspects of group is the opportunity to move from silence to sharing in the context of connection.

BEARING WITNESS

I join a lunch table where I see a man sitting alone and two other women speaking. I introduce myself as a psychologist who has worked with survivors, whose two friends have suffered loss from suicide, and who comes each year to be one of the leaders. The women introduce themselves and share their losses of a few years ago. The man watches. When his young adult daughter arrives, she speaks for both about the loss of her mother a month earlier and the refusal of her brother to speak about it. What will unfold from this informal table discussion as more survivors fill the table is normalization of the fear of coming to such an event and validation of the difficulty of dealing with a suicide.

What will become apparent is the reality of different family reactions and intergenerational conflict regarding loss and expressions of grief. People will reveal anger toward family members who criticized them for coming, of the family pressure to keep suicide a secret, and of the relief of speaking with others who have lived through violent loss by suicide.

PSYCHOEDUCATION AND MEDIA

Media can serve an important role in trauma group work. They not only provide psychoeducation that facilitates normalizing, validating, and self-reflection, they invite identification at a safe distance. They model the power of verbal exchange and permission for differences. As such, they stimulate narrative. Each year, I observe members in the afternoon breakout groups refer to the survivor group in the film as a preface to bringing up a topic like the holidays, children, and so forth, or as a point of comparison with their own experience.

CONTAINMENT

As in other trauma groups, homogeneity fosters cohesion as a function of the commonality of experience. I have observed that such groups allow containment of details, images, and graphic descriptions with less overt retraumatization than heterogeneous groups, particularly in the acute stage of trauma. In the homogeneous groups of parent, sibling, and spouse suicide survivors, there is an invitation for members to say what they have not shared anywhere else. It is implicit in the modeling of those who have been there before that the group is a safe place. In the face of the graphic descriptions of a loved one's suicide, members hold each other with their eyes and often respond with tears that give support and permission to share and be held emotionally. Hearing about another's loss by suicide seems to make it possible to reconsider what they have faced and find a place for what they cannot quite believe.

GIVING VOICE

Suicide is a violent act that resonates in different ways with those who knew and loved the person lost. In my experience, a group that has benefited from this program includes the siblings of a brother or sister who has died by suicide. In their research with siblings, Dyregrov and Dyregrov (2005) call them "the forgotten bereaved" (p. 714). These researchers report that siblings in this situation rarely share outside the home for fear of stigma and rejection. In the home, they often restrain themselves from mentioning the death even though they have a need to speak with and be comforted by their parents.

Sitting together in a group on Suicide Survivor's Day, siblings talk about the fear of upsetting their bereft parents as well as the difficulty of being silent. Often they express anger toward the sibling who has died by suicide for creating such pain for everyone. They wonder if they were even loved or trusted by that brother or sister. Many register the fear of being like the sibling and possibly getting that desperate, asking, "Could I do that?"

As the leader to the sibling group, I have listened and at times invited clarification or interpretation of the non-verbal cues of members that seem to validate the shared feelings. Sometimes, I have invited group consideration of differences or confusion. Sometimes, I have used psychoeducation to clarify a topic like the causes of suicide and the psychic pain that it reflects. Although unknown to each other, sibling survivors embrace the opportunity to ask questions to learn what others have faced and how they have responded. Often, they reveal for the first time in these groups that they knew something about their sibling they feel they should have shared or acted upon. At such times, there is often mutual support for feelings of guilt, as well as validation of the common but unrealistic notion that they could have prevented the suicide. Stolorow (2007) would describe this group process as forming "a connection with a brother or sister who knows the same darkness" (p. 49).

ALTRUISM

The behavior of the quiet father at the lunch table mentioned above is an example of the power of group process in a one-day group experience. As it happens, this quiet father was in my breakout group that afternoon, and in stepping up to care for someone else, he became one of the most verbal members. On hearing another man with a frozen face share without emotion that his wife had taken her life the week before, the quiet father broke his silence to disclose the details and pain of his own wife's public suicide. The message of this unexpected disclosure seemed to be, "It feels unbearable, I know, but somehow we will find a way." He added that he appreciated that this was a group of spouses because he could finally speak without his children having to hear or cope with what he had seen. The others nodded in agreement. As happens in a group, the giving and getting is often unexpected but powerful and mutual.

International Survivors of Suicide Day is not unlike other full-day group programs offered in the aftermath of trauma, such as Care of Caregivers, Couples Connection, and Family Resiliency Programs for which there have been qualitative evaluations of effectiveness in reducing the primary and secondary impact of trauma (Klein & Phillips 2008; Underwood, 2008). What is important to consider is the transformative potency of group programs that may only last for a day. While many people will need more intervention to integrate violent trauma, reaching out in a group that requires one day of involvement may be a risk many can handle, one that holds potential for starting a healing process.

BREAKING THE MILITARY CODE OF SILENCE

When asked by organizations to offer informal groups for military women to facilitate their readjustment from military to civilian life, I intended to give those women an opportunity to come together and discuss related issues. I knew from the literature (Benedict, 2009; Caplan, 2011; Katz, Bloor, Cojucar, & Draper, 2007) and my own experiences speaking with and writing about military women, that reentering civilian life was a jolt. There was the need to make up for lost time away from children, the strain of redefining relationships, and the difficulty of putting aside all that they carried in order to be physically and emotionally present (Buchele & Spitz, 2004; Phillips, 2012a, 2012b, 2013; Phillips & Kane, 2008). For these groups, I had prepared some psycho-educational and humorous talking points, but I never used them.

The women who came together did not know each other. They spanned years and service from WW II to Desert Storm and Kuwait, as well as to Operation Iraqi Freedom and Operation Enduring Freedom in Afghanistan. Most were veterans; a few were active reservists. They were a mix of single, married, and divorced women. The rationale for the group was to offer them a place to be with other veterans or military women who understood issues of reintegration to civilian life. What unfolded across different groups was unexpected. They seemed captivated by each others' stories and patient with the latecomers who interrupted or members who walked around with agitation, returning only to respond to someone's issue from across the room. As the facilitator, I was mostly an empathic listener whose presence served to hold the group psychologically, facilitate sharing, and offer validation and support, if needed. I was struck with the way they seemed to search out who they were in the eyes and comments of the others. It is what I had seen in other homogeneous trauma groups, the wish to know and be known by others who have journeyed in a similar way. It is also the need of survivors, for whom violence has disrupted and altered the original sense of self, to have a safe place to find a voice and find self again.

Military women are often placed separately from each other when serving, and so for many, these groups were giving them a female military cohort that they had never experienced. How could they reintegrate into a civilian life without first connecting their experiences with other female veterans? I should not have been surprised that, as they found their commonalities and validated each other's issues, they found a voice for the military sexual trauma that many had suffered, denied, disowned, or acted upon. Having worked with rape victims over many years, I understood the assault to body and mind, the inability to make sense or put words to what had occurred, and the inability to forgive self for being a victim of rape. What was palpable here was the complicated silence that makes MST different from civilian sexual trauma.

As shown in *The Invisible War* (Ziering et al., 2012), when a man or women in the military has been raped, they feel that there is no safe place. There is no one to trust with the horror and often no way to put an end to it, as one fears gossip, retaliation, ostracism, or career destruction. What became striking in these informal group experiences was that in the course of talking about a range of topics, one person often broke the silence about sexual violence by sharing a story she had never told. At these times, the others listened, some with tears, some validating with similar situations, some saying nothing. A testament to them was their ability to make room for disclaimers and minimize personal experiences by some group members. In one case, a member who had been quiet when the topic was first raised waited until a few groups later to ask if her former homelessness and substance abuse might be connected to the sexual abuse she had put out of her mind and never mentioned.

The benefit of this type of group experience, which invited members to meet informally every few months to have lunch and speak, was actually unexpected. Very different from on-going treatment groups, or even weekly groups with open membership, the occasional gatherings of women seemed to allow them to consider issues on their own terms and time without expectations. They were just talking, and as group facilitator, I was listening, empathizing, noting commonalities, and supporting their connection. Maybe it was this very arrangement that made breaking the silence about military sexual trauma possible.

In trauma response, we understand that often we must adapt to the culture and bring our services to those in need (Klein & Phillips, 2008). One of the realities about female veterans, particularly mothers who feel they have been away from their children too much, is that they take very little time or help for themselves when they return from service. In this case, we were adapting to their culture. Perhaps it lowered the barriers of resistance to meet them on their time and schedule. What was illuminating was that although as veterans some had sought outside private therapy or used the VA for other services, most had never addressed military sexual abuse. Perhaps providing them with a cohort of military women with the overall goal of helping each other was both a trigger for memory and a safe place to share the pieces of the sexual violence suffered.

Surprising for me as a clinician, and perhaps something that is more likely to emerge when military women are meeting together, was an additional, unexpected reason for silence about MST. In addition to the horror, fear, ostracism, and self-blame, it became clear that some women colluded with the silence because they believed they could not own the betrayal of sexual trauma and feel proud of their service at the same time. They loved the military. They saw it as a definition of self, even as veterans. In one or two cases, there was even talk of staying in the reserves. To own the abuse and get help was to lose something they believed in: "You shut your mouth and pretend it didn't happen because you wanted this your whole life and if you let it get to you—it will be ruined." The challenge for some was not just breaking the silence about the sexual violence, but reconciling to it without disqualifying pride in serving.

There are many things that cannot happen in informal military women's groups that meet over many months. We have no formal evidence of completing the stages of establishing safety, remembering, mourning, and connecting that foster recovery from trauma (Herman, 2007). What we do have is a reflection of enough safety and connection to break the silence of violence in small steps, to verbalize the fears and conflicts, to give voice to what was never said or owned, and to bear witness to these in others. If this was a step closer to dealing with trauma and connecting with organizations that help military members, then it was a step away from violence.

SUMMARY

Somewhere in the space between violence and trauma is dangerous silence. Silence intensifies the impact of trauma and trauma that goes unspoken, unwitnessed, and unclaimed and it often "outs itself" as more violence to self and/or others. One only has to consider the relevant empirical evidence to confirm this tragic cycle. Crucial to addressing the danger of silence in this cycle is understanding of the centrality of silence existentially, neuropsychologically, psychologically, developmentally, interpersonally, and culturally.

The bridge to voicing and assimilating the unspeakable is empathic connection with others. This can take place in varying group contexts, such as a one-day group experience like International Survivors of Suicide Day or an informal group like the military women's groups described above. In varying configurations, group offers a holding environment without shame or stigma in the aftermath of the unspeakable. There, one is heard without words; one hears others and finds words; and it is safe enough to feel like a victim until one can become a survivor. A group experience has the potential to begin, expand, and facilitate a healing process. As such, group can respond to the dangerous role of silence in the relationship of trauma and violence.

"Without the integration of traumatic events into cultural discourses, individuals as well as society in general stay traumatized" (van der Merwe & Gobodo-Madikizela, 2008, p. 58).

REFERENCES

Alvarez, L., & Sontag, D. (2008, February 25). When strains on military families turn deadly. *New York Times*. Retrieved from http://www.nytimes.com/2008/02/15/us/15vets.html?pagewanted=all

Benedict, H. (2009). *The lonely soldier: The private war of women serving in Iraq*. Boston, MA: Beacon.

Bloom, S. L., & Reichert, M. (1998). *Bearing witness: Violence and collective responsibility*. New York: Haworth.

Boulanger, G. (2007). *Wounded by reality: Understanding and treating adult onset trauma*. New York: Psychology Press.

Breschisci, A. (2013, September 19). Silent anti-bullying short film "Strain" speaks volumes. *Newsday*. Retrieved from http://www.newsday.com/long-island/li-life/silent-anti-bullying-short-film-strain-speaks-volumes-1.6105628

Brison, S. J. (2002). *Aftermath: Violence and the remaking of a self*. Princeton, NJ: Princeton University Press.

Bromberg, P. (2011). *The shadow of the tsunami and the growth of the relational mind*. New York: Routledge.

Buchele, B. J., & Spitz, H. I. (2004). *Group interventions for treatment of psychological trauma*. New York: American Group Psychotherapy Association.

Caplan, P. J. (2011). *When Johnny and Jane come marching home: How all of us can help veterans*. Cambridge, MA: MIT Press.

Caruth, C. (1996). *Unclaimed experience: Trauma, narrative, and history*. Baltimore, MD: Johns Hopkins University Press.

Cerel, J., Padgett, J. H., & Reed, G. A. (2009). Support groups for suicide survivors: Results of a survey of group leaders. *Suicide and Life-Threatening Behavior, 39*(6), 588-598.

Chang, Y., Havener, D., & Armstrong, C. (2012). *Strain* [Motion picture]. Los Angeles, CA: LeliMelo Productions.

Cozzens, D. B. (2002). *Sacred silence: Denial and crisis in the church*. New York: Liturgical Press.

Dyregrov, K., & Dyregrov, A. (2005). Siblings after suicide—"The forgotten bereaved." *Suicide and Life Threatening Behavior, 35*(6), 714–724.

Feigelman, W. J., Jordan J. R., McIntosh, J. L., & Feigelman, B. (2012). *Devastating losses: How parents cope with the death of a child to suicide or drugs.* New York: Springer.

Fein, R. A., & Vossekuil, B. (1999). Assassination in the United States: An operational study of recent assassins, attackers, and near-lethal approaches. *Journal of Forensic Sciences, 44*(2), 321-333.

Freud, S. (1958). Introductory lectures on psycho-analysis. In J. Strachey (Ed. & Trans.), *The standard edition of the complete psychological works of Sigmund Freud* (Vol. 15, pp. 1-240). London: Hogarth Press (Original work published 1916-1917).

Fritz, P. A. T., Slep, A. M. S., & O'Leary, K. D. (2012). Couple-level analysis of the relation between family-of-origin aggression and intimate partner violence. *Psychology of Violence, 2*(2), 139-153.

Garvin, C. (1997). *Contemporary group work* (3rd ed.). Needham Heights, MA: Allyn and Bacon.

Harber, K. D., & Pennebaker, J. W. (1992). Overcoming traumatic memories. In S. A. Christianson (Ed.), *The handbook of emotion and memory: Research and theory* (pp. 359-387). Hillsdale, NJ: Erlbaum.

Hargarten, J., Burnson, F., Campo, B., & Cook, C. (2014). Suicide rate for veterans far exceeds that of civilian population. Retrieved from http://www.publicintegrity.org/2013/08/30/13292/suicide-rate-veterans-far-exceeds-civilian-population

Herman, J. (2007). *Trauma and recovery: The aftermath of violence from domestic violence to political terror*. New York: Basic Books.

Hoge, C. W., Auchterlonie, J. L., & Milliken, M. S. (2006). Mental health problems, use of mental health service, and attrition from military service after returning from deployment to Iraq or Afghanistan. *Journal of the American Medical Association, 295*, 1023-1032.

Iverson, K. M., Dick, A., McLaughlin, K. A., Smith, B. N., Bell, M. E., Gerber, M. R., et al. (2012). Exposure to interpersonal violence and its associations with psychiatric morbidity in a U.S. national sample: A gender comparison. *Psychology of Violence, 3*(3), 273-287. doi:10.1037/a0030956

Kang, H., Dalager, N., Mahan, C., & Ishii, E. (2005). The role of sexual assault on the risk of PTSD among Gulf War veterans. *Annals of Epidemiology, 15,* 191-195. doi:10.1016/j.annepidem.2004.05.009

Katz, L. S., Bloor, L. E., Cojucar, G., & Draper, T. (2007). Women who served in Iraq seeking mental health services: Relationships between military sexual trauma, symptoms, and readjustment. *Psychological Services, 4*(4), 239-249. doi:10.1037/1541-1559.4.4.239

Killgore, W. D. S., Cotting, D. I., Thomas, J. L., Cox, A. L., McGurk, D.,Vo, A. H., et al. (2008). Post-combat invincibility: Violent combat experiences are associated with increased risk-taking propensity following deployment. *Journal of Psychiatric Research, 42*(13), 1112-1121. doi:10.1016/j.jpsychires.2008.01.001

Kim, Y., & Leventhal, B. (2008). Bullying and suicide: A review. *International Journal of Adolescent Medical Health, 20*(2), 133-154.

Kimerling, R., Street, A., Pavao, J., Smith, M., Cronkite, R. C., Holmes, T. H., & Frayne, S. (2010). Military-related sexual trauma among Veterans Health Administration patients returning from Afghanistan and Iraq. *American Journal of Public Health, 100,* 1409-1412. doi:10.2105/AJPH.2009.171793

Klein, R., & Phillips, S. B. (2008). *Public mental health service delivery protocols: Group interventions for disaster preparedness and response.* New York: American Group Psychotherapy Association.

Klein, R. H., & Schermer, V. L. (2000). *Group psychotherapy for psychological trauma.* New York: Guilford.

Lubin, H., & Johnson, D. R. (2008). *Trauma-centered group psychotherapy for women: A clinician's manual.* New York: Haworth.

Mendelsohn, M., Herman, J., Schatzow, E., Kallivayalil, D., Levitan, J., & Coco, M. (2011). *The trauma recovery group: A guide for practitioners.* New York: Guilford.

Miller, A. (2014). Threat assessment in action. *Monitor on Psychology, 45*(2), 37-42.

O'Brien, T. (2009). *The things they carried.* New York: Mariner.

Paymar, M. (2000). *Violent no more: Helping men end domestic abuse.* Alameda, CA: Hunter House.

Phillips, S. (2012a). Military mothers: Reflections of trauma and triumph. *Psych Central.* Retrieved February 10, 2014, from http://blogs.psychcentral.com/healing-together/2012/05/military-mothers-reflections-of-trauma-and-triumph/

Phillips, S. (2012b). Finding the way home from war: A promise and a process. *Psych Central.* Retrieved February 10, 2014, from http://

blogs.psychcentral.com/healing-together/2012/11/finding-the-way-home-from-war-a-promise-and-a-process/

Phillips, S. (2013). Parents of our military: Supporting their care and courage. *Psych Central*. Retrieved February 10, 2014, from http://blogs.psychcentral.com/healing-together/2013/11/parents-of-our-military-supporting-their-care-and-courage/

Phillips, S. (2014). No innocent bystanders: The role we play in reducing violence. *Psych Central*. Retrieved February 10, 2014, from http://blogs.psychcentral.com/healing-together/2014/01/no-innocent-bystandersthe-role-we-play-in-reducing-violence/

Phillips, S., & Kane, D. (2008). *Healing together: A couple's guide to coping with trauma and post-traumatic stress*. Oakdale, CA: New Harbinger.

Raine, N. V. (1999). *After silence: Rape and my journey back*. New York: Three River Press.

Schwab, G. (2010). *Haunting legacies: Violent histories and transgenerational trauma*. New York: Columbia University Press.

Shengold, L. (1989). *Soul murder: The effects of childhood abuse and deprivation*. New Haven, CT: Yale University Press.

Shneidman, E. S. (1972). Foreword. In A. C. Cain (Ed.), *Survivors of suicide* (pp. ix–xi). Springfield, IL: Charles C. Thomas.

Stolorow, R. (2007). *Trauma and human existence: Autobiographical, psychoanalytic, and philosophical reflections*. New York: Analytic Press.

Taft, C. T., Monson, C. M., Hebenstreit, C. L., King, D. W., & King, L. A. (2009). Examining the correlates of agression among male and female Vietnam veterans. *Violence and Victims, 24*, 639-652.

Underwood, M. M. (2008). Children and families dealing with a traumatic event. In R. H. Klein & S. B. Phillips (Eds.), *Public mental health service delivery protocols: Group interventions for disaster preparedness and response* (pp. 1-21). New York: American Group Psychotherapy Association.

United States Department of Justice, Office of Justice Programs. (2004). *Veterans in state and federal prison*. Retrieved from http://www.ojp.usdoj.gov/bjs/abstract/vsfp94.htm

van der Merwe, C. N.-M., & Gobodo-Madikizela, P. (2008). *Narrating our healing: Perspectives on working through trauma*. Newcastle, UK: Cambridge Scholars Publishing.

Vossekuil, B., Fein, R. A., Reddy, M., Borum, R., & Modzeleski, W. (2002). The final report and findings of the Safe School Initiative: Implications for the prevention of school attacks in the United States. Washington, DC: United States Secret Service & United States Department of Education. Retrieved from http://www.secretservice.gov/ntac/ssi_final_report.pdf

Weiner, J., Richmond, T. S., Conigliaro, J., & Wiebe, D. J. (2011). Military veteran mortality following a survived suicide attempt. *BMC Public Health, 11,* 374. doi:10.1186/1471-2458-11-374

World Health Organization. (2003). World report on violence and health. Retrieved from http://www.who.int/violence_injury_prevention/violence/world_report/en/

World Health Organization. (2008). The global burden of disease. Retrieved from http://www.who.int/topics/global_global_burden_of_disease/en

Ziering A., & Barklow, T. K. (Producers), Kirby, D., (Writer/Director). (2012). *The invisible war* [Motion picture]. New York: Cinedigm.

There's Always a Villain to Punish: Group Processes Contributing to Violence and Its Remediation

NINA K. THOMAS, PH.D., ABPP, CGP

ABSTRACT

This paper considers the widespread use of violent metaphors, such as "combat" and "war," to represent the current social, psychological, and political problems within the United States. I apply Lakoff and Johnson's (1980) thesis that metaphor shapes thought, policy, and behavior. I examine how use of such metaphors inclines the national consciousness toward violence and punishment for it. In addition, I discuss shame and humiliation as psychological precursors of violence, particularly as these play out in the exclusion and extrusion via group scapegoating of individuals and whole groups from active participation in an esteemed or powerful other group. Included within the concept of "violence" are those harmful social policies that invalidate the experiences of disempowered people within the United States. I consider the role of group processes in resolving the injuries wrought by violence, particularly as these operate within such restorative justice projects as the Glencree Ex-Combatants Programme in Northern Ireland. Lessons emerge from restorative justice projects installed internationally for ameliorating conflict within and between "victim" groups in the United States.

[The] universal language is violence.
–Stopford, 2014

Nina K. Thomas is Clinical Associate Professor, Postdoctoral Program in Psychotherapy and Psychoanalysis, New York University.
I gratefully acknowledge the suggestions made by several colleagues, including Ghislaine Boulanger, Hal Strickland, and of course the editors of this special edition, Robert Klein and Victor Schermer.

VIOLENCE IN AMERICA

There is a deep and disturbing paradox within American culture. We pursue peace and security, search for cures, and strive to right social injustice while utilizing the language of violence: the war on terror; the war on drugs; the war on poverty. We typically say that a person with a disease "battles" her illness, that in addressing a problem we utilize our "armamentarium," that controversy becomes a "firestorm." We use the language of violence to effectively sanction its use in *opposing* violence. Such linguistic turns are not causally implicated in what many in the U.S. experience as an increase in life threatening events. I do, however, subscribe to and will detail Lakoff and Johnson's (1980) formulation that the language in which we cast a problem shapes how we understand and approach a solution.

Embedded within the language of violence are the binaries of victim and perpetrator, good and bad, right and wrong, a Manichean universe in which there is always a villain to punish. Splitting and the projective mechanisms that underlie such a moral division of the world contribute to violence. This is particularly the case when that split is concretized in the face of threats to security or self-esteem and the "other" is not just different but becomes the "enemy." In casting the world as a choice only between good and bad, us and them, our attention is distracted from the originating cause of such "wars" referred to above. That these wars reflect sociopsychological processes deriving from vectors of violence is easily disavowed when our environment is defined primarily in Manichean terms. I refer here to U.S. society's exclusion of non-dominant values and ideals, the withering of the social safety net, and to a host of other policies that severely constrict opportunities for marginalized groups. When the recourse to violence is acknowledged (more often it is denied), the group in power justifies its use by harking back to an event or period in which it "suffered." The rationale for violent practices is thereby established.

In this paper, I examine the multiple ways in which violence occurs within U.S. culture. Thousands are held incommunicado in black sites run by the United States and its allies around the world putatively to protect its citizens. Draconian drug laws incarcerate hundreds of thousands of mostly young African-American and Latino men on "three strikes and you're out" laws purportedly designed to combat illegal drug use and crime. Those dependent on social supports for their survival are denigrated and dehumanized with such labels as "welfare queens." Thus violence informs social policy in the United States. Relentless use of the term "illegal aliens" dehumanizes undocumented immigrants in the nation's consciousness. What is dissociated by such labels is that people deemed "aliens" are husbands, wives, mothers, fathers, sons and daughters, and members of communities. We attack the self constructs and dehumanize the subjects who are so labelled. Equally, we constrict our approach to what many within the United States and other countries deem problematic. Politics is simple; understanding the factors contributing to violence is complex. That complexity is overridden in the metaphors we utilize for the sociopsychological issues confronting us. We create an environment so conceptually narrow that attention is focused on punishment as the only appropriate response to violence and crime. To explore all the forces that operate in creating a violent society is beyond the scope of this paper. Rather, as Klein and Schermer substantively detail in their introduction to this issue, violence lies at the core of America's history and culture, whether we consider the genocide of native Americans, slavery and the multitude of laws that continue to effectively impoverish people of color even after the "official" end to slavery, the mythic vigilante heroes of the "Wild West," or more contemporary examples in "Jim Crow," "stand your ground," and "stop and frisk" laws. Each of these contains elements of what Volkan (1997, 2001; Volkan & Itzkowitz, 2000) has referred to as the society's "chosen glory" or "chosen trauma" that I will expand on below. In addition, I present the case for applying the practices implemented in other nations to address the problem, utilizing community-based rather than nationally formulated processes. I will elaborate on the "doer–done to" phenomenon articulated by Benjamin (2004) as underlying such community projects and propose that "restorative" justice practices are far more useful than the "retributive" justice so profoundly installed within our society.

I briefly review the concepts of narcissistic rage (Kohut, 1972), apocalyptic despair (Strozier, 2002; Strozier & Boyd, 2010), splitting, projective identification, and paranoia (Klein, 1935, 1946) as these contribute to the recourse to violence. When understood from a psychological perspective, restorative justice draws on group processes by which to re-humanize those, both "doer" and "done to," who previously confronted one another as "enemies." This facilitates an intersubjective perspective in response to injury to break the cycle of violence—that is, developing the capacity for mentalization (Fonagy, 2001), holding another's mind in mind—in those formerly in conflict with one another. If we conceptualize violence as a social pandemic, then it seems appropriate that social-psychological approaches incorporating group processes and practices best serve our efforts to intervene.

PSYCHOLOGICAL PRECURSORS OF VIOLENCE

Most mental health practitioners acknowledge our inability to accurately predict *who* will commit violence. Psychological theorists and students of violence focus on several vectors operant in creating the psychic state that motivates a person to *commit* violent acts (Klein, 1935; 1975; Kohut, 1972; Leary, Kowalski, Smith, & Phillips, 2003; Strozier, 2002; Strozier et al., 2010). The dominant commonalities among them include shame and humiliation. Narcissistic assaults, coexisting with an environment in which the individual is powerless to repair his self-esteem, contribute to violence as the only potential solution for him (most of those who have committed large scale violent acts are male; cf. Muenster & Lotto, 2010, p. 72).

Muenster and Lotto (2010) among others (Lindner, 2001; Margalit, 1996), systematically deconstruct the role humiliation plays in acts of violence, noting in particular the association of humiliation with retaliatory behavior "even at additional cost to the retaliator" (p. 72). That humiliation involves the public extrusion from a group is part and parcel of the retaliatory fuel felt by the subject. Social rejection has been deemed "the most significant risk factor for adolescent violence, stronger than gang membership, poverty or drug use" (Leary, Twenge, & Quinlivan, 2006, p. 111). Contributing is the retaliator's perception of having been morally wronged. Blaming the other, particularly where the individual feels his safety to be threatened, further justifies, to him, his resort to violence.

VIOLENCE IN AMERICA

While some may be copycat events, the kinds of violence that occurred in the school shootings at Columbine, Sandy Hook, Virginia Tech, in fact, 44 others between the Sandy Hook tragedy of December 2012 and February 2014 (Strauss, 2014), exemplify what Strozier (2002) has referred to as "apocalyptic despair," alienation and social isolation amongst many contemporary adolescents. Boys and guns is hardly a new phenomenon, however. It is noteworthy that a report in the *Los Angeles Herald* of September 11, 1874, cited the death of a 16-year-old boy as follows:

> This boy lost his life through the too common habit among boys of carrying deadly weapons. We do not know that this habit can be broken up. We do not know that school teachers have the right, or would exercise it if they had, of searching the pockets of their pupils, but it seems almost a necessity that some such rule be enforced...Nearly every school-boy carries a pistol, and the power of these pistols range from the harmless six-bit auction concern to the deadly Colt's six-shooter. (Boys and pistols, 1874)

The news item could just as well have been written at any time between the 1870s and today with similar effect. The concern becomes mired in conflict, as for example the persistent debate within the United States over gun control laws and Americans' right to defend themselves.

It is impossible to know if what Strozier terms "apocalyptic despair" was in play in the incident reported in 1874. He applies the concept to the Columbine shootings of April 1999 and similar ones both before and after in a comprehensive study of terrorist violence (Strozier & Boyd, 2010). By "apocalyptic," Strozier (2002) means "any idea or image that is total, absolute, and world ending while at the same time part of a yearned-for process of renewal" (p. 278). In the case of Columbine, he notes the shooters' identification with a virulently hostile right-wing ideology as imagined antidote to the extrusion they experienced from the social group of their high school community. According to a tape made by the shooters, and suggestive of their identification, the event was timed to occur on Hitler's birthday.

As in many similar events, the shooters had been exiled to the social margins of teenagers who were their peers. Socially shunned, ridiculed, in sum narcissistically assailed by others, in

Strozier's words, they "took refuge in [an] immersion in the religion of hate and right wing ideology of Neo Nazism" (2002, p. 286). In agreement with Volkan (1997), Strozier asserts that the humiliated subject attaches to an ideology, and often to a charismatic leader, in the belief that doing so will magically restore his intactness and that vengeance will redress his humiliation. Klebold and Harris imagined reversing their social abasement as the "unwanted others" among their high school peers through their violent attacks.

Strozier (2002; Strozier et al., 2010) and Stopford (2014) address the marrow-penetrating hopelessness about the future in young adolescent and adult men as a result of protracted experiences of marginalization or shunning, preventing those affected from seeing beyond the immediate moment. Such despair is not without external justification, as both authors detail. Young men of color also have severely foreshortened prospects for life beyond drugs, prison, and surviving as they can. As Stopford (2014) points out: "Similar to the apparently self-destructive behavior of abuse (such as self-mutilation, disordered eating, drug abuse, risky sexual encounters) drug abuse and so called 'black on black violence' is both a symptom and an enactment of national historical and contemporary relational trauma" (p. 211).

The kinds of violence in events like those, as well as the less reported ones in inner-city environments, are of a form Kohut has termed "narcissistic rage" (1972), to be differentiated from other forms of aggression. The "shame prone person" responds to narcissistic insult with action to produce a similar narcissistic injury on others.

> The need for revenge, for righting a wrong, for undoing a hurt by whatever means, and a deeply anchored, unrelenting compulsion in the pursuit of all these aims which gives no rest to those who have suffered a narcissistic injury—these are features which are characteristic for the phenomenon of narcissistic rage in all its forms and which set it apart from other forms of aggression. (p. 379)

Finally, Klein's (1935, 1975) theories of splitting and the paranoid-schizoid position are integral to a psychoanalytic perspective on the processes at work in those who commit violent acts.

In her theorizing, the hallmark of the paranoid world view is an inability to contain both good and bad aspects of self and other. The bad parts of ourselves are evacuated and projected into others; the good is retained in the self. It is, however, an uneasy balance when any injury or rebuff may be construed as an attack on self-esteem and confirmation of our "badness." In such an internal world of persecutory part objects that are projected outward, the individual lives in a persistent state of hatefulness directed both at the self and others. Under certain conditions, the perception of others' actions as attacks can motivate aggressive retaliation. Klein's formulation of projective identification (1946) is usefully applied when thinking about group processes connected to violence. In a group's unwillingness to take responsibility for injuries they cause or persistence in finding others to blame, the scapegoated "other" becomes the source of insecurity or diminished sense of self. The "other" in this exchange then comes to hold our own despised qualities and often identifies with them in such a way as to be similarly driven to expel them. It is this ricocheting exchange that contributes to violence as an attempted solution. It is often easy to forget what Simone Weil said: "I have the germ of all possible crimes, or nearly all, within me" (1951, p. 48).

GROUP PSYCHOLOGY AND VIOLENCE

Certainly, there have been critiques of the applicability of individual psychological theorizing to group behavior (Terman, 2010). Sheidlinger's (1984) discussion of individual and group analytic theorizing is a valuable resource. There is a more recent robust literature on violence and group, including Alderdice (2007), Gampel (2000), and Hopper (2002) among others. Taking account of the group's experience in terms of its history, identity, and perceived threats to security and self-esteem is fundamental. The oft-cited instance of Germany's humiliation in the Versailles treaty ending World War I as contributing to World War II or the gang warfare in urban environments as a response to being "dissed" are examples of how the group may be galvanized to violence in response to perceived shame and humiliation. Under circumstances in which members of a group feel vulnerable, a chosen trauma may be readily used as the basis for aggression to restore the group's sense of identity, or to imaginatively and magically erase the humiliation of defeats. A group's history is portrayed in stories told between and among generations, in commemorations of significant events, and more and more, as reported in the media. A group's "chosen trauma," while not willed but rather selected from its collective past, is what Volkan calls "a collective memory of a catastrophe" (1997, p. 48), an event that carries special resonance for group history, consciously and unconsciously becoming an organizing dimension of the group self. With its clear boundaries between historical enemies and friends, a chosen trauma contributes to the cohesion of the group, whether a nation, family, or, in urban settings, a "gang."

The attacks of 9/11 are one example of a national "chosen trauma" in the consciousness of the United States and the world used to justify our role in the wars in Iraq and Afghanistan. Characterization of these wars is replete with the kinds of metaphors about which Lakoff and Johnson (1999) construct their premise that language links to the workings of our minds, "structure[s] our reasoning, our experience, and our everyday language" (p. 47).

HOW METAPHOR SHAPES THINKING

The cognitive linguist George Lakoff and his philosopher coauthor Mark Johnson (1980) elegantly detail the ways in which metaphor—"understanding and experiencing one thing in terms of another" (p. 5)—shape our thinking, indeed structure our thinking as well as our actions. Take for an example the regular use of the metaphors of combat in our everyday language of politics, business, media, news, sports, and entertainment. To stimulate your associations on this topic, I offer a brief matching exercise. Choose the best match for who said, "I killed him":

1. One tennis champion who stunningly outplayed the other.
2. A driver who plowed down a pedestrian.
3. A lawyer who argued a difficult case and won.

An expression like "I killed him" might be used in any of the three examples. Sports is "combat" and the person we play with is an opponent; so too is a legal defense "combat," and safe driving is "defensive driving." Lakoff and Johnson (1980) assert that not only do we speak about an abstraction, as one example, in physical imagery of combat, but we conceive of it in that way. "Shock and awe." "Collateral damage." "Friendly fire." Metaphors such as these narrow our attention to the bugle-blaring of war and express its cost in exsanguinated language that keeps the true meaning behind the metaphor hidden from view (Lakoff, 1980; Lakoff & Johnson, 1980). Their use distracts us from registering the impact of war on civilians and military alike. Even the diagnostic term *PTSD* obscures the effect on individuals' and families' lives and relationships by making it a medicalized phenomenon.

A powerful example of how violence suffuses our culture refers back to the example earlier in this paper, the label "illegal aliens." When we speak of people in such terms, we are saying that they do not warrant our consideration as part of humanity. They are outside our moral universe and are objects to be feared. They have broken the law in entering this country; therefore, they are "capable," if not "programmed," to commit even more serious crimes. In being "alien," they are effectively our "enemy." Reasoning in this way may then be used to justify building a border fence to prevent continued illegal entry and, should situations require it, the death of undocumented entrants. The use of "illegal alien" for those who are in the United States without valid documentation collapses the possibility of thinking about the multiple dimensions involved in living on the fringes of society, escaping life-threatening circumstances in their home countries, fearing deportation, worrying about becoming ill or injured, or providing education and food for their families.

Metaphors, particularly those used by pundits and politicians to cast a problem, become the basis for individual and societal thinking and discourse. For example, inner city violence becomes "black on black violence," thereby overlooking poverty and multiple other factors underlying the phenomenon. While social scientists have studied these problems in depth, my focus is on the collapse of complexity in the social mind when metaphors project causality onto those who might be viewed as victims.

A further example of how metaphor shapes our thinking lies in what Lakoff and Johnson (1999) refer to as "moral accounting" (pp. 290-334); that is the moral imperative that someone who has done harm must "pay" for what he or she has done. It is this moral accounting, "paying one's debt to society," "balancing the books," that is challenged in the restorative justice projects in various parts of the world.

RESTORATIVE JUSTICE

There is a belief within some African cultures that to punish someone is to dismember the community. Restorative justice approaches the redress of injury from the vantage point of establishing responsibility for the injury sustained, promoting mutual understanding of its causes and effects, and developing a process for making amends (Olson & Dzur, 2003). Community members[1] are involved in repairing the harm wrought by crime. In a nation that has the highest rate of imprisonment in the world (Beale, 2003), in which one in three black men can look forward to being incarcerated at some point and "1 in every 15 African-American children has a parent who is currently in either prison or jail" (Kellson, 2014), it may be hard to envision a restorative justice approach. Whole regions of the United States are dependent on a prison economy for employment and commerce. Yet restorative justice efforts currently are in use in several parts of the United States, including the offenses of juveniles and in victim-offender mediation. It is a more robust part of the justice system within other countries, Canada, New Zealand, Australia, Germany, among them. Despite the many critiques of restorative justice, the outcomes in those countries implementing the approach (Poulson, 2003; Strang & Braithwaite, 2001) suggest we would do well to expand it.

Those international efforts often have been part of the larger sociopolitical aim of rebuilding trust and security following protracted violent conflicts. Most often they combine reconciliation with restoration of communities. The project I draw on works to repair the long-term sequelae of the violence in Northern Ireland during what is referred to as "The Troubles." The Glencree Sus-

---

1. The notion of "community" is critiqued by Weisberg, a contributor to the *Utah Law Review*'s symposium on restorative justice (2003). I understand "community" to mean a group that defines itself *qua* group of people who share similar interests and concerns.

tainable Peace Network, now enveloped within the Glencree Centre for Peace and Reconciliation, has, since 2002, worked within communities to rebuild relationships between those previously estranged by politics, economics, religion, and a long history of violence. Bringing together groups who have always characterized one another as "enemies" has manifold challenges, not least, the willingness to trust other participants and facilitators.

Breaking the cycle of violence requires the ability to see beyond the labels of "doer" and "done to" (Benjamin, 2004) and the "hierarchy of suffering" (Hamber, 2009b), being able to experience the other as having her own center of subjectivity. In the context of a history of violence, too often one person is subjected to the other's violence in what Benjamin (2004) terms "a one-way street." Such experiences make repair and reconciliation an extremely difficult process. The Glencree programs are well attuned to these challenges.

> Seeing the human side is very difficult...they were perceived as enemies but were also human beings; it was human beings you were killing, it is human beings who are grieving, that's hard to see, that's a big mountain to climb. (anonymous participant, Hamber, 2009a)

An early part of the Glencree Centre's efforts involved taking small groups from all sides of "The Troubles" on two wilderness trips, one to South Africa where they spent two weeks together camping in the bush. One participant remarked: "There were more fears to be overcome in the bush than fears of each other" (anonymous, Hamber, 2009a). The wilderness was chosen to support reconciliation and repair since it meant undisturbed time for reflection and required cooperative efforts for basic survival.

Among other elements, participants had nightly patrols during which they were armed against possible animal attacks. Being able to sleep soundly while someone who had been your enemy roamed the boundary of your camp under arms was a significant achievement. The wilderness experience was not the sole component of Glencree's work to restore the communities of former combatants in Northern Ireland. It involved extensive group work building out from these early encounters to train community leaders committed to seeing beyond labels of victim and enemy, undoing the history of retribution for past wounds. Since space precludes, I end with another quotation from a participant, an anonymous former Ulster Volunteer Forces member: "I felt physically fit, but the mountains yesterday nearly killed me. These mountains are metaphors. It is a real challenge to face the questions of my children: 'Why did you abandon me?' 'Why did you take this conflict on?'" (Hamber, 2009a).

Restorative justice is predicated on acknowledging the injury caused, its wrongfulness, and the readiness of both offender and victim to make amends and accept the reparation and apology offered. "Injury" and "victim" include not only legal "crime" but injuries to groups disadvantaged by discriminatory social policies and legislation. Here, I would include women, gender-variant people, people of color, and non-dominant religious members.

An excellent multinational meta-analysis of restorative justice programs was conducted by Poulson (2003), in which he presents significant results gleaned from seven studies involving 4602 respondents ("1297 victims in restorative justice, 1189 victims in court, 1077 offenders in restorative justice, and 1039 offenders in court" p. 169). Space permits only a brief summary of his findings, but notable is that victims were 3.4 times more likely and offenders two times more likely to find the restorative justice model more fair than court proceedings (p. 178). Similarly significant findings (though without the robust differences between restorative justice and court proceedings) exist in the satisfaction of victims and offenders with how their cases were handled. Both found the restorative justice model to hold offenders accountable at a rate "4.9 times more likely for victims and 4.8 times more likely for offenders" (p. 187) than was true for the court model. In fact, approximately three out of four offenders apologized to victims in the restorative justice model as compared with three out of four offenders who did not apologize in court (Poulson, 2003, p. 189). Also worthy of note is that in one study, victims' and offenders' perceptions of each other improved.

Findings from other studies commented on by Poulson show additional significant dimensions favoring the implementation of the restorative justice model, particularly for juvenile offenders. One study of restorative justice as compared with court proceedings found that 63% of youth in the sample who committed suicide had been referred to the juvenile justice system (Poulson, 2003, p. 202). With more than eight referrals, the suicide rate increased five times. Finally, restorative justice shows significant effects on recidivism rates, in fact a 32% decrease in recidivism (p. 199). Although there are no comparative data for restorative justice, these robust results make it urgent that restorative justice be implemented more widely.

GROUP'S CONTRIBUTION TO RESTORATIVE JUSTICE UNDERTAKINGS

Those who participated as facilitators in the restorative justice programs which Poulson reports on varied considerably in their training and expertise. They varied from police officers who received three days of training in family conferencing to volunteers who received 30–40 hours and supervised apprenticeships and observations. The Glencree program, on the other hand, was designed and led by, among others, a seasoned clinical psychologist with significant experience from work with the South African Truth and Reconciliation Committee who was well versed in group processes and the difficulties that might arise.

Given the importance of the outcome, trust is a significant factor. As mentioned earlier, in the Glencree Program participants were confronted with potentially life-threatening circumstances to test their willingness to rely on former enemies and their new leaders. Trust is built slowly through repeated experience of the strengths and frailties of other participants, all contributing to the recognition of shared humanity. Although the details in Poulson's (2003) report are thin in this respect, his finding that each party reported an improved perspective on the other is hopeful. The ability to alter one's view of the other aids in redefining the experience of injury and potentially interrupts the cycle of violence.

A recent example within the United States provides a powerful example of the utility of restorative justice. On August 15, 1999, 22-year-old Cornealius "Mike" Anderson and another young man held up a Burger King night manager making a night deposit at a bank in St. Charles, Missouri, a suburb of St. Louis. Shortly afterward they were arrested. Ten months later in June 2000 Anderson was released on $25,000 bond, his lawyers having filed a post-conviction appeal. At a final appeal hearing Anderson was not present. When the judge asked where Anderson was, his attorney responded that he was out on bond. The prosecuting attorney "jumped up in court and said, 'Oh no… We checked this morning. He's in Fulton Correctional Facility'" (Lussenhop, 2013). In fact, Anderson was living in his original community and in training to become a master carpenter. Although legal procedure would have had him re-arrested and returned to jail, the warrant for his arrest was never issued.

For 13 years, Anderson remained in the same community, owned a contracting business, married, had children, was active in his church, and coached his son's football team. He remained in his community until July 25, 2013. It was only on the date he was to have been released from prison, had he been there, that the Department of Corrections realized he had never been incarcerated. At 6:00 a.m. on that July morning, a phalanx of marshals with helmets, shields, and machine guns blocked off the suburban street he lived on with his wife and children and roused him from sleep to serve his original sentence. Anderson was held, 22 hours a day, in a cell in Fulton Correctional Facility. The cost to Missouri taxpayers for housing Anderson was $20,000 a year, the cost to him and his family incalculable. Anderson was finally released in May 2014 after a judge determined his behavior over the preceding 13 years had been exemplary of a model citizen.

Despite significant sequelae of the ordeal he had experienced, the victim of Anderson's crime, in an interview with National Public Radio said:

> [T]he more I thought about it, it was like, what you're doing to him is not right. He wasn't out robbing other people, doing this, that, and the other. He seemed to have gotten his life together. You've got to give the guy a little bit of slack. I mean, yeah, he screwed up when he was little. But the law dropped the ball. The law ought to drop it completely. They need to leave the man alone. (Glass, 2014)

There cannot be a better example of the appropriateness of restorative justice, from the beginning of the judicial process that wound its relentless and costly way, both financial and psychological, trying, appealing, and incarcerating Anderson. As Olson and Dzur (2003) argue, if the goal of criminal justice is to restore "ruptured human relationships" (p. 62), it is far more successfully achieved when all parties—victim, offender,,and community—are involved, as the Anderson case demonstrates. It appears as well that U.S. public opinion is growing in support of processes that address the social problems underlying crime rather than those that support harsher prosecution. Sixty-two percent of those polled in 2000 were seen "favoring solving social problems as compared with 27% who favored spending more money on prisons, police and judges" (Beale, 2003, p. 423).

Considering the burgeoning prison population, the often inhumane treatment of prisoners, and the threat of bankrupting state budgets, restorative justice appears to be well timed to grow beyond its limited implementation within the United States. Currently, these programs are funded through grants, religious or community organizations, or, on a lesser scale, state funding. Diverting funds from criminal prosecution is both possible and practical despite the political obstacles set up most often by those whose interests lie in the "business" of punishment.

Prior to initiating its statewide program for victim-offender mediation, Vermont ran focus groups to determine community receptivity to such programs and received marked evidence of support (Olson & Dzur, 2003). This preparatory work offers useful lessons for involving the larger community in an alternative to incarceration. Vermont's use of focus groups helped educate the public and took the pulse of the community. State leaders were able to lay the groundwork in the public consciousness for a new approach to crime and violence. If monies were spent advocating for community voices on issues of crime and punishment, communities would be educated to the social and psychological benefits of alternatives to prosecution and incarceration.

These examples of a program to reconstitute the social relationships of former enemies (Northern Ireland), and the justice projects that are an alternative to court proceedings (multi-national), have significantly different histories. The complexities of the former are plentiful, and in the latter there are significant levels of bureaucracy and "stakeholders." To build on these examples requires funding, well-developed inroads into the communities, and follow-through. Stopford (2014) makes a powerful case for how counterproductive efforts at amelioration of violence are when "outsiders" to a community fail to maintain relationships. Local stakeholders are vital to the success of such programs.

CONCLUSION

Klein's theorizing about projective identification is central to conceptualizing individual and group dynamics as precursors of violence. If we can "finger" another as the cause of our vulnerability, shame, and fearfulness, we are relieved of having to examine our own participation in violence in individual, societal, or small group contexts. Volkan's work, too, powerfully describes the role of group identity and history as contributing to violent practices.

The restorative justice efforts I have described incorporate group processes for developing approaches to ameliorate the violence wrought by fingering particular communities and by incarceration. The leaders of these undertakings work with an awareness of the challenges for groups in building trust. They involve community leaders as well as victims and offenders to acknowledge the injury caused and accept responsibility. There are significant results that alter the perceptions of victim and offender and lower recidivism of offenders.

Violence is an ever-present surround in the uncertainty of our lives. The psychological precursors of violence are often the deeply felt humiliation and shame that a person may experience at the hands of those by whom he or she is shunned or made to feel inferior. Violence lies as well within the language we use to think about a subject, as Lakoff and Johnson (1980) elaborate. By failing to deconstruct the metaphors that form the basis of our thinking, we may perpetuate the violence we ostensibly aim to remediate. Undertakings that restore intersubjectivity in relationships and aim to install the capacity for viewing the other as influenced by our interactions hold the most possibility for repair of violent outcomes. Restorative projects like those underway internationally, as well as the limited efforts in the United States, are valuable alternatives to the "eye for an eye" systems that guide our penal institutions, policies, and practices.

REFERENCES

Alderdice, Lord J. (2007). The individual, the group and the psychology of terrorism. *International Review of Psychiatry, 19*(3), 201-209.

Beale, S. S. (2003). Still tough on crime? Prospects for restorative justice in the United States. *Utah Law Review, 2003*, 413-437.

Benjamin, J. (2004). Beyond doer and done to: An intersubjective view of thirdness. *Psychoanalytic Quarterly, 73*, 5-46.

Boys and pistols. (1874, September 11). *Los Angeles Herald.* p. 2.

Fonagy, P. (2001). *Attachment theory and psychoanalysis.* New York: Other Press.

Gampel, Y. (2000). Reflections on the prevalence of the uncanny in social violence. In A. C. G. M. Robben & M. M. Suarez-Orozco (Eds.), *Cultures under siege: Collective violence and trauma* (pp. 48–69). Cambridge, UK: Cambridge University Press.

Glass, I. (Producer & host). (2014, February 14). Except for that one thing: This American life [Radio broadcast]. Retrieved from http://www.thisamericanlife.org/radio-archives/episode/518/except-for-that-one-thing

Hamber, B. E. W. (2009a). *Glencree Sustainable Peace Network.* Unpublished presentation in possession of the author.

Hamber, B. (2009b). *Transforming societies after political violence: Truth, reconciliation and mental health.* New York: Springer.

Hopper, E. (2002). *The social unconscious: Selected papers.* London: Jessica Kingsley.

Kellson, J. (2014). Going up the river: Solving social problems. *Technician Online.* Retrieved from http://www.technicianonline.com/opinion/article_d887d0bc-b62b-.

Klein, M. (1935). A contribution to the psychogenesis of manic-depressive states. *International Journal of Psycho-Analysis, 16*, 145-174.

Klein, M. (1946). Notes on some schizoid mechanisms of defense. *International Journal of Psycho-Analysis, 27*, 99-110.

Klein, M. (1975). *Envy and gratitude and other works 1946–1963.* London: Hogarth and the Institute of Psycho-Analysis.

Kohut, H. (1972). Thoughts on narcissism and narcissistic rage. *Psychoanalytic Study of the Child, 27*, 360-400.

Lakoff, G. (1980). The metaphorical structure of the human conceptual system. *Cognitive Science, 4*, 195-208.

Lakoff, G., & Johnson, M. (1980). *Metaphors we live by.* Chicago: University of Chicago Press.

Lakoff, G., & Johnson, M. (1999). *Philosophy in the flesh: The embodied mind and its challenge to Western thought.* New York: Basic Books.

Leary, M. R., Kowalski, R. M., Smith, L., & Phillips, S. (2003). Teasing, rejection, and violence: Case studies of the school shootings. *Aggressive Behavior, 29*, 202-214.

Leary, M. R., Twenge, J. M., & Quinlivan, E. (2006). Interpersonal rejection as a determinant of anger and aggression. *Personality and Social Psychology Review, 10*(2), 111-132.

Lindner, E. G. (2001). Humiliation—Trauma that has been overlooked: An analysis based on fieldwork in Germany, Rwanda/Burundi, and Somalia. *Traumatology, 7*(1), 46-68.

Lussenhop, J. (2013, September 12). An oversight allowed a convicted man to walk free for thirteen years. Now the justice system, wants to restart the clock. *St. Louis Riverfront Times*. Retrieved from http://www.riverfronttimes.com/2013-09-12/news/cornealious-anderson-prison-mistake-fugitive-missouri-the-extremely-long-and-sometimes-forgetful-arm-of-the-law/full

Margalit, A. (1996). *The decent society*. Cambridge, MA: Harvard University Press.

Muenster, B., & D. Lotto. (2010). The social psychology of humiliation and revenge. In C. B. Strozier, D. W. Terman, J. W. Jones, & K. A. Boyd (Eds.), *The fundamentalist mindset: Psychological perspectives on religion, violence, and history* (pp. 71-89). New York: Oxford University Press.

Olson, S. M., & Dzur, A. W. (2003). The practice of restorative justice: Reconstructing professional roles in restorative justice programs. *Utah Law Review, 2003*, 57-89.

Poulson, B. (2003). A third voice: A review of empirical research on the psychological outcomes of restorative justice. *Utah Law Review, 2003*, 167-203.

Robinson, P. H. (2003). The virtues of restorative processes: The vices of "restorative justice." *Utah Law Review, 2003*, 1-15.

Scheidlinger, S. (1984). Psychoanalytic group psychotherapy today—An overview. *Journal of the American Academy of Psychoanalysis, 12*, 269-284.

Stopford, A. (2014). "There's no trust in anything:" Psychosocial perspectives on trauma in a distressed African American neighborhood In M. O'Loughlin & M. Charles (Eds.), *Fragments of trauma and the social production of suffering* (pp. 201-222). Lanham, MD: Rowman & Littlefield.

Strang, H., & Braithwaite, I. (2001). *Restorative justice and civil society*. Cambridge, UK: Cambridge University Press.

Strauss, V. (February 14, 2014). At least 44 shootings since Newtown—new analysis. *Washington Post*. Retrieved February 14, 2014, from http://

www.washingtonpost.com/blogs/answer-sheet/wp/2014/02/13/at-least-44-school-shootings-since-newtown-new-analysis/

Strozier, C. B. (2002). Youth violence and the Apocalyptic. *American Journal of Psychoanalysis, 62*, 285-298.

Strozier, C. B., & Boyd, K. (2010). The psychology of apocalypticism. *Journal of Psychohistory, 37*(4), 276–295.

Strozier, C. B., Terman, D. M., Jones, J. W., & Boyd, K. A. (Eds.). (2010). *The fundamentalist mindset: Psychological perspectives on religion, violence and history.* New York: Oxford University Press.

Terman, D. M. (2010). Theories of group psychology, paranoia, and rage. In C. B. Strozier, D. M. Terman, J. W. Jones, & K. A. Boyd (Eds.), *The fundamentalist mindset: Psychological perspectives on religion, violence and history* (pp. 16-28). New York: Oxford University Press.

Volkan, V. D. (1997). *Blood lines. From ethnic pride to ethnic terrorism.* New York: Farrar, Straus & Giroux.

Volkan, V. D. (2001). September 11 and societal regression. *Mind and Human Interaction, 12*(3), 196-216.

Volkan, V. D., & Itzkowitz, N. (2000). Modern Greek and Turkish identities and the psycho-dynamics of Greek-Turkish relations. In A. C. G. Robben & M. M. Suarez-Orozco (Eds.), *Cultures under siege: Collective violence and trauma* (pp. 227-247). New York: Cambridge University Press.

Weil, S. (1951). *Waiting for God.* New York: Putnam.

Weisberg, R. (2003). Restorative justice and the danger of "community." *Utah Law Review, 2003*, 343-374.

Voices of Violence Video Series

BILL ROLLER, M.A., FAGPA

The relative absence of live-to-camera, unscripted, spontaneous group therapy training videos for various theories and techniques is understandable. Few clinicians wish to expose themselves and their skills to the whims of chance or risk the criticisms of colleagues. This is somewhat ironic since the practice of group psychotherapy necessarily makes the mistakes of group leaders and co-leaders highly visible to patients. Such vulnerability marks the career of group psychotherapists. Those videos that have met this challenge have carved out a special niche in the educational video market. The producers of this video series, The Voices of Violence, are to be commended for showing even a small unscripted segment of therapists working with their group members.

However, the group members and the context in which they are treated are not part of the typical practice of most group therapists. The videos present the therapeutic treatment of males incarcerated for the violent crimes of murder, rape, and aggravated battery in two different prisons, one in the United States, the other in England. The choice of presenting two different treatment programs is wise because it allows the viewer to compare and contrast the cognitive behavioral approach of the Resolve to Stop Violence Project in San Francisco jails with the psychodynamic approach of the Grendon Therapeutic Prison in Britain. Both programs use group therapy or group work as a fundamental element of education and treatment. Both tolerate

---

Bill Roller is president of the Berkeley Group Therapy Education Foundation, a Life Fellow of the American Group Psychotherapy Association, and past co-chairman of the Group Therapy Symposium, Department of Psychiatry, University of California School of Medicine, San Francisco. He maintains a private practice in Berkeley, California, as psychotherapist and organization consultant.

no violence from participants and strive to create a safe environment in which the men can explore the feelings and dynamics of their behavior. Both start from the premise that we as a society ought to invest in the psychological treatment of prisoners and not the exclusively punitive measures meted out in most prisons. The common rule is to treat the men with respect, allow them their dignity, and let them feel listened to.

Part one of the series lays out the theoretical basis for understanding the behavior of the incarcerated men. An impressive array of experts examines the early childhood experiences of violent offenders, highlighting the disturbed parent-child attachment styles, their destructive thought processes, and their distorted social perceptions. The common experience for many of these men is sexual and physical abuse, emotional bullying, and parental neglect. Of particular import is the insecure attachment and the chaotic emotional climate that exist in violent families. The goals of treatment are helping the men to identify the progressive levels of violent thinking and to interrupt the progression of their violent thoughts. Five levels of violent cognition are enumerated: (1) the paranoid-suspicious, (2) the persecuted misfit, (3) the self-deprecating and pseudo-independent posture, (4) the overtly aggressive, and (5) thoughts of self-aggrandizement and predatory narcissism (Firestone & Firestone, 2008). The therapists apply appropriate interventions in both group and individual treatment to interrupt these thought processes. The video consists of prisoners individually voicing their personal histories and therapists giving their interpretations of how to understand the prisoners' inner world. Sometimes the narrator or therapist introduces a topic and then an individual prisoner elaborates on the theme with his own personal experience and memories. This alternating structure allows the viewer time to absorb the painful and horrific subject matter that is introduced. Gradually, we come to understand the intense shame and misreading of social situations that plague these men and make it difficult for them to regulate their emotions.

One of the more disturbing yet familiar patterns of their behavior is the tendency to identify with the aggressor—or to act out what was done to them. These men have identified with their angry, violent parent instead of with their scared, abused child. This can take the form of reactive violence (responding as they saw others respond) or predatory violence (planning destructive and harmful acts). The disorganized attachment they experience leads them to read the intentions of others incorrectly—for example, seeing malevolence where there is none—and responding with aggression. These men have little capacity to envision the mental states of others and so fall back on primitive defenses when frightened or confused. Therapists teach the prisoners to distinguish between what they call the authentic self and the anti-self, a concept somewhat reminiscent of the ideas of biophilia and necrophilia of Erich Fromm (1963). The goal is to allow the life- and self-loving self to predominate over the death- and self-loathing self. At one point, the narrator points out the close relationship between violence toward others and the urge to suicide—which reminded this reviewer of Albert Camus' (1956) observation that suicide and murder both originate in the emotion of despair.

Part two of the video series concerns the treatment programs for violent individuals at two sites—Grendon Prison in England and the Resolve to Stop Violence Project (RSVP) in San Francisco jails. Both programs have been found to be highly effective in treating violent individuals, reducing the risk of re-offending by 80%, compared to similar violent males living in standard prison conditions. Both programs call for a re-conceptualization of incarceration, focusing on treatment and rehabilitation. Both programs teach prisoners to challenge their destructive thoughts and maladaptive beliefs through voice therapy which involves five steps: (1) Verbalize the destructive inner voice in the second person, taking distance from it, (2) Identify the source of this inner voice, (3) Talk back to the inner voice, (4) Notice how the inner voice influences behavior, and (5) Take action against what the inner voice tells you to do.

This approach is similar to the therapy practiced by clinicians who identify the parental introject as the voice that gives negative attributions and injunctions to the individual. The steps taken to address this voice closely parallel the steps followed in Redecision Therapy, a creative combination of Gestalt and Transactional Analysis (Roller, 1997).

The Resolve to Stop Violence Project provides an intensive 6-day per week, 12-hour per day involvement in systematic working groups, each focused on a different aspect of human psychology, across a 12-month period (Gilligan & Lee, 2005). This program includes a discussion group that questions the assumptions of what is called the Male Role Belief System. This approach echoes the work of Terry Kupers and others who describe prisoners as acting as scapegoats upon whom the dark and hurtful sides of masculinity can be projected (Sabo, Kupers, & London, 2001). Another group listens to the first-person narratives of how victims have been impacted by violence. A third group writes and acts in one-act plays, looking for a critical turning point in growing up where a fateful decision to be violent was made.

The Grendon Prison program cultivates a therapeutic community that allows a therapeutic relationship to develop between inmates and prison staff over time. It will take from 18 months to several years to see the benefits of the program in the changed behavior of the imprisoned men. It was opened in 1962 and designed as an experiment in the psychological treatment of exceedingly violent males, the majority of whom are severely personality disordered, including many psychopaths. The treatment program consists of daily group therapy sessions where the men explore their past, take responsibility for their crimes, and learn ways to avoid re-offending. A large percentage of these men have been sexually and physically abused, traumatic events that are pertinent to their ongoing violent behavior. The men recall and relate their abusive experience in group and work through the emotional aftermath. Although the video clips of spontaneous group process are brief—approximately 5 minutes for each program—they are highly revelatory.

No physical restraints or "cages" are used to control group therapy members in either program. This is significant to show since many prisons nationwide, including California Corrections, put prisoners in what are euphemistically called "therapeutic cubicles" during group therapy sessions, ostensibly to protect the prisoners and their group therapists (Roller & Zimbardo, 2013). The enlightened treatment shown in both programs contradicts the supposed necessity for such abusive practices. As one therapist says in the video, "If we want to reduce the level of violence in society, starting with the most violent people we have...nothing is more important than to make sure not to strip them of their human dignity." Also, the interaction among group members, especially in the psychodynamic group, seemed sophisticated in terms of cohesion and psychological astuteness. The participants were attuned and well adapted to the requirements of group membership.

It would be helpful to the viewer if more of the actual group interaction in both the San Francisco and Grendon programs were shown. What is shown is effective, but more would have been gained if additional live action were captured on video. A third DVD, focusing on the interactions of group members and interventions by therapists in both programs, would considerably heighten the value of this excellent video series and ought to be considered by the producers. Such a video could track the development of one group across several months or years and demonstrate how prisoners change behavior over time. Commentary by the group therapists could then interpret and point out the salient features of what is happening in each group and make real for a skeptical audience the powerful changes these therapy groups can have on their members.

The production quality of the video series is generally high, the audio clear, and the narrative statements by prisoners captured candidly and movingly. However, one comment about editing is warranted. A few of the soft cuts and transitions work well in presenting the prisoners' comments, but straight cuts would be more effective for most of the edits, rather than slow dissolves of prisoners' faces that just seem blurry and amateurish.

There is a lot of information conveyed in this series, and repeated viewings will reward the student with a deeper understanding of the subject matter. The instructor's manual that comes with the set of DVDs is well written and will prove helpful for instructors in pacing the learning process in college and university classrooms. This video series challenges the status quo of the criminal justice system and presents a new perspective that ought to be considered by therapists, teachers, administrators, police, and guards who work within that system.

A final personal note seems appropriate. As a beginning group therapist 35 years ago, I co-led a weekly therapy group for male prisoners for a year at San Quentin prison in California. All group members had killed at least one person and had extremely violent backgrounds. I wish we had had a video series like this back then to help us understand our patients better and give us a picture of the depth of treatment possible in a comprehensive therapeutic community.

This video series is truly inspiring, not just for its insights to help clinicians in the treatment of violent offenders but because it gives us a vision of the kind of society we could be if we could resist the urge to scapegoat persons both within and beyond our national boundaries.

REFERENCES

Camus, A. (1956). *The rebel: An essay on man in revolt.* New York: Knopf.

Firestone, R. W., & Firestone, L. (2008). *Firestone Assessment of Violent Thoughts professional manual.* Lutz, FL: Psychological Assessment Resources.

Fromm, E. (1963). *War within man: A psychological enquiry into the roots of destructiveness.* Philadelphia: American Friends Service Committee.

Gilligan, J., & Lee, B. (2005). The Resolve to Stop the Violence Project: Reducing violence in the community through a jail based initiative. *Journal of Public Health, 27,* 143-148.

Roller, B. (1997). Redecision therapy. In The promise of group therapy: *How to build a vigorous training and organizational base for group therapy in managed behavioral healthcare* (pp. 78-92). San Francisco: Jossey-Bass/Simon & Schuster.

Roller, B., & Zimbardo, P. (2013, July 14). *Group therapy can be a solution for over-crowded prisons rather than a technique of shame at California prisons.* Retrieved from http://Thepromiseofgrouppsychotherapy.wordpress.com

Sabo, D., Kupers, T., & London, W. (Eds.). (2001). *Prison masculinities.* Philadelphia: Temple University Press.

Voices of Violence Series. *The Roots of Violence* (Part One), and *Effective Treatment of Violent Individuals* (Part Two). Produced by psychotherapy.net. 2 DVDs, 60 minutes each. Includes instructor's manual. $298 for educational institutions.

Toward Understanding and Treating Violence in America: Some Contributions From Group Dynamic and Group Therapy Perspectives

Introduction to Part II

ROBERT H. KLEIN, PH.D., ABPP, CGP, DLFAGPA
VICTOR L. SCHERMER, M.A., L.P.C., LFAGPA

ABSTRACT

The co-editors of the journal's two special issues on "Violence in America" from group psychotherapy and mental health standpoints review the articles in Part I and introduce the articles in Part II. The latter includes articles on anger management in groups, group psychotherapy for domestic violence, domestic "homegrown" terrorism, and two general commentaries. The co-editors provide broad reference points for the focus on clinical concerns, levels of treatment, variations in types of perpetrators, screening for groups, and the group-as-a-whole, relational, and social contexts of violence. Whether in small therapy groups, social interventions, or society's management of violence, empathy, boundaries, holding, and containment must be provided in such a way that they prevent violent acts while healing the hurts and shame that underlie violence in all its forms. Therapists' familiarity with these issues in their work can contribute fruitfully to treatment efforts and addressing a pressing social problem.

Robert H. Klein is a Clinical Faculty member at the Yale School of Medicine and is in private practice in Westport and Milford, Connecticut. Victor L. Schermer is in private practice in Philadelphia, Pennsylvania.

VIOLENCE IN AMERICA

In Part I of the special issue of this journal, we (Klein and Schermer, 2015) introduced a series of articles addressing the prevalence of violence in America and how group therapists can contribute to its understanding and amelioration through treatment, prevention, and social change. We pointed out several concerns: (1) the history and patterns of violence in our culture, (2) parallels (isomorphy) between the dynamics of therapy groups and those of society at large, (3) the process of addressing aggression, perpetrators, and victims in groups and society, and (4) the contribution that group therapists and mental health workers can make to the national dialogue about curbing the pandemic of violence in the United States and elsewhere.

In Part I, our authors elaborated upon the violence-potentiating roles of paranoia, fight-flight group dynamics, and scapegoating (Rice, 2015); social disconnection and loss of empathy (Gottlieb, in Schermer, 2015; Phillips, 2015); shame and guilt (Phillips, 2015; Roller, 2015; Thomas, 2015); violence implicit in language and social institutions (Thomas, 2015); silence, non-communication, and the bystander effect (Phillips, 2015); and social neglect and marginalization (Thomas, 2015). Our authors agreed in principle that: (a) violence is often an outcome of untreated psychological trauma, (b) the competitive and stressful culture in which we live plays an unspoken but important role, and (c) with key exceptions (for example, psychopathy, genetic tendencies, neurological abnormalities), many if not most offenders are wounded, shame-based individuals for whom violence is an act of desperation and sometimes a misguided effort at "justice" for perceived past slights, injuries, and wounds suffered at the hands of others. To a considerable extent, violence is a disease of affect dysregulation that results from broken and disrupted attachments in the history of the individual, the group, and past generations.

Now, in Part II, we continue to explore the causes, dynamics, and alleviation of unbridled aggression in its diverse forms, while focusing the clinical and theoretical microscope on two important aspects: (1) the group treatment process and (2) selected special populations in which violence is a key element. Our authors here consider the levels and effectiveness of psychoeducational, cognitive-behavioral, and relational-psychodynamic interventions and treatment models. The populations they examine include group members with anger control problems (Gerhart, Holman, Seymour, Dinges, & Ronan, 2015); domestic violence (Lothstein, 2015); and homegrown terrorism (historically and in the new millennium), especially the "lone-wolf" terrorists fueled by the Internet (Post, 2015). Included are two commentaries (Buchele, 2015; Green, 2015) summing up and assessing the contributions.

The emphases in Part II thus consist of (1) the nature of treatment and prevention efforts and (2) the characteristics of perpetrators of violence and their group and relational contexts. By way of introduction, we now provide a broad perspective on these issues.

BASIC CONSIDERATIONS OF THE TREATMENT AND PREVENTION OF VIOLENCE

Empathy and Boundaries; Holding and Containment

Because violence by its very nature is life-threatening and self-perpetuating, it must be preemptively forbidden, both in therapy groups and in society-at-large. A strong boundary must be enforced which rules out violence. Societies have laws against violence, and therapy groups have rules that prohibit it. While many violations of group rules (such as lateness, failure to pay fees, and contact outside of group) can be tolerated and analyzed, violence in therapy is a sufficient reason to consider removing the transgressor from the group. Violence feeds upon itself, so even a slap or shove which does no overt harm usually cannot be tolerated in a therapy group that requires expressing thoughts and feelings in words.

Such prohibitions against violent acts, however, are all too often inappropriately projectively identified and generalized onto persons and groups who are then "profiled" and scapegoated as incorrigibly violent. While individuals who are likely to repeat violent acts need to be at least temporarily prevented from doing harm through incarceration, hospitalization, or restraining orders, many if not most acts of violence are committed by people who are otherwise ordinary or even good members of society and can benefit from various kinds of interventions. The process of labeling, blaming, and shaming perpetrators is fueled by fear that leads to misunderstanding, scapegoating, stereotyping, and other factors that put a distance between perpetrators or other marginalized individuals and those who might help them to change and integrate within the society. In such a climate of stereotyping and excommunication, empathy is lost, help cannot be given or received, and, as individuals become concretized as objects or things rather than sentient beings, violence is perpetuated.

Thus, those hoping to ameliorate violence through psychotherapy, education, and prevention must negotiate a difficult path between (1) empathic understanding of the person who commits the violence and (2) boundary-regulation that sends a clear message that violence is impermissible and has consequences. The problem of reconciling these two requirements is further complicated by the fact that fantasies, words, and games that ventilate aggression are necessary to mental health. As the psychoanalyst Theodore Reik wryly put it, "A thought murder a day keeps the psychiatrist away" (Robertz, 2007). Helpers, whether they are therapists, parents, teachers, or interventionists, must allow healthy outlets for aggression while prohibiting violence as such. When we consider that for some individuals (and almost all of us under extreme conditions) angry thoughts and emotions can translate into violent acts, the task of combining empathic understanding with boundary-keeping can become daunting and complex.

Fortunately, there are psychotherapy concepts and techniques that deconstruct the opposition between empathy and boundaries. Two of the most important ways of reconciling human understanding with firm boundaries (mercy and justice) are holding and containing—that is, the therapist's caregiving functions that parallel the mother's care for her infant. Holding (Winnicott, 1960) consists of providing an optimal interpersonal environment for psychological development. In childrearing, it involves the mother's "good enough" responsiveness to the infant's needs. In therapy, holding takes the form of attention, listening, and empathic attunement to the patient or group. Containing (Bion, 1963) is similar to holding but emphasizes the thought process and emotions by: (1) including and processing instead of denying, projecting, and evacuating anger, and (2) interposing delay of gratification and facilitating the mediation and transformation of powerful impulses by subjecting them to higher-order thought processes. By "containing" the infant's projective identifications, the mother helps the infant to retain these mental contents and to develop the capacity for cognition and self-regulation (Schore, 2003). Violence is often the result of interpersonal derailment (Stern, 1977, p. 9). Thus, holding and containing the hurt and rage that provoke violence become ways to help people modulate their affects, relate better to others, and hence become less violence-prone.

From the standpoint of holding/containing, it becomes clear that empathy and boundaries, far from opposing one another, are mutual aspects of a facilitating environment. When, for example, the group therapist holds the members by listening attentively and being emotionally available and responsive, he also becomes a role model for attunement and empathic communication as an alternative to acting out. When he contains the members' projective identifications through effective understanding and interpretation, he helps them contain their hurt and rage and transform their raw emotions into metaphors and ideas that can be communicated and utilized for interpersonal problem-solving. Effective holding and containing include both empathy and boundary-setting in the multidimensional and sometimes challenging process that Bass (2006) aptly called "the strangeness of care."

For example, in an inpatient substance abuse therapy group, a big, brawny man with a hair-trigger temper exacerbated by recent withdrawal from alcohol, announced his entry into the group with a cynical denunciation of the treatment process and the staff, and a threat to "beat the hell out of" the therapist. The therapist's immediate thought was to discharge him from the hospital for making an overt threat. However, feeling protected by the men in the group, with whom he had formed a strong alliance, and empathically sensing something "soft" in the patient, he calmly told the patient that threats and violence were grounds for immediate dismissal but that he, the therapist, understood that the patient must be feeling very scared and vulnerable to want to strike a person and leave a group who could help him. The group supported the therapist and urged the patient to talk about what he was going through. The patient was moved to tears, and spoke about a series of hurts and losses, including his mother's recent death. Holding and containment, which included boundary-setting along with empathy, transformed the patient's rage into disclosure of his experience, expression, and understanding (Strasser, 1985), which in turn helped him bond with the other members and express his grief.

Holding and containment are resources that therapists can contribute not only to treatment, but to all levels of social interaction in which there is a potential to heal and ameliorate violence. For example, if the psychiatrists and other mental health workers who had treated Adam Lanza, the Newtown Sandy Hook Elementary School shooter, for several years had had the resources to engage his family and community in a process of holding and containment of this severely mentally ill young man, for example by providing an ongoing support system, his deteriorating condition might have been better monitored and contained and a disaster averted. Instead, he was unattended as he withdrew into his room and the dark part of his mind while his mother set no limits either to his use of weapons or his total isolation (Griffin, 2013). Speck (Speck & Attneave, 1973) used a "town hall" meeting to facilitate the treatment of a schizophrenic. Therapists in New York City provided group support to those traumatized by 9/11. There are models for community intervention that could be more widely used to hold and contain the sorts of regressions that potentiate violent behavior.

In addition, the social, economic, and political climate, as well as the new technologies such as the Internet, social networking, and smartphones, can either potentiate or alleviate violence. Anything from the way that politicians phrase their speeches to the way that parents talk to their children, to Facebook, to school policies, to television shows and computer games can serve the purpose of containing and holding with empathy and boundaries, or they can subtly or overtly encourage bullying, scapegoating, profiling, and acts of aggression. Therapists can bring to the society at large the lessons they have learned from their work to influence social policy, attitudes, and the way people in our society relate to one another on a daily basis.

Our authors in both Parts I and II, all of whom have intensively studied and/or worked with the potential for violence, suggest a variety of strategies for holding and containing the potential for violence in our culture. For example, in Part I, Gottlieb spoke of the need for social action to restore the kind of empathy that brings people together rather than reinforcing the current social "disconnect." Rice held that a process of group mourning and reparation has the potential to alleviate scapegoating and the perpetual reenactment of "chosen trauma." Thomas pointed out that the language and metaphors that accompany social marginalization and neglect potentiate violence, and that less emphasis on punishment and more on "restorative justice" that redeems rather than isolates individuals can create a climate and language of reconciliation. Phillips called for openness and disclosure of our hurts and wounds rather than remaining silent about them. In Part II, Lothstein suggests the importance of remediating faulty or traumatic attachment patterns that lead to violent reactions in domestic quarrels. Gerhart and colleagues incorporate interpersonal learning and social skill sets into their work with anger-prone individuals. The common thread running through these articles is that interpersonal relatedness and connectedness promotes self-regulation of rage, fear, and other traumatic affects that, when unattended, can lead to violence.

Levels of Treatment and Intervention

Group therapists are aware that treatment can occur at levels of education, support, cognitive-behavioral therapies, and exploration of existential, developmental, and interpersonal components of the personality and the group-as-a-whole (Yalom & Leczyz, 1995). They also know that some patients benefit from time-limited and change-oriented groups, while others are helped by open-ended groups that emphasize interpretation of dynamics and interpersonal relationships. Patients with anger management problems and/or violent histories present special problems regarding the choice of treatment modalities and the extent of uncovering deeper conflicts. The choice of approach is crucial because we don't want to provoke anger and violence by our interventions (iatrogenic, treatment-induced illness). Strategies may vary depending on the diagnoses and other characteristics of the treatment population. Violence-prone individuals are a heterogeneous group. We want to tailor treatment to each patient's complex needs, not just symptoms as such.

In this respect, our authors offer treatment protocols at several levels. Gerhart and colleagues offer a group-based violence-reduction training program (VRTP), a cognitive-behavioral approach focused on management of aggression. Lothstein, by contrast, proposes a three-tiered model for treating domestic violence in particular.

According to Lothstein, up until now, two tiers, psychoeducational and cognitive-behavioral, have been the most often used approaches to treating domestic violence. Lothstein proposes a third tier, a dynamic-relational approach that more deeply addresses the underlying trauma, shame, and other developmental factors that perpetuate the violent response to stress and conflict. Importantly, he also incorporates findings from interpersonal neuroscience which suggest the way the brain processes human interactions, so that the therapist can help patients improve by using therapy to enhance neurosynaptic connections and other brain structures and functions, since there is evidence that trauma causes brain changes and that therapy can restore some of the deficient biochemical and structural factors (Cozolino, 2002, 2006).

Thus, Lothstein addresses the biological, cognitive, and relational components of anger management and violent tendencies, all while providing appropriate supports—what he calls a "multimodal, integrative model." His approach is a step forward not only for psychotherapy, but potentially for social interventions to curtail violence as well. For example, court-mandated programs for domestic violence are typically limited to psychoeducational support, which may be effective in the short run by establishing clear boundaries and consequences. However, empathy, holding, and containment tend to take second place in such contexts. Therapy that includes the underlying developmental causes and offers a facilitating environment for recovery can potentially reduce recidivism over the long-term.

It should be added that not only therapists but society as a whole, including its family, community, legal, political, and socioeconomic institutions, must address the problems of violence at multiple levels as well as their underlying causes. Therapists, working along with social scientists, can begin to define the interventions and social changes that minimize violence as a solution to and outcome of the many dilemmas of human existence.

PERPETRATORS OF VIOLENCE AND THEIR GROUP AND RELATIONAL CONTEXTS

Since levels of intervention and care may vary for different individuals and groups, and since screening and assessment are essential to group psychotherapy, it becomes important to ask, "Who among us is likely to throw the first stone?" That is, which individuals are likely to become violent offenders, and what are their characteristics? A simple predictor is history. A prior record of violence, or being exposed to violence, is likely to be a strong prognostic indicator of future violence. However, since we want to prevent violence before it happens, we need to consider which personality types, developmental histories, genetic constitutions, and environmental exposures identify and predict those who need care.

The Complexity and Diversity of Violent Acts and Perpetrators

Taken together, the articles in both Parts I and II suggest the impossibility of pigeon-holing violence and violent offenders as a general personality type. A serial killer, a mass shooter, a terrorist, a thief with a gun, a traumatized war veteran, and a spouse who abuses his partner are very different from one another. Moreover, the potential for aggression is present in everyone, so in addition to personal history, genetics, and so on, stressful situations, precipitating events, and social contexts rather than personality may be determining factors that result in untoward actions.

Thus, our authors, largely depending on the populations they are considering, arrive at conclusions that are different and not easily integrated. For example, with regard to terrorists, Post, based on his review of many studies, concludes that, "there is no psychological characteristic or psychopathology that separates terrorists from the general population. Rather it is group dynamics, with a particular emphasis on collective identity that helps explain terrorist psychology." If we combine seemingly contradictory findings with what we know about comorbidity (e.g., drug abusers, borderline personalities, and bipolar patients are noted for their anger-management problems), it becomes clear that it is difficult to integrate these findings into a simple prognostic formula. The problem of identifying and categorizing potentially violent personalities is further complicated by the nature/nurture controversy. Recent research suggests that a particular gene (MAOA), dubbed the "warrior gene," contributes to aggressive tendencies, especially under high provocation (McDermott, Tingley, Cowden, Frazzetto, & Johnson, 2009). However, such research has yet to determine the percentage of variance in aggression attributable to genetics versus environmental factors.

It would thus appear from the views of our authors as well as the findings on aggression from a host of other sources that violence as a "symptom" is a function of multiple characteristics of development, for example, trauma, personality type, and diagnoses. Defining these factors is especially important in screening for group members, including participants for interventions at the societal level. There is no single thread that is going to solve all the problems of aggression in our groups and in society, any more than there is one treatment approach or type of therapy group that is most effective for all patients with anger-management difficulties. The group therapist, in particular, needs to be very aware of the specific composition and populations of the groups he or she conducts as well as the specific goals and objectives for treatment and intervention.

Group Relations and Violence

Bion often used visual perception as a model for the therapist's "in-sight" into his patient's conflicts and personality. For example, he remarked that just as the perceived distance of an object is enhanced by "binocular vision," that is, the input from the two eyes in depth perception, so too is the therapist's view of the patient enhanced by having multiple vertices or theories which, taken together, add dimensionality and depth to the therapist's understanding (Grotstein, 2014). To carry the visual analogy a step further, in ordinary thinking and discourse about social issues such as violence, the mind tends to "see" concrete images, just as the retina of the eye takes in the light that impinges directly upon it. In visual perception, the retinal image is called the "proximal stimulus." It takes considerable information processing in the brain to perceive the environmental situation, the "distal stimulus" that constitutes the outer reality that calls for a response. If all we "see" is the retinal image, it would be a flat pattern of colors with no meaning or utility. The brain constructs the "big picture" of the external world from the small amount of information that enters the visual system.

Similarly, when it comes to violence on a societal scale, most of the social and media discourse tends to center on the concrete images that are "proximal" to the violent act. The focus recently, for example, has been on "guns" and "perpetrators" and attempts to control them. It takes considerable mental effort and expertise to see the "distal" causes of violence, that is, the interpersonal and group dynamic factors that lead up to the violence and provide a ground and context that allow it to occur. The "eyes" and binocular vision that allow society to recognize the relational context of violence must partly come from group psychologists whose particular vertices or theories allow them to "see" the group-as-a-whole reality above and beyond the concrete objects and images. If lasting changes are to be made, input about group and social dynamics is a necessary part of the national conversation about violence.

Thus, an important purpose of these special issues is to examine the social context that makes violence a more or less acceptable solution to human frustration and conflict. In various ways, our authors are saying that whether it is a small group, a community, or a society, there are particular conditions and contexts that potentiate violence and those that lead to non-violent solutions and attitudes.

In Part I, these conditions and contexts were explored. In the interview with Dan Gottlieb, he contended that fear, mistrust, and loss of empathic relations among human beings escalates anger. Rice showed how leadership stirred up or reduced aggression in an inpatient community meeting. He suggested that a paranoid fight-flight group climate or one of panic leads to scapegoating and victimization. He touched on some features in American culture and history such as stereotyping and profiling of minority groups that create a climate of hostility and provocation. He showed how a nation's "chosen trauma" perpetuates violence across generations. Thomas argued that the vocabulary and metaphors of a society contain aggressive connotations. She showed how marginalization and institutional neglect create desperation and separatism. She gave illustrations of the difference between retaliatory and restorative justice that makes the difference between perpetuation and amelioration of violence. Phillips discussed the sources of silence, suppression, non-disclosure, and the bystander effect that prevent the healing of psychological trauma and the aftermath of abuse. In general, they all made clear how group climates of shame and fear fuel anger and aggression, which in turn leads to more shame and fear in a vicious cycle. They gave examples of how unresolved mourning and internalized wounds potentiate a desire to "right the wrong" through violence against the aggressor. By contrast, healing of loss and trauma ameliorates the recurrence of resentment, anger, and violence.

Thus, a common factor underlying violent tendencies is broken or traumatic attachment. Generally, when people feel held and cared for, responded to empathically, feel understood, and form secure attachments, they are less likely to become violent. But America has a long history of marginalization, dislocation, persecution, inequalities, war, and homegrown terrorism that have led to broken family bonds, life upheavals, protracted mourning, and feelings of injustice sufficient to traumatize much of the population. We see such traumatic histories in our therapy groups as well as in the statistics on murder, suicide, domestic abuse, and the prevalence of anxiety disorders and depression.

In Part II, the role of context is further elaborated. Lothstein points to the pandemic character of domestic violence, suggesting that shame-based interpersonal relations and damaged attachments so pervasively create tensions between domestic partners that it becomes a national problem. Roller, in the previous issue, suggested that stereotyping prison inmates as incorrigible interferes with humane treatment efforts. He cited the startling fact that up until recently, some group therapy sessions with violent offenders housed them in individual cages to prevent them from harming one another! Surely, there is no clearer example of boundary-setting that fosters shame rather than holding, self-regulation, and healing. We don't know how many people in the society at large are put in metaphorical cages that similarly limit their freedom and creative potential in ways that fuel burning aggression and perpetual shame within each of them.

Post contends that group dynamics rather than personality factors lead to homegrown terrorism such as the Boston Marathon bombing by two disenchanted siblings who were exposed to terrorist ideology and the Fort Hood massacre by an army psychiatrist who had contacts with terrorists via Internet "communities." Terrorism in the United States has a long history. Post traces terrorism in America to the nineteenth century, explores the changing face of terrorist activity aimed at social change, and points to intergenerational conflicts between terrorists and their parents' generation as a recurring feature. He shows how terrorist leaders in foreign countries are able to fuel terrorist activity in the United States via the Internet by promoting a religious agenda in which those who do not conform become enemies. Post theorizes that a cross-generational group dynamic reinforces dependence on the leader and fight/flight and paranoid projection with respect to "outsiders."

By far, the bulk of human bloodshed has consistently over the course of history resulted from group forces and dynamics where certain individuals become vivid personifications. (The individual is the perpetrator, but he represents the group.) Thus, group therapists are among those who possess special insights about how groups function that can be of great value in promoting peace and healing at the level of communities and society.

SUMMARIES OF CONTRIBUTIONS TO PART II

Part II explores issues about violence in America as they pertain primarily to therapy groups and to lesser extent support groups, situational interventions, and societal issues. As mentioned, there is an emphasis on psychotherapy process and specific types of violence and offenders: specifically anger-management patients, domestic partners, homegrown terrorists, and the prison population. Because of the complexity of the problems, the co-editors had to be selective in both topics and approach. We regret, for example, that we were unable to include concerns about minorities such as African Americans, Latinos, and the LGBT community. Most of our authors utilize psychodynamic and group dynamic approaches. There are many other ways to think about violence and its treatment. We see these two special issues not as the final word or a comprehensive "handbook," but the beginning of an extended dialogue that opens up to new perspectives. The following brief summaries to the articles in this issue may help the reader orient himself to their content.

Part II begins with a model of group psychotherapy for patients with anger-management difficulties. Gerhart, Holman, Seymour, Dinges, and Ronan propose an evidence-based approach utilizing cognitive-behavioral techniques. They describe a group-based violence-reduction training program (VRTP) for helping patients to manage frustration and stress from frustration-aggression and social problem-solving frameworks. They regard the group process itself as the vehicle for growth and change. They highlight the importance of dealing with anger-infused group relations. Importantly, they are proceeding with a meta-analysis and study of the variables that affect outcome in groups where anger and its management are emphasized. Empirical research on aggression, especially when the group process is a factor, has been neglected until now, and their work represents a much-needed step forward.

Lothstein goes deeper into the underlying causes of violence within the specific context of domestic violence. He documents the complex and costly problem of domestic violence in the United States, citing shocking statistics that suggest it is of "pandemic" proportions. He notes that domestic violence involves both men and women as perpetrators and critically examines the lack of success associated with the use of the "Duluth model," a primarily psychoeducational, feminist-based, court-ordered intervention. He argues that domestic violence is rooted developmentally in early traumatic exposure to interpersonal violence involving shame, humiliation, and powerlessness. The damaged self-structures that are formed lead to subsequent painful vulnerabilities and tragic reenactments. He proposes a comprehensive, in-depth treatment model based primarily on a creative synthesis of psychodynamic, object relations, and self-psychology theory that also takes into account newer developments in the neurosciences.

Post, a political psychologist, examines a problem that has stimulated recent thought and debate: terrorism with a revolutionary intent, which today is taking place along religious lines. He states that there are no psychological characteristics or diagnoses that separate terrorists from the general population. Rather it is group dynamics, with a particular emphasis on collective identity that helps explain terrorist psychology. Terrorist group dynamics manifest Bion's (1961) basic assumption group cultures. Post gives a history of terrorism in the United States from the nineteenth century to the new millennium and offers an historical understanding of "four waves" of terrorism from group dynamic and intergenerational perspectives. He argues that with the communications and Internet revolution, a new phenomenon is emerging which may presage a fifth wave: lone wolf terrorists who through the Internet are radicalized and feel they belong to the virtual community of hatred.[1] He explores the motives and group processes that fuel the lone wolf phenomenon.

Part II concludes with commentaries from two distinguished colleagues from the group therapy and group dynamics fields, respectively: Buchele and Green. We hope you find these contributions stimulating and fruitful, and that you will help to continue and extend the questioning, the dialogue, and the work that our authors have begun.

REFERENCES

Bass, A. (2006). *Interpretation and difference: The strangeness of care*. Stanford, CA: Stanford University Press.
Bion, W. R. (1963). *Elements of psychoanalysis*. New York: Basic Books.
Bion, W. (1961). *Experiences in groups*. London; Tavistock.
Buchele, B. J. (2015). Commentary on "Toward Understanding and Treating Violence in America: Some Contributions From Group

---

[1]Post wrote his article over a year prior to publication of this issue. As of now, his prediction has become a troubling reality of worsening proportions.

Dynamic and Group Therapy Perspectives," *International Journal of Group Psychotherapy, 65*(2), 273-283.

Cozolino, L. (2002). *The neuroscience of psychotherapy: Building and rebuilding the human brain.* New York: Norton.

Cozolino, L. (2006). *The neuroscience of human relationships: Attachment and the developing social brain.* New York: Norton.

Gerhart, J., Holman, K., Seymour, B., Dinges, B., & Ronan, G. F. (2015). Group process as a mechanism of change in the group treatment of anger and aggression. *International Journal of Group Psychotherapy, 65*(2), 181-208.

Green, Z. G. (2015). Commentary on "Toward Understanding and Treating Violence in America: Some Contributions From Group Dynamic and Group Therapy Perspectives," *International Journal of Group Psychotherapy, 65*(2), 285-294.

Griffin, A. (2013, December 28). Lanza's psychiatric treatment revealed in documents. *Hartford Courant.* http://articles.courant.com/2013-12-28/news/hc-lanza-sandy-hook-report1228-20131227_1_peter-lanza-adam-lanza-nancy-lanza

Grotstein, J. (2014). Foreword. In V. L. Schermer (Ed.), *Meaning, mind, and self-transformation: Psychoanalytic interpretation and the interpretation of psychoanalysis* (pp. xiii-xix). London: Karnac.

Klein, R. H., & Schermer, V. L. (2015). Toward understanding and treating violence in America: Some contributions from group dynamic and group therapy perspectives. Introduction to Part I. *International Journal of Group Psychotherapy, 65*(1), 1–28.

Lothstein, L. M. (2015). A multi-tiered group therapy model to identify and treat the root causes of domestic violence: A proposal integrating current social neuroscience findings. *International Journal of Group Psychotherapy, 65*(2), 211-240.

McDermott, R., Tingley, D., Cowden, J., Frazzetto, G., & Johnson, D. D. (2009). Monoamine oxidase A gene (MAOA) predicts behavioral aggression following provocation. *Proceedings of the National Academy of Sciences U.S.A., 106*(7), 2118-2123.

Phillips, S. B. (2015). The dangerous role of silence in the relationship between trauma and violence: A group response. *International Journal of Group Psychotherapy, 65*(1), 65-87.

Post, J. M. (2015). Terrorism and right-wing extremism: The changing face of terrorism and political violence in the 21st century: The virtual community of hatred. *International Journal of Group Psychotherapy, 65*(2), 243-271.

Rice, C. A. (2015). A group therapist reflects on violence in America. *International Journal of Group Psychotherapy, 65*(1), 41-62.

Robertz, F. J. (2007). Deadly dreams: What motivates school shootings? *Scientific American: Mind and Brain.* http://www.scientificamerican.com/article/deadly-dreams/?page=2.

Roller, B. (2015). The Voices of Violence Series. *International Journal of Group Psychotherapy, 65*(1), 109-114.

Schermer, V. L. (2015). Violence, threat, and emotional "malnourishment": An interview with Dr. Dan Gottlieb. *International Journal of Group Psychotherapy, 65*(1), 31-39.

Schore, A. N. (2003). *Affect regulation and disorders of the self.* New York: Norton.

Speck, R. V., & Attneave, C. L. (1973). *Family networks.* New York: Pantheon.

Stern, D. (2002). *The first relationship: Infant and mother.* Cambridge, MA: Harvard University Press.

Strasser, S. (1985). *Understanding and explanation.* Pittsburgh, PA: Duquesne University Press.

Thomas, N. K. (2015). There's always a villain to punish: Violence in America. *International Journal of Group Psychotherapy, 65*(1), 89-107.

Winnicott, D. W. (1960). The theory of the parent-infant relationship. *International Journal of Psycho-Analysis, 41,* 585-595.

Yalom, I. D., & Leszcz, M. (1995). *The theory and practice of group psychotherapy* (5th ed.) New York: Basic Books.

Group Process as a Mechanism of Change in the Group Treatment of Anger and Aggression

JAMES GERHART, PH.D.
KRISTA HOLMAN, PH.D.
BAILEY SEYMOUR, B.A.
BRANDY DINGES, B.A.
GEORGE F. RONAN, PH.D.

ABSTRACT

Angry reactions can present unique challenges to the process of conducting group therapy, especially when providing group treatment to participants who have histories of angry or aggressive behavior. This article briefly reviews relevant literature and describes a group-based violence reduction training program (VRTP). The VRTP conceptualizes anger and aggression from a frustration-aggression framework and employs treatment derived from research in the area of social problem-solving. An emphasis is placed on how fostering group experiences consistent with Irving Yalom's classic work on the theory and practice of group therapy can reinforce skill acquisition and general treatment responsiveness. Management of the group process is a plausible mechanism of change in group treatment of anger. We highlight the challenges and benefits of dealing with anger-infused communication while ensuring the integrity of the overall group process. Case examples are provided for illustration of VRTP. Future research can answer important questions about group process and mechanisms of change in group-based treatments for anger and aggression.

James Gerhart is with the Department of Behavioral Sciences at Rush University Medical Center in Chicago. Krista Holman, Bailey Seymour, Brandy Dinges, and George F. Ronan are with the Department of Psychology at Central Michigan University in Mount Pleasant.

VIOLENCE IN AMERICA

THE IMPORTANCE OF PROCESS IN THE GROUP TREATMENT OF ANGER

Anger and the expression of anger are central to the human experience and occur cross-culturally. Anger is often conceptualized as a negative emotional response to stress and provocation (DiGiuseppe & Tafrate, 2007; Gardner & Moore, 2008). The expression of anger in humans is thought to vary based on biological, environmental, and psychological vulnerabilities (DiGiuseppe & Tafrate, 2007; Gardner & Moore, 2008). Contemporary definitions posit three facets of human anger that include angry affect and emotion, hostile attitudes and beliefs, and aggressive verbal and physical behavior. Mild forms of anger may be experienced as annoyance or irritability, whereas more intense forms of anger may be experienced as hatred or rage. Increases in the intensity of anger are often accompanied by changes in physiological arousal resulting from activation of the sympathetic component of the autonomic nervous system (Barefoot, Dodge, Peterson, Dahlstrom, & Williams, 1989).

Because anger serves multiple functions, some have argued that the response is best understood within context (Ollendick, 1996). Although the subjective experience of anger is often unpleasant and humans often seek to decrease such negative internal states, anger when properly channeled can motivate persistence in the face of frustrating situations. At times, however, negative internal states can propel humans to behave in an impulsive or suboptimal manner. Anger that does not match contextual cues or leads to a degradation in functioning is viewed as maladaptive. While the maladaptive display of anger can still serve to reduce the immediate internal distress of the person expressing the anger, poorly regulated anger can interfere with effective problem-solving and can elicit distress in other individuals (Ronan, Dreer, Dollard, & Ronan, 2004; Ronan, Gerhart, Bannister, & Udell, 2010). Poorly regulated anger has also been associated with general problems in the areas of health maintenance, pain regulation, and relationship dissatisfaction that may motivate individuals to seek psychological treatment (Brosschot & Thayer, 1998; Bruehl, Burns, Chung, Ward, & Johnson, 2002; Gerhart, Seymour, Maurelli, Holman, & Ronan, 2013; Ronan et al., 2004).

Basic research has identified several key components associated with the lack of a match between angry responses and contextual cues. Aggressive attitudes and hostile attribution biases have been shown to predispose individuals to interpret contexts as more threatening or frustrating than warranted (Huesmann, 1998). Anger-related activation of the fight/flight response has been associated with impulsive and aggressive responding (Bongard, Al'Absi, & Lovallo, 1998). The use of ineffective conflict management strategies during episodes of anger and aggression predicts less prosocial outcomes (Ronan et al., 2004).

While available treatments vary with regard to theoretical orientation in the strategies used for treating anger and aggression, the vast majority of empirically evaluated programs have included behavioral, cognitive, or cognitive-behavioral methods (Beck & Fernandez, 1998; DiGuiseppe & Tafrate, 2007). Most empirically investigated anger and aggression programs emphasize the restructuring of angry attitudes, reducing physiological arousal, enhancing problem-solving, and improving interpersonal communication, and evidence suggests that treatments employing multiple components may have added benefit for sustained change after treatment (DiGuiseppie & Tafrate, 2007; Saini, 2009). This added benefit of multicomponent treatments may be attributable to the complexity of anger and aggression, both between and within individuals, and the need for a diverse skill set to regulate anger and aggression.

Mechanisms of Change

As meta-analytic work supporting the efficacy of psychotherapy accumulates, important research questions are shifting away from asking *which* treatments work, to asking *how* and *why* specific treatment contexts and mechanisms enable treatments to work (Gibbons et al., 2009; Kazdin, 2007). This approach suggests that identifying mechanisms of change will allow clinicians to be more effective in guiding clients through the process of change. More research is needed to identify mechanisms responsible for change in anger and aggression treatments, and the common factors in psychotherapy suggest plausible contexts and mechanisms of change including client background and engagement, along with the therapeutic alliance and skill acquisition via the group therapy process (Leszcz & Kobos, 2008).

It is well recognized that the client plays an active role in response to treatment, as it is the client that must engage and learn from the therapeutic experience (Tallman & Bohart, 1999). Client background and developmental history provide an important context for understanding response to treatment. For instance, treatment responsiveness for anger and aggression tends to vary depending on static client factors such as exposure to traumatic stress and personality traits because the client must integrate new learning with past experience and behavior (Gerhart, Ronan, Russ, & Seymour, 2013; Marshall et al., 2010). Dynamic client factors also play a role in treatment response. Participants enter treatment with varying levels of motivation, confidence, and commitment to change. A key goal of early treatment is helping clients identify the consequences of their angry behaviors and build hope and confidence for change, as these changes are associated with better response to treatment (McMurran, 2009; Ronan, Gerhart, Bannister, & Udell, 2010).

As is often the case when dealing with emotionally taxing issues, the quality of the therapeutic alliance predicts treatment responsiveness, and it is also one plausible mechanism of change in anger and aggression interventions (Sparks, Duncan, & Miller, 2008). Establishing a sound therapeutic alliance can be especially challenging when interacting with people who have evinced poorly controlled anger and aggression (Howells & Day, 2003). Our experience suggests that clients who seek help with managing anger and aggression often do so at the prompting of significant others or components of the legal system. Clients who enter treatment to please others may disagree with the assessed need for treatment or the treatment goals, and disagreements about the basics of treatment can result in ruptures in the therapeutic alliance (DiGuiseppe, Tafrate, & Eckhardt, 1994). Client anger can also result in anxiety or angry reactions from the treatment provider, and these emotions, in turn, may increase defensiveness or avoidant therapeutic styles (Sharkin, 1989). Burns and colleagues (1999) found that client irritability interacted with other emotional states to erode the therapeutic alliance. Given that anger may present unique challenges to the clinician, some have argued that clinicians benefit from specific training in responding to client anger and facilitating readiness to change (Hess, Knox, & Hill, 2006; McMurran, 2009).

Treatments for anger and aggression are frequently delivered in group settings to maximize cost effectiveness, with the resulting social dynamics adding multiple layers of complexity (Butler & Fuhriman, 1983; Long & Cope, 1980; Yalom, 1970). Nevertheless, group therapy for forensic populations can be helpful for a variety of reasons that are well integrated into the group therapy literature (e.g., Yalom 1970; 1975; 1995). Group therapy process has been generally defined as the events and interchanges that occur in the group treatment session, such as participant learning, the processing of emotional material, modeling of effective interpersonal behavior, and the development of cohesion among group members (Yalom & Leszcz, 2005). Group therapy provides clients with opportunities to learn from others with similar backgrounds, interact with others who experience similar concerns, practice and enhance interpersonal skills, and obtain feedback from like-minded group members (MacDevitt & Sanislow, 1987; Morgan, Ferrell, & Winterowd, 1999; Winterowd, Morgan, & Ferrell, 2001). Positive group interactions can be particularly helpful for offenders in restricted settings who otherwise would have limited opportunity to practice effective interpersonal skills in a safe, therapeutic environment. Although these group processes often serve to enhance treatment outcome, failure to form a cohesive and cooperative group can magnify challenges for providers. Conflict and disagreement between a portion of group members can interfere with the overall group effectiveness; however, if properly managed, group tension and conflict can be harnessed to promote behavioral change (Yalom & Leszcz, 2005).

The literature on group therapy suggests that the therapeutic process itself is a plausible mechanism of change in the group treatment of psychosocial concerns (Corsini & Rosenberg, 1955). Researchers have distilled three group-based mechanisms of change that have been categorized as involving cognitive, emotional, or behavioral components (Erdman, 2009). At the cognitive level, group participants learn that anger, frustration, and stress are universal experiences. This change in understanding can serve to reduce the stigma of anger and emotional distress.

Participants learn to challenge unhelpful thought patterns, such as catastrophic thinking, that tend to escalate angry arousal. As participants learn more about the psychology of anger and aggression, they are better prepared to discriminate angry emotion from aggressive behavior and to regulate their anger by taking into account others' perceptions of anger and aggression. At the emotional level, participants learn to accept and process emotional distress. This learning can result from group members sharing simple techniques for the expression of pent-up emotional distress and the development of more complex mechanisms for processing emotion or the habituation of strong physical reactions (Jaycox, Foa, & Morral, 1998; Stewart, Villatte, & McHugh, 2012). As such, the reduction of angry arousal enables the participant to reduce urges to engage in impulsive and aggressive responding, and to adopt more altruistic and empathic attitudes toward others. Finally, at the behavioral level, group participants can learn new skills in interpersonal contexts that may mimic the situations where their anger occurs. Verbal instruction on anger regulation can help therapist and group members to model effective anger-regulation behaviors, and immediate feedback can directly reinforce effective anger regulation or extinguish ineffective aggressive behaviors.

By describing a group-based intervention for violent offenders, our goal is to enhance the efforts of clinicians who provide group-based treatments for angry and aggressive clients. We review the program's conceptual foundations and research results and provide illustrative case examples. We hope that this will not only guide clinicians to utilize plausible mechanisms of change in group treatment for anger and aggression but also direct attention to emerging empirical methods of the analysis of mechanisms of change.

VRTP Overview

The Violence Reduction Training Program (VRTP), located at a midwestern university, is a group-based program for adults with difficulty regulating anger and aggression. The majority of VRTP participants are court-ordered to treatment after being convicted of violent offenses such as aggravated assault, assault, assault and battery, and domestic violence. A smaller percentage of participants are self-referred for help managing anger and aggression in community, occupational, or family settings. Similar to other clinical samples of angry and aggressive individuals, it is not uncommon for group membership to be heterogeneous, with participants ranging from emotionally withdrawn to emotionally volatile and situationally angry to antisocial (Babcock, Miller, & Siard, 2003; Holtzworth-Munroe & Stuart, 1994).

The angry, aggressive, and violent behaviors of VRTP participants are conceptualized as ineffective strategies for resolving real-life problems. As such, the VRTP seeks to expand participants' social problem-solving repertoires for addressing life problems (D'Zurilla & Goldfried, 1971; Nezu, 2004). Working with offenders can be challenging, given that a significant portion of participants enter treatment with low readiness to change (Ronan, Gerhart, Bannister, & Udell, 2010) and may utilize angry problem-solving strategies in group sessions. Despite these challenges, ongoing research indicates that participation in the VRTP is associated with enhanced social problem-solving skills and reduction of ineffective conflict management strategies.

Conceptual Foundations of VRTP

The VRTP has its conceptual foundations in the modern reformulation of the frustration-aggression hypothesis (Berkowitz & Harmon-Jones, 2004) and social problem-solving theory (D'Zurilla & Goldfried, 1971; Nezu, 2004; Skinner, 1984). These conceptual foundations provide the clinician with a framework for understanding basic mechanisms of change for anger and aggression. The frustration-aggression hypothesis maintains that anger and aggression are often triggered by exposure to aversive, stressful, and frustrating events (Berkowitz, 1989; Berkowitz & Harmon-Jones, 2004). The anger-provoking effects of common stressors such as discomfort, pain, goal thwarting, insults, and resource loss tend to be ubiquitous.

Social problem-solving theory provides an explanation for why some individuals are more aggressive in reaction to frustration and stress (D'Zurilla & Goldfried, 1971; Nezu, 2004). The social problem-solving process involves attitudinal components, including positive and negative attributions about problems; decision-making components that include how to identify effective solutions; and behavioral components that include how to inhibit impulsive responding and approach rather than avoid problems. Anger-regulation problems are conceptualized to occur in relation to deficits in social problem-solving. For instance, an individual is expected to be more likely to react to life problems with poorly regulated anger if he or she tends to make hostile attributions towards others, or impulsively reacts to problems without considering all viable solutions.

Anger, in comparison to other emotions, is especially detrimental to social problem-solving because it tends to motivate individuals to directly confront problems (Carver & Harmon-Jones, 2009), but it is also associated with a probability of impulsive responding and a decrease in the ability to delay gratification (Gerhart, Heath, Fitzgerald, & Hoerger, 2013). When confronted by real-life problems, angry individuals are more likely to act in verbally and physically aggressive ways to change the behavior of others. These impulsive reactions may be reinforced to the extent that they provide short-term escape from aversive emotional states and tension, but they often complicate objective problems and amplify interpersonal conflict (Gardner & Moore, 2008).

The VRTP targets both frustration-aggression reactions and social problem-solving deficits. Anger is reduced by preventing the occurrence of future stressful events, reducing cognitive reactivity to stress through cognitive challenging, and enhancing the relaxation response through breathing retraining, guided imagery, and progressive muscle relaxation. Aggression is further reduced by training participants in more effective communication strategies, such as active listening and conflict management skills.

Intake Evaluation

Clients complete an intake evaluation and risk-assessment lasting approximately 75 minutes. The primary goals are to clarify the reason for referral, assess risk of violence, and foster a working alliance with the participant. The intake is also helpful for identifying special learning styles that may require accommodation during treatment, and for determining whether participants are appropriate for group-based treatment (Yalom & Leszcz, 2005). For example, individuals with learning disabilities may require additional accommodations to informational materials to enhance skill acquisition. Participants may dictate out-of-session assignments to accommodate writing difficulties. In some instances, the intake procedures reveal that an individual is not amenable to group treatment, or that more intensive and/or individualized services are required because they exhibit hyperactive or disruptive behaviors that would interfere with the group process. Individualized treatment protocols are developed for clients who are not deemed appropriate for group treatment.

Several structured procedures are used to screen potential group members. The Historical-Clinical Risk Management-20 (HCR-20; Webster, Douglas, Eaves, & Hart, 1997) is a structured interview that asks clients a series of questions to quantify static (unchanging) and dynamic (changing) factors relevant to understanding past aggression and predicting future aggression. A paper-and-pencil version of the Structured Interview for DSM-IV Personality Module (SCID-II; First, Gibbon, Spitzer, Williams, & Benjamin, 1997) is used to screen for the presence of personality traits that are queried during the interview to assess for the presence of formal personality disorders. Finally, components of the Psychopathy Checklist (PCL-R; Hare, 1991) are administered to assess traits associated with psychopathy, such as aggressive narcissism, lack of remorse, callousness, and impulsivity (Douglas, Ogloff, Nicholls, & Grant, 1999). When warranted, the clinician may review available legal documents to corroborate participant reports.

Treatment Summary[1]

Treatment is delivered in 13 90-minute sessions. Typically, 10–12 participants are recruited for each group, but group size depends on the flow of community referrals. Because many cli-

---

1. Electronic copies of a *Violence Reduction Training Program Therapist Manual*, a *Violence Reduction Training Program Client Manual*, and all accompanying video clips can be obtained by sending a request to George F. Ronan, Ph.D., ABPP, Director, Violence Reduction Training Program, Carls Center for Clinical Care, Health Profession Building, Central Michigan University, Mount Pleasant, MI 48858 or an e-mail to George Ronan at ronan1gf@cmich.edu.

ents are mandated to treatment by either the legal system or significant others, motivation to actively engage can be suboptimal. The first two sessions present a series of 5-minute videos developed for the VRTP to enhance readiness to change (Prochaska & DiClemente, 1983). These video clips guide group members through a critical evaluation of statements made by protagonists who minimize the negative consequences of their aggressive behavior, acknowledge the negative consequences of their aggressive behavior, or actively learn skills to decrease their aggressive behavior. The gender and race of the perpetrators, as well as the context of the aggression, were intentionally varied to ensure relevance for a diverse clinical sample. Motivational interviewing strategies are employed to elicit and reinforce increased readiness to change (Miller & Rollnick, 2002). These discussions are referred to periodically through the group sessions to foster a group process that promotes readiness to change.

Session three provides psychoeducation on the VRTP conceptualization of anger and aggression. Clients are taught to distinguish angry thought and emotion from aggressive behavior and to learn about the role that frustration plays in anger and aggression. A critical goal of this third session is for participants to begin to separate angry cognition and emotion from aggressive and violent behavior, so that they can experience subjective anger without feeling the need to suppress it to maintain self-control or, conversely, to behave aggressively when feeling aroused. To generalize this distinction to daily life, participants are asked to complete out-of-session diaries of anger arousal and to detail reactions to strong anger and aggressive outbursts.

Sessions four through seven concern the social problem-solving model. Session four emphasizes the process of problem identification, and participants are encouraged to separate facts from assumptions and identify tangible stressors like financial problems or relationship issues that evoke anger and aggression in their lives. A key goal is for clients to begin to distinguish facts and evidence from opinions and assumptions about their problems. For instance, a client may begin to separate the fact that her partner behaved in a hostile manner from her assumption that she is no longer loved. In this example, the goal is to restructure the interpretation to reduce time spent ruminating on fears of rejection and abandonment while empowering the client to focus on a rational goal of reducing hostile communication. Session five continues to describe problem identification, and instruction is given in breathing retraining to regulate physiological arousal that may interfere with problem-solving (Hazaleus & Deffenbacher, 1986). Sessions six and seven train clients to set clear behavioral goals to problem-solve, brainstorm, and select and implement possible solutions.

Sessions eight and nine emphasize strategies to overcome common barriers to problem-solving. Session eight revisits the impact of physiological arousal on problem-solving in greater detail. Participants discuss the contribution of anger and anxiety to impulsive and avoidant coping styles. Participants are guided to rehearse deep muscle relaxation (McCallie, Blum, & Hood, 2006) and visual imagery (Hall, Hall, Stradling & Young, 2006). For example, one visual imagery exercise invites participants to imagine being at the beach, incorporating all five senses to enhance their engagement with the imagery. Session nine addresses the contribution of thinking errors to angry emotion and aggressive behavior. Participants learn to use thought records to identify and correct common cognitive distortions that amplify distress and anger (Beck, 1971).

Sessions 10 through 12 emphasize communication problems that may interfere with problem-solving. Session 10 provides instruction in effective listening skills. Participants role-play high-conflict scenarios while practicing effective nonverbal (e.g., good eye contact and posture) and verbal communication (e.g., reflective listening). Session 11 emphasizes attitudes and behaviors needed to engage in effective assertive communication. Participants practice stating wants and needs in a respectful manner, repeating their wishes, discussing and resolving breakdowns in communication, and communicating about roles and boundaries. Session 12 emphasizes confrontation management. Participants learn fair-fighting rules and explore high-conflict issues that arise in interpersonal relationships at work and at home. These sessions involve significant behavioral rehearsal, and participants role-play the use of each skill set. Session 13 provides a review of the overall program and allows participants to learn material they may have missed due to absences. At the end of session 13, participants respond to the first post-treatment assessment by completing paper-and-pencil measures. Longer-term follow-up data are collected through surveys and legal document reviews.

Managing Anger in Group Sessions

Yalom (2008) viewed conflict as a necessary part of group process, and clinically relevant expressions of anger are common when treating aggression in a group format (Nadelson, 1977). Group members often experience increased affect when discussing difficulties or recounting prior anger episodes. Given that anger and aggression tend to occur within the context of interpersonal relationships, it is expected that these reactions will periodically generalize to the treatment context if the client becomes frustrated or disappointed with the treatment or the clinician (Kohlenberg & Tsai, 1991; McCullough, 2006; Nadelson, 1977). In these situations, participants often display physiological correlates of anger, such as a flushed face, tense posture, and angry affect, as well as low-intensity aggressive behaviors, such as verbal bellicosity or door slamming.

The direct confrontation of participant anger can be challenging and, at times, perceived as threatening (Hess et al., 2006). Whereas some clinicians experience shame and anger when their clinical abilities are challenged by angry participants (Hahn, 1995), others experience frustration when working with hostile clients who behave aggressively or ambivalently (Groves, 1978). While it is true that the most data about optimal clinician response to client hostility are anecdotal, there has been a growing recognition that clinician emotional reactions to participant anger can be used tactfully to enhance treatment responsiveness. For instance, a survey study by Dalenberg (2004) found that clients were attuned to clinician responses to anger and reported greater treatment satisfaction when concern and compassion were used. VRTP practitioners are encouraged to internally acknowledge their emotional reactions to client hostility and to redirect that emotional reaction toward fostering the group member's well-being. Because the clinical formulation is built on principles of behavior that apply to both VRTP participants and practitioners, in-session expressions of anger are viewed as unique opportunities for practitioners to model, prompt, and directly reinforce effective problem-solving responses *in vivo*.

Group leaders are trained to model self-control and empathic listening skills which set the stage for effective problem-solving. Active listening statements such as, "It sounds like you're ticked off right now; let's talk and see if we can figure this out" convey both an interest in the group member's well-being and a willingness to calmly address, rather than avoid or impulsively confront, angry affect. A positive and thoughtful reaction opens the door to the problem-definition step of problem-solving. Directly dealing with client anger also provides an opportunity for the group leader to model empathy and the direct validation of the angry participant's experience when responding to anger. The goal is to have participants imitate similar strategies in their day-to-day living (Bandura, 1969; Yalom, 1995). If needed, additional steps of the problem-solving model may be explored.

Using clinical judgment, practitioners may also decide to periodically model effective anger regulation by self-disclosing examples of their own effective anger-regulation strategies, such as sharing a personally frustrating situation that evoked anger and the use of relaxation techniques or cognitive reframing. Used strategically, such self-disclosures may facilitate the group process and build rapport, but care should be taken not to inadvertently burden group participants (Dies, 1973). Clinical judgment should be used with caution, as cognitive biases have been shown to compromise clinical decision making (Garb, 2004). In our clinical experience, we find that self-disclosure is most effective when the clinician first reflects on what material to disclose with co-therapists and supervisors, but this topic has not been explored empirically. We also find that a foundational understanding of social problem-solving principles enables the clinician to seize on therapeutic opportunities as they unfold in the here-and-now of group process.

VRTP practitioners also enhance skill acquisition through process statements that shape and reinforce problem-solving behaviors. Process interpretations can call attention to a specific behavior or process during treatment and explicate the function or consequence of behavior in the form of an if-then rule. A VRTP practitioner might state, "It sounds like you feel relieved now that you've brainstormed some options. I'm glad we took the time to look at the problem and some possible solutions." This guides the participant's attention to the reinforcing results of problem-solving, in this case, a sense of emotional relief. The goal is for participants to learn to use their own process interpretations to resolve a conflict.

Although the problem-solving theory underlying VRTP encourages the resolution of problems, participants also learn that there are times when anger arousal is overwhelming and problem-solving should be delayed until arousal decreases and "cooler heads prevail." In such a case, the participant learns to signal a time-out period so that anger reactions and fight/flight responses can run their course. Periodically, similar situations will arise in the course of group treatment, and if the practitioner judges that discussion may escalate to impulsive anger reactions, the group leader may help participants temporarily disengage from the problem at hand. Such a strategy is critical for regulating physiological arousal; however, if used inflexibly, disengagement may also encourage avoidant coping. Therefore, practitioners need to highlight these process interventions by making a statement such as, "It sounds like we feel strongly about this topic. Let's take a break, and come back to this idea later." Whereas process interpretations increase the salience of group communication, *process interventions* direct and modify behaviors as they occur. Process interventions are especially useful for de-escalating high-conflict group interactions.

Practitioner Training

The VRTP was developed and implemented within the clinical psychology training program at Central Michigan University. Most practitioners are trainees completing their doctoral degrees in clinical psychology. Training is delivered in accord with the general foundations of cognitive-behavioral clinical training programs (Klepac et al., 2012), and the supervisory process gives special attention to the unique challenges associated with dealing with frequent participant anger and aggression. In addition to the rote learning of treatment principles and protocols, trainees shadow experienced practitioners, receive regular weekly supervision, and consult with the supervising psychologist on an as-needed basis. The shadowing experience is an especially valuable training experience because veteran practitioners serve as models and debrief on their subjective reactions to the group process. Such training is also beneficial for helping trainees and clinicians normalize and accept common reactions to challenging group interactions, such as frustration and self-doubt. Direct clinical supervision provides an opportunity for trainees to process their reactions to stressful group processes, problem-solve, and role-play effective responses under supportive conditions to mitigate the use of reactive or avoidant responses to the group process (Hess et al., 2006). The emphasis is placed on helping the trainee or clinician model effective problem-solving skills, even during their own emotional reactions to the group process.

Case Vignettes: Anger Evoked in Session

Certain situations inherent in the therapeutic context are more likely to trigger clinically relevant behaviors, including anger. Kohlenberg and Tsai (1991) offer several examples, such as time structure, fees, practitioner mistakes, and emotional expressions that may evoke problem behaviors, such as anger. In our experience with VRTP, participant anger tends to be triggered by frustrating circumstances, such as inconvenient hours, inability to pay fees, and disagreements over treatment progress. Some examples from VRTP clients are highlighted below.

Reporting Attendance and Participation to Parole and Probation Officers. It is common practice for parole and probation officers to receive regular updates on the attendance and progress of court-ordered offenders. Typically, a weekly letter is mailed to the probation officer with a brief note about the participant's compliance with treatment. While probation officers are not provided with information regarding what the person said, they receive information about attendance, participation, and homework completion. This reporting process can generate concerns, as exemplified by the case of Trevor, a middle-aged male who was court-ordered to treatment after an altercation at a local bar. While engaged in treatment, Trevor worked in the food service industry, and his work schedule interfered with his ability to attend sessions. A mid-treatment review resulted in Trevor being informed that he would need to make up portions of the treatment protocol because he had only completed four of seven sessions, and had failed to turn in several homework assignments. Trevor became visibly angry at the news, exhibiting a flushed red face and stiff posture, and he raised his voice to yell that he had been treated unfairly. The practitioner immediately addressed the anger with active listening skills: "It sounds like you're frustrated that you won't be able to pass this section. Tell me what concerns you the most. I want to make sure I understand."

Through continued problem-definition, it became apparent that Trevor was scared of being re-arrested. He became less agitated as he discussed his concerns. To support his independent problem-solving, Trevor was encouraged to check his facts and assumptions: "That does sound scary. What evidence do you have that you'll be rearrested?" Trevor explained that a family member had been arrested for failing to enroll in court-ordered treatment. Trevor was coached to proactively approach the problem and contact his probation officer the next day when he felt calm enough. Although he appeared preoccupied during the remainder of session, he contacted his probation officer as planned and arranged to remediate his missed attendance and poor homework completion. In this case, the compromise was agreeable for all parties. Trevor was able to avoid extra jail time, and the practitioner and probation officer could be flexible without ignoring the rules and potentially reinforcing Trevor's avoidance of treatment.

Disagreement Resulting in Group Escalation. In week six, the video vignette at the beginning of the session portrays a scenario in which a woman takes a day off from work to plan a surprise birthday party for her husband. When the husband calls her at work, he is told that she has taken a personal day. Without knowing about the plans for his party, he suspects that she is being unfaithful and confronts her, becoming physically aggressive. The woman tells him about the party and leaves. While discussing the vignette, the group members were skeptical of the wife's explanation. The group leader reviewed the distinction between facts and assumptions and prompted the clients to consider alternative explanations. The situation escalated quickly; group members raised their voices, and each emphatic claim that the wife was cheating fueled the other group members' level of arousal.

Rather than assuming an adversarial stance, the group leader chose to roll with resistance by redirecting their attention to another example. The group members responded better to this example and were able to distinguish the facts and assumptions in the situation. When the level of arousal in the room had returned to baseline, the group leader revisited the scenario from the video vignette. After calming down and learning to identify assumptions using another example, the group members were able to view the wife's suspected infidelity as an assumption rather than a fact, and thus were better able to separate facts from assumptions when formulating problems.

Expressing Emotion and Challenging Hot Thoughts. The VRTP devotes several sessions to cognitive challenging, during which clients discuss common thinking errors that lead to anger. It is helpful when examples generated from their own lives are used to illustrate the concepts. For example, Joan, a middle-aged female client, often engaged in conflict with her roommate, a woman in her early twenties, and she was referred to VRTP following an altercation. Joan found her roommate to be incredibly frustrating, stating that she could not even perform basic household tasks correctly. The group leader helped Joan identify some "hot thoughts" related to her roommate, such as, "She is stupid" and "She is lazy." Through further discussion, Joan revealed that the young woman had grown up in a neglectful household. Joan was eventually able to challenge these hot thoughts by considering that her roommate may not have been taught any basic skills. She began to view herself as a positive role model and reconceptualized their living situation as an opportunity to help the young woman learn how to perform certain basic household tasks. Although Joan still became frustrated at times, her new conceptualizations led her to interpret her roommate's behavior as less intentional. Joan became less frustrated and angered by her roommate's behaviors.

Threatening and Aggressive Behavior. Participants undergo a risk assessment prior to enrollment in the VRTP, and all participants are informed that the program has zero tolerance for violence.

Participants who engage in physical aggression or violence within treatment sessions will face appropriate legal consequences. Several policies and procedures are used to enhance participant and practitioner safety. For example, the clinic doors automatically lock so that individuals who leave a group session cannot return without authorized access. VRTP groups are always co-led so that one practitioner may leave to contact public safety officers in case of a threat.

Periodically, participants will exhibit high intensity anger and threatening behaviors. These responses tend to be the exception rather than the rule, but they can be among the most challenging responses to manage in a session. For instance, paranoid and hostile ideation may lead some participants to misperceive treatment goals or intent. In these volatile situations, practitioners strive to model effective conflict-management skills. This entails maintaining open and non-threatening body language, speaking in an assertive but calm voice, and empathically rolling with resistance (Miller & Rollnick, 2002). The practitioner may also explore and validate underlying fears or frustration related to the anger. If conflict management strategies fail, the individual is encouraged to leave. From time to time, individuals have become verbally aggressive, displaced anger by throwing papers and slamming doors, and stormed out of the session.

Trent was a young adult referred by his probation officer after making threatening remarks about his ex-girlfriend. During the intake session, he presented as behaviorally agitated and suspicious about the need to complete psychosocial questionnaires. Trent was certain that his referral to treatment stemmed from false accusations by his "jealous" ex-girlfriend who "was just trying to get attention." Because of his frustration with his ex-girlfriend, motivational interviewing techniques were used to roll with his resistance toward treatment. Results of the evaluation suggested that Trent exhibited a mix of narcissistic and dependent personality traits, and his behavioral history was positive for threatening remarks towards friends and family.

Trent appeared agitated during the first group treatment session a week later. He squirmed in his chair and glared at the other participants. Trent's agitation peaked early on when participants introduce themselves and, if willing, discuss the factors leading up to their participation. Two participants disclosed their reasons for referral: domestic assault and child abuse. When the discussion came to focus on Trent, he jumped from his seat, pointed at the lead clinician, and stated, "I'm sick of being interrogated about this. You know very well that this is all a bunch of BS, and if you keep it up, you'll all pay. I'm out." Trent threw his client manual in the direction of the lead clinician and stormed out of the treatment room.

So as not to further escalate the situation, the lead clinician did not interfere with the participant leaving, but followed behind to see that he left the clinic and that the clinic door was securely locked. The lead clinician then contacted campus security and the participant's probation officer to inform them of the incident. The co-clinician remained in the room to resume the group process. When a group member leaves in anger, the situation is processed by the remaining group members. The focus is often on the underlying skill sets that might have resulted in a different outcome. Participants who leave a group session under these circumstances undergo a subsequent individual screening to determine whether they will continue in the program. If safety concerns remain, then the appropriate persons are notified. Group interactions involving high volatility are reviewed by the VRTP team. In this case, the probation officer deemed that Trent had violated his probation, and he was sentenced to treatment while incarcerated.

Research From VRTP

Self-report and reoffense data gleaned from court records provide support for the feasibility and effectiveness of VRTP. Following treatment, program completers demonstrated enhanced social problem-solving skills and a higher ratio of positive to negative strategies for managing high-conflict situations (Ronan, Gerhart, Bannister, & Udell, 2010). As such, participants who complete treatment are expected to exhibit more adaptive thinking about stressful life situations, and to reduce avoidant and impulsive reactions to frustration. Participants also demonstrate an enhanced ability to identify effective solutions for resolving conflicts, such as talking through problems and communicating assertively about wishes and desires. This study also found that approximately 31% of VRTP participants failed to complete treatment, although treatment dropout was unrelated to pretreatment readiness to change.

As noted, VRTP participants are often heterogeneous with regard to referral reasons, background factors, and developmental history. A significant proportion present to treatment with longstanding interpersonal problems and problematic self-concepts. Although participants with antisocial, borderline, and histrionic traits reported using higher levels of negative conflict-management strategies than other VRTP clients at pretreatment, those individuals with Cluster B personality traits decreased their use of negative strategies during treatment (Gerhart, Ronan, Russ, & Seymour, 2013). This provides evidence that VRTP can be beneficial for participants whose anger and aggression are related to longstanding interpersonal problems.

At present, more research is needed to fully evaluate long-term effects of VRTP and its mechanisms of change. While the three-year VRTP follow-up data are not yet published, offenders who completed similar programming in jail were less likely to reoffend over a three-year period when compared to jailed offenders who failed to complete treatment (Ronan, Gerhart, Dollard, & Maurelli, 2010). This line of research has also hinted at plausible mechanisms of change in VRTP, including enhanced social problem-solving and enhanced readiness to change (Ronan, Gerhart, Bannister, & Udell, 2010); however, more comprehensive assessments across the full course of treatment are needed.

New Directions in Assessing Mechanisms of Change

The need for more comprehensive assessment of mechanisms of change in VRTP and related treatments has been made salient by meta-analytic work comparing the effects of bona fide treatments for psychosocial conditions. A number of studies have found that bona fide treatments, or active non-placebo treatments, produce similar outcomes across protocols and treatments for a variety of psychological concerns (Cuijpers et al., 2012; Wampold et al., 1997; Wampold, Minami, Baskin, & Callen Tierney, 2002). The treatments studied often represent diverse theoretical approaches to psychotherapy, and propose unique explanations and causes for treatment outcomes, calling into question whether specific or common mechanisms of change are at work across the various modes of psychotherapy. At present, the treatment outcome literature is composed primarily of pre-to-post treatment comparisons and randomized control trials that have not been designed to evaluate mechanisms of change (Burns et al., 2015; Kazdin, 2007).

Kazdin (2007) offered several recommendations for clinicians and researchers interested in answering questions about why and how treatments work by indentifying causes or mechanisms of change in psychotherapy. Potential mechanisms are basic psychological processes that may plausibly explain changes in the target outcome variable. In the case of group treatment for anger, a researcher may be interested in understanding changes in interpersonal learning or hostile attitudes related to changes in aggressive behaviors. These mechanisms must be operationalized and measured during the course of treatment, with specific attention to the timeline of change in mechanisms and outcome variables. As noted by Burns and colleagues (2015), a substantial change in the mechanism (e.g., interpersonal learning, hostile attitudes) should precede and be statistically correlated with a substantial change in the outcome (e.g., verbal aggression, frequency of violence); however, a change in the outcome variable should not precede change in the mechanism. Frequent measurements of potential mechanisms and outcomes at each treatment timepoint would enable a more fine-grained analysis of the timing of change (Kazdin, 2007).

Based on these recommendations, the VRTP is moving forward to assess theoretical mechanisms of change in violence reduction based on social problem-solving theory and alternative models. Weekly assessments of hostile problem attitudes and aggressive behaviors will be analyzed to determine whether VRTP is effective in reducing aggression by first reducing hostile thinking and enhancing readiness to change. Alternative, but plausible competing mechanisms such as anger suppression and avoidance will also be explored (Gardner & Moore, 2008). Mechanisms of change can then be linked to specific intervention components by assessing the timeline of change and conducting more fine-grained analysis of intervention techniques. For instance, it is expected that the initial treatment sessions should have the greatest impact on readiness to change, as these sessions target treatment-related attitudes. In contrast, the mid to later treatment sessions should have a more substantial impact on hostile thinking, as problem-solving attitudes and cognitive distortions are addressed at this time. Behavioral coding of recorded sessions is needed to ascertain how specific treatment techniques and group processes, such as cohesion, impact change in mechanisms and key outcomes.

CONCLUSION

The treatment of anger, aggression, and violence has moved away from a reliance on theories of psychotherapy toward a reliance on basic research that has identified relevant variables and mechanisms of change. The VRTP is a group-based protocol designed to enhance the ability of clients to regulate the expression of their anger and to reduce their frequency of aggressive and violent responding. Research on frustration-aggression models underpins the protocol which targets social problem-solving and other skills to enhance client ability to resolve frustrations in a nonviolent manner. Research indicates that participation in the VRTP is associated with enhanced problem-solving skills and a reduction in negative conflict strategies. Although structured risk assessments are used to rule out clients who are too violent or otherwise unsuitable for the VRTP, client expression of clinically relevant anger is common. Dealing with the direct expression of client anger can be challenging even for experienced clinicians. A sound working alliance, an accurate clinical formulation, and sensitivity to group process increase the probability of being successful when providing services to this difficult population.

REFERENCES

Babcock, J. C., Miller, S. A., & Siard, C. (2003). Toward a typology of abusive women: Differences between partner-only and generally violent women in the use of violence. *Psychology of Women Quarterly, 27*(2), 153-161.

Bandura, A. (1969). *Principles of behavior modification.* New York, NY: Holt.

Barefoot, J. C., Dodge, K. A., Peterson, B. L., Dahlstrom, W. G., & Williams, R. B. (1989). The Cook-Medley hostility scale: Item content and ability to predict survival. *Psychosomatic Medicine, 51*(1), 46-57.

Beck, A. T. (1971). Cognition, affect, and psychopathology. *Archives of General Psychiatry, 24,* 495-500.

Beck, R., & Fernandez, E. (1998). Cognitive-behavioral treatment of anger: A meta-analysis. *Cognitive Therapy and Research, 22,* 63-74.

Berkowitz, L. (1989). The frustration-aggression hypothesis: An examination and reformulation. *Psychological Bulletin, 106,* 59-73.

Berkowitz, L., & Harmon-Jones, E. (2004). Toward an understanding of the determinants of anger. *Emotion, 4*(2), 107-130.

Bongard, S., Al'Absi, M., & Lovallo, W. R. (1998). Interactive effects of trait hostility and anger expression on cardiovascular reactivity in young men. *International Journal of Psychophysiology, 28*(2), 181-191.

Brosschot, J. F., & Thayer, J. F. (1998). Anger inhibition, cardiovascular recovery, and vagal function: A model of the link between hostility and cardiovascular disease. *Annals of Behavioral Medicine, 20*(4), 326-332.

Bruehl, S., Burns, J. W., Chung, O. Y., Ward, P., & Johnson, B. (2002). Anger and pain sensitivity in chronic low back pain patients and pain-free controls: The role of endogenous opioids. *Pain, 99*(1-2), 223-233.

Burns, J. W., Higdon, L. J., Mullen, J. T., Lansky, D., & Wei, J. M. (1999). Relationships among patient hostility, anger expression, depression, and the working alliance in a work hardening program. *Annals of Behavioral Medicine, 21*(1), 77-82.

Burns, J. W., Nielson, W. R., Jensen, M. P., Heapy, A., Czlapinski, R. & Kerns, R. D. (2015). Specific and general therapeutic mechanisms in cognitive-behavioral treatment of chronic pain. *Journal of Consulting and Clinical Psychology, 83*(1), 1–11. doi:10.1037/a0037208

Butler, T., & Fuhriman, A. (1983). Level of functioning and length of time in treatment variables influencing patients' therapeutic experience in group psychotherapy. *International Journal of Group Psychotherapy, 33*(4), 489-505.

Carver, C. S., & Harmon-Jones, E. (2009). Anger is an approach-related affect: Evidence and implications. *Psychological Bulletin, 135*(2), 183-204.

Corsini, R. J., & Rosenberg, B. (1955). Mechanisms of group psychotherapy: Processes and dynamics. *Journal of Abnormal and Social Psychology, 51*(3), 406-411.

Cuijpers, P., Driessen, E., Hollon, S. D., van Oppen, P., Barth, J., & Andersson, G. (2012). The efficacy of non-directive supportive therapy for adult depression: A meta-analysis. *Clinical Psychology Review, 32*(4), 280-291.

Dalenberg, C. J. (2004). Maintaining the safe and effective therapeutic relationship in the context of distrust and anger: Countertransference and complex trauma. *Psychotherapy: Theory, Research, Practice, Training, 41*(4), 438-447.

Dies, R. R. (1973). Group therapist self-disclosure: Development and validation of a scale. *Journal of Consulting and Clinical Psychology, 41*(1), 97-103.

DiGiuseppe, R., & Tafrate, R. (2007). *Understanding anger and anger disorders.* New York, NY: Oxford University Press.

DiGiuseppe, R., Tafrate, R., & Eckhardt, C. (1994). Critical issues in the treatment of anger. *Cognitive and Behavioral Practice, 1,* 111-132.

Douglas, K. S., Ogloff, J. R., Nicholls, T. L., & Grant, I. (1999). Assessing risk for violence among psychiatric patients: The HCR-20 violence risk assessment scheme and the Psychopathy Checklist: Screening Version. *Journal of Consulting and Clinical Psychology, 67*(6), 917-930.

D'Zurilla, T. J., & Goldfried, M. R. (1971). Problem solving and behavior modification. *Journal of Abnormal Psychology, 78*(1), 107-26.

Erdman, S. A. (2009). Therapeutic factors in group counseling: implications for audiologic rehabilitation. *Perspectives on Aural Rehabilitation and Its Instrumentation, 16*(1), 15-28.

First, M. B., Gibbon, M., Spitzer, R. L., Williams, J. B. W., & Benjamin, L. S. (1997). *Structured Clinical Interview for DSM-IV Axis II Personality Disorders (SCID-II).* Washington, DC: American Psychiatric Press.

Gardner, F. L., & Moore, Z. E. (2008). Understanding clinical anger and violence: The anger avoidance model. *Behavior Modification, 32*(6), 897-912.

Garb, H. N. (2004). Clinical judgment and decision making. *Annual Review of Clinical Psychology, 1,* 67-89.

Gerhart, J. I., Heath, N. M., Fitzgerald, C., & Hoerger, M. (2013). Direct and indirect associations between experiential avoidance and reduced delay of gratification. *Journal of Contextual Behavioral Science, 2*(1-2), 9-14.

Gerhart, J. I., Ronan, G. F., Russ, E. U., & Seymour, B. (2013). The moderating effects of cluster B personality traits on violence reduction training: A mixed model analysis. *Journal of Interpersonal Violence, 28*, 45-61.

Gerhart, J. I., Seymour, B., Maurelli, K., Holman, K., & Ronan, G. F. (2013). Health and relationships in violence reduction participants: Indirect effects of angry temperament. *Journal of Forensic Psychiatry and Psychology, 24*(2), 179-191.

Gibbons, M. B. C., Crits-Christoph, P., Barber, J. P., Wiltsey Stirman, S., Gallop, R., Goldstein, L. A., ... Ring-Kurtz, S. (2009). Unique and common mechanisms of change across cognitive and dynamic psychotherapies. *Journal of Consulting and Clinical Psychology, 77*(5), 801-813.

Groves, J. E. (1978). Taking care of the hateful patient. *New England Journal of Medicine, 298*(16), 883-887.

Hahn, W. K. (1995). Therapist anger in group psychotherapy. *International Journal of Group Psychotherapy, 45*, 339-347.

Hall, E., Hall, C., Stradling, P., & Young, D. (2006). *Guided imagery: Creative interventions in counseling & psychotherapy*. Thousand Oaks, CA: Sage.

Hare, R. D. (1991). *The Hare Psychopathy Checklist – Revised*. Toronto, ON: Multi-Health Systems.

Hazaleus, S. L., & Deffenbacher, J. L. (1986). Relaxation and cognitive treatments of anger. *Journal of Consulting and Clinical Psychology, 54*(2), 222-226.

Hess, S. A., Knox, S., & Hill, C. E. (2006). Teaching graduate trainees how to manage client anger: A comparison of three types of training. *Psychotherapy Research, 16*, 282-292.

Holtzworth-Munroe, A., & Stuart, G. L. (1994). Typologies of male batterers: Three subtypes and the differences among them. *Psychological Bulletin, 116*(3), 476-497.

Howells, K., & Day, A. (2003). Readiness for anger management: Clinical and theoretical issues. *Clinical Psychology Review, 23*(2), 319-337.

Huesmann, L. R. (1998). The role of social information processing and cognitive schema in the acquisition and maintenance of habitual aggressive behavior. In R. G. Geen & E. Donnerstein (Eds.), *Human aggression: Theories, research, and implications for policy* (pp. 73-109). New York, NY: Academic Press.

Jaycox, L. H., Foa, E. B., & Morral, A. R. (1998). Influence of emotional engagement and habituation on exposure therapy for PTSD. *Journal of Consulting and Clinical Psychology, 66*(1), 185-192.

Kazdin, A. E. (2007). Mediators and mechanisms of change in psychotherapy research. *Annual Review of Clinical. Psychology, 3*, 1-27.

Klepac, R. K., Ronan, G. F., Andrasik, F., Arnold, K. D., Belar, C. D., Berry, S. L., ... Strauman, T. J. (2012). Guidelines for cognitive behavioral training within doctoral psychology programs in the United States: Report of the Inter-organizational Task Force on Cognitive and Behavioral Psychology Doctoral Education. *Behavior Therapy, 43*(4), 687-697.

Kohlenberg, R. J., & Tsai, M. (1991). *Functional analytic psychotherapy: A guide for creating intense and creative therapeutic relationships.* New York, NY: Plenum.

Leszcz, M., & Kobos, J. C. (2008). Evidence based group psychotherapy: Using AGPA's practice guidelines to enhance clinical effectiveness. *Journal of clinical psychology, 64*(11), 1238-1260.

Long, L. D., & Cope, C. S. (1980). Curative factors in a male felony offender group. *Small Group Behavior, 11*(4), 389-398.

MacDevitt, J. W., & Sanislow, C. (1987). Curative factors in offenders' groups. *Small Group Behavior, 18*(1), 72-81.

Marshall, A. D., Martin, E. K., Warfield, G. A., Doron-Lamarca, S., Niles, B., & Taft, C. T. (2010). The impact of antisocial personality characteristics on anger management treatment for veterans with PTSD. *Psychological Trauma: Theory, Research, Practice, and Policy, 2*(3), 224-231.

McCallie, M. S., Blum, C. M., & Hood, C. J. (2006). Progressive muscle relaxation. *Journal of Human Behavior in the Social Environment, 13*(3), 51-66.

McCullough, J. P., Jr. (2006). *Using disciplined personal involvement to treat chronic depression: CBASP.* New York, NY: Springer.

McMurran, M. (2009). Motivational interviewing with offenders: A systematic review. *Legal and Criminological Psychology, 14*(1), 83-100.

Miller, W. R., & Rollnick, S. (2002). *Motivational interviewing: Preparing people for change* (2nd ed.). New York, NY: Guilford.

Morgan, R. D., Ferrell, S. W., & Winterowd, C. L. (1999). Therapist perceptions of important therapeutic factors in psychotherapy groups for male inmates in state correctional facilities. *Small Group Research, 30*(6), 712-729.

Nadelson, T. (1977). Borderline rage and the therapist's response. *American Journal of Psychiatry, 134*, 748-751.

Nezu, A. M. (2004). Problem solving and behavior therapy revisited. *Behavior Therapy, 35*(1), 1-33.

Ollendick, T. (1996). Violence in youth: Where do we go from here? Behavior therapy's response. *Behavior Therapy, 27*, 485-514.

Prochaska, J. O., & DiClemente, C. C. (1983). Stages and processes of self-change of smoking: Toward an integrative model of change. *Journal of Consulting and Clinical Psychology, 51*(3), 390-395.

Ronan, G. F., Dreer, L. E., Dollard, K., & Ronan, D. W. (2004). Violent couples: Coping and communication skills. *Journal of Family Violence, 19*(2), 131-137.

Ronan, G. F., Gerhart, J. I., Bannister, D., & Udell, C. (2010). Relevance of a stage of change analysis for violence reduction training. *Journal of Forensic Psychiatry and Psychology, 21*, 761-772.

Ronan, G. F., Gerhart, J. I., Dollard, K., & Maurelli, K. (2010). An analysis of survival time to re-arrest in treated and non-treated jailed offenders. *Journal of Forensic Psychiatry and Psychology, 21*(1), 102-112.

Skinner, B. F. (1984). The evolution of behavior. *Journal of the Experimental Analysis of Behavior, 41*, 217-221.

Sparks, J. A., Duncan, B. L., & Miller, S. D. (2008). Common factors in psychotherapy. In J. L. Lebow (Ed.), *Twenty-first century psychotherapies: Contemporary approaches to theory and practice* (pp. 453-497). Hoboken, NJ: Wiley.

Stewart, I., Villate, J., & McHugh, L. (2012). Approaches to the self. In L. McHugh & I. Stewart (Eds.), *The self and perspective taking: Contributions and applications from modern behavioral science* (pp. 3-35). Oakland, CA: Context Press.

Tallman, K., & Bohart, A. C. (1999). The client as a common factor: Clients as self-healers. In M. A. Hubble, B. L. Duncan, & S. D. Mille (Eds.), *The heart and soul of change: What works in therapy* (pp. 91-131). Washington, DC: American Psychological Association.

Wampold, B. E., Minami, T., Baskin, T. W., & Callen Tierney, S. (2002). A meta-(re)analysis of the effects of cognitive therapy versus "other therapies" for depression. *Journal of Affective Disorders, 68*(2), 159-165.

Wampold, B. E., Mondin, G. W., Moody, M., Stich, F., Benson, K., & Ahn, H. N. (1997). A meta-analysis of outcome studies comparing bona fide psychotherapies: Empirically, "all must have prizes." *Psychological Bulletin, 122*(3), 203-215.Webster, C. D., Douglas, K. S., Eaves, D., & Hart, S. D. (1997). *HCR-20: Assessing risk for violence* (version 2). Burnaby, BC: Simon-Fraser University, Mental Health, Law, and Policy Institute.

Winterowd, C. L., Morgan, R. D., & Ferrell, S. W. (2001). Principal components analysis of important goals for group work with male inmates. *Journal for Specialists in Group Work, 26*(4), 406-417.

Yalom, I. D. (1970). *The theory and practice of group psychotherapy.* New York, NY: Basic Books.

Yalom, I. D. (1975). *The theory and practice of group psychotherapy* (2nd ed.). New York, NY: Basic Books.

Yalom, I. D. (1995). *The theory and practice of group psychotherapy* (4th ed.). New York, NY: Basic Books.

Yalom, I. D., & Leszcz, M. (2005). *The theory and practice of group psychotherapy* (5th ed.). New York, NY: Basic Books.

Multi-tiered Group Therapy Model to Identify and Treat the Root Causes of Domestic Violence: A Proposal Integrating Current Social Neuroscience Findings

LESLIE M. LOTHSTEIN, PH.D., ABPP

ABSTRACT

Domestic violence (DV) is a national public health crisis. The leading treatment model, the Duluth Model, has failed to reduce or prevent DV. New models of treatment for DV are needed. In this paper, an emphasis is placed on an integrated multimodal approach to treating DV, integrating the current psychological science on the neurobiology and brain science of human violence with recent findings in the neurobiology of group relationships to present a treatment program for DV employing a group therapy model. This group therapy treatment approach moves away from the treatment of symptoms to the treatment of the root causes of violence. The two-tier Duluth model (a community teaching model of psychoeducation and court-mandated behavioral therapies for male perpetrators) is expanded to include a third tier. This is a psychological science-driven model that identifies and treats the root causes of DV using a group process and group systems-oriented approach.

Leslie M. Lothstein is affiliated with the Department of Psychiatry at Yale University and Case Western Reserve University.
The author would like to thank all of his cotherapists, specifically Ben Katz, MSW, Jany Keat, Ph.D., Psy.D, and Alexandra Harley, M.A.

INTRODUCTION AND BACKGROUND

In this paper I emphasize the importance of employing a multimodal approach to treating domestic violence, integrating a psychological science model on human violence (Raine, 2013) and using group therapy and recent findings in the neurobiology of group process (Gantt & Badenoch, 2013) as the treatment choice for domestic violence (DV). I have expanded the two-tier Duluth model using a community teaching model of psychoeducation and court-mandated behavioral therapies for male perpetrators. I introduce a tier-three stage as a psychological science-driven model identifying and treating the root causes of DV in order to reduce recidivism and curb DV. I use a relational approach to treatment in the context of group therapy, embodying recent curative factors in the neurobiology of therapy groups and the neurobiology of violence.

These ideas are based on 45 years of clinical work with adolescent and adult groups, inpatient and outpatient. I run three open-ended weekly therapy groups for sexually violent individuals, two intensive outpatient groups for men and women struggling with boundary issues at home and work, and forensic work with violent patients, many with histories of DV and damaged attachment styles and with serious psychiatric illnesses.

WHY A "ONE SIZE FITS ALL" MODEL DID NOT WORK

Until recently, treating domestic violence (DV)—also known as interpersonal violence (IV), intimate partner violence (IPV), family violence (FV), and relational violence (RV)—has focused on the Duluth model, a feminist-based ideologically driven model that included a two-tiered approach to treatment that was community-based and included safe houses for victims. This approach failed in its mission to curb all DV and reduce recidivism (Babcock, Green, & Robie, 2004; Feder & Dugan, 2002; Murphy & Baxter, 1997) as it excluded women as perpetrators of DV (Bowen, 2009) and was based on an ideological model that was not scientifically informed (Corvo & Dutton, 2008; Dutton & Corvo, 2006; Feder & Wilson, 2005; Ganley, 2006; Gondolf, 1997). It failed almost all clinical research outcome studies for efficacy (Babcock et al., 2004; Feder & Dugan, 2002; Feder & Wilson, 2005; Ganley, 2006; Gondolf, 1997; Murphy & Baxter, 1997) despite many intervention strategies (Roberts, 2002). Moreover, when constructing the Duluth model, many ethical issues surrounding forced, mandated, or coerced treatment were overlooked (Caplan, 2006). Future approaches to DV suggest including the role of genetics, evolutionary biology, and neurobiology in the organization and activation of violence, focusing on the possible neurobiological roots of violence and the reality of female violence and female perpetrators, and viewing DV as the final common pathway of environmental and genetic pathways.

In order to understand the complexities of DV and why the Duluth model failed, consider the following vignette in a group therapy session. Would an ideological one-size-fits-all approach work here? The group treatment takes places in an intensive outpatient treatment program using an expressive, relational approach to group therapy.

"S-MOTHERING": THE GROUP ON THE RUN FROM THE ABANDONING MOTHER

This group consisted of eight patients, four men and four women, and two leaders (a male and a female). There was a long silence, one that usually portends powerful urges and despair/ depression in the group. Brian began talking. He had an intense, battle-weary look, perhaps due to his current chaotic domestic situation and to early childhood exposure to abandonment. He addressed the group earnestly about his need to have his ex-girlfriend stop texting him. He seemed unsure how to deal with this issue as he felt harassed by her. Although he had left her, she texted him daily, sometimes many times a day. He noted, "I recently ended a year-long relationship with her and there are weird boundaries." He added, "I don't want to cut her off at the knees. I want to remain on good terms with her, to still stay connected to her in a way that is safe to me. But I am ambivalent. I feel smothered by her, but my ambivalence landed me in the hospital." His metaphor "cut her off at the knees" and not wanting to feel smothered reverberated in the group through themes of aggression-dependence from other patients that surfaced out of the silence.

Mabel identified with Brian's ex and said, "I am a texter." She talked about a relationship she had that ended with her feeling as if "I wanted to die." She related this to her early developmental trauma in a family that was violent and ruthless. She said, "I hated my childhood and I married my father," her first husband. At the wedding, she had had cold feet and tried to drop out of the ceremony since she did not love her intended husband. As she was walking away, her father threatened her and pushed her back towards the altar, telling her she had to go through with the marriage and marry a man she didn't love. She went to her marital bed in a stupor. In a short time, a son was born and she emotionally connected to him and viewed him as her savior, a Jesus baby, to rescue her from her internal world of cruelty and ruthlessness. The marriage soon ended, and ten years after the divorce she met Alan and their relationship had a spark that soon became an engulfing flame of love. She had never felt such happiness, lust, and merriment. Her heart sang with joy. But at her apogee of love and enthrallment Alan ran off, abandoning her and his stepson. Mabel was in a state of emotional chaos and could not get him out of her mind, talking as if she were going to emotionally stalk him. She said, "I can't breathe"; she felt dead when he abandoned her. She wanted his love back and tried to pressure him to love her through her emotional texting. Her world of childhood domestic violence and physical abuse had had a reprieve with her son and with Alan. She was now obsessed with having Alan back and began to stalk him, an aggressive and potentially dangerous behavior. She identified with Brian and his fear of being smothered and wondered whether her need to smother had driven Alan away.

Arnold chimed in, noting that his mother had also abandoned the family when he was 12 to move up to Maine with another man. He felt numb and dead, having lost his mother forever. In his marriage, he always feared his wife would leave him, and he threatened her with abandonment and violence. The initial silence of the group was now uncovering the intense emotionality in the group that was related to powerful abandonment issues, emotional chaos in childhood, wishes to reconnect with the lost parent, and the outright aggression and violence of the parent toward the child now verbalized as vengeance toward the marriage partner.

At this point, Darlene said that like Mabel, she too wanted to die. She turned to Arnold and said, "I feel sorry for you. My mother took off when I was three and I saw her again when I was 16 and a second time when I was 25." Darlene felt ignored, abandoned, and unloved and identified with Brian and Mabel. She took her anxieties about attachment into her marriage, threatened to leave her marriage and child, and had no insight into how angry and violent she was toward her husband and child. Sean, in a state of despair, reported that he now wanted to vomit, saying he was "skimming along the bottom of a deep depression."

The triadic themes of abandonment, feeling smothered, and obsessed with death and dying surfaced as the silence ebbed, coalescing into a chaos of abandonment and cruelty. These themes were taken into the patients' relationships or marriages and acted out in ways similar to their experiences in their families of origin. In this context, two female patients who had remained silent now presented themselves as having perfect family lives, blissful marriages, and happy childhoods and did not see how they belonged in this group. There was a Pollyanna-ish quality to the organization of their disclosures of not fitting in, as if they did not want to speak truthfully in the group or were overwhelmed by the openness of other patients. The subgroup was entertaining feelings of joy and happiness in the dustbowl of the group's misery. The bipolarity of affect reflected the use of defensive splitting as a primary defense mechanism in the group.

Would reframing the issues as related solely to a patriarchal model of male power and control address and treat the violent issues arising in the group? Would simply changing a patient's thinking about texting or about how men are inherently violent resolve the deeper issues of each group member?

Applying a psychological-science model of DV deepens our understanding. The clinical data suggest that we need to employ multiple perspectives to understand the violent attachments involved in DV situations. We have to incorporate the findings of psychological science by appealing to developmental process, attachment styles, early childhood exposure to family violence and abandonment, hate and rage in the core nuclear family, and the repetition compulsion. In the vignette above, all of these issues are percolating in the group, and a relational/dynamic model of group therapy is a better conceptual fit to address the complex issues. Moreover, the group-as-a-whole system is a microcosm of the family of origin and provides a framework for working with all of the patients' relational issues of violence stemming from impaired attachment systems.

HISTORICAL MODELS OF TREATMENT FOR DV

While there are many models of care to treat DV, few have involved an integrated and multimodal approach that references cultural, gender, and biological differences in the experience and expression of violence. The representative theories that have been researched include feminist theories (Anderson, 1997; Yllo, 2005); object relations theory, attachment theory, and trauma theory (Bowlby, 1969, 1976, 1988; Fonagy, 1999; Fonagy & Target, 1995; Karr-Morse, Wiley, & Brazelton, 2007); psychoanalytical theory (McWilliams, 2004; Welldon, 2011; Yakeley, 2010; Yakeley & Meloy, 2012); developmental theory (Karr-Morse et al., 2007; Karr-Morse & Wiley, 2012); social theories of violence (Lawson, 2012), and family theory and family systems theories (Daly, 2003).

More recently, a body of literature on what really works in psychotherapy suggests that it is not the theory or techniques employed but common factors across theories of psychotherapy that lead to successful therapeutic outcomes. Norcross (2002) and Shedler (2010) suggested that it is not the theoretical orientation that leads to change, but the core common factor involving the therapeutic relationship and therapeutic alliance. Additionally, genetic and neuroimaging data from the neurosciences have elucidated important information regarding the evolutionary roots and neurobiology of attachments that can lead to violent attachments and DV. In this vein, the social neurosciences have postulated the importance of recognizing the human brain as primarily a social one in which social connectedness is a primary drive (Lieberman, 2013) and aggression and violence are inherent aspects of human neurobiology (Raine, 2013).

VIOLENCE IN AMERICA

FROM IDEOLOGY TO PSYCHOLOGICAL SCIENCE

According to Gilligan (1996) and Motz (2008, 2014), DV begins in the cauldron of the original group, the child's home, destroying families and traumatizing children. Historically, DV has been identified as a social disease (Alpert, 2002; Gilligan, 1996) and as a major public health crisis (Black et al., 2011; Department of Justice, 2011; Eckhardt et al., 2013; National Center for Injury Prevention and Control, 2003; Hamel, 2012). DV has been hypothesized to be an intergenerational problem that leads to millions of emergency room visits per year (primarily by women) and untold hundreds of millions of lost dollars in productivity (National Center for Injury Prevention and Control, 2003).

The triggers for DV, IPV, or RV are complex but usually relate to the following: humiliation and shame (Gilligan, 1996), threat of loss and abandonment (Lothstein, 2013), despair or the wish for revenge (Motz, 2014), an immature need to possess a love object exclusively, and emergence of pathological jealousy and control strategies that sometimes reach levels of catathymic rage (Meloy, 1997; Yakeley, 2010). DV can also be triggered by alcohol- or substance-induced rage (National Institutes of Health, 1997) and abnormal cerebral functioning due to multiple causes (Raine, 2013). Essentially, DV is triggered by complex forces where relational systems are under threat. Violence expressed as DV is the result of a breakdown in social connectivity and a sense of being expelled from the group. And it is within the context of group therapy that human connectivity can be reestablished.

An explanation of DV has to be multimodal and reference functional and structural psychological factors involved in all human brain-behavior systems. Approaching any complex psychological problem from ideology alone is bound to fail. Psychological science, such as data from randomized controlled studies, meta-analyses, and single case studies, provides the research foundations for understanding and treating the complexities of DV.

The three-tier approach I am advocating focuses on a linear progression from tiers 1 and 2 to a third tier employing a comprehensive psychology science model searching for the root causes. Root cause analysis seeks to determine the fundamental elements of a recurrent issue by employing ever more particular methods to develop a specific treatment method.

Tier 3 treatment integrates the findings of psychological science from such diverse areas as evolutionary psychology (Raine, 2013), attachment theory (Bowlby, 1969, 1976, 1988), developmental trauma (van der Kolk, 2002), family systems theory (Motz, 2014; Scharff & Scharff, 2011; Schnarch, 2009), group systems theory (Agazarian, 2004; Rutan, Stone, & Shay, 2007), and the neuro- and social sciences findings on human violence (Cozolino, 2006, 2010; Doige, 2007; Glenn & Raine, 2014; Lieberman, 2013; Raine, 2013). The tier-three model focuses on the relational aspects of violence that are part of the root causes of DV (Motz, 2014; Scharff & Scharff, 2011; Schnarch, 2009). All this is done within the framework of a group therapy approach to repairing damaged self-structures to occur within a relational model of group therapy that is nonjudgmental. The therapy group best approximates the family and community in which early behavioral strategies of human connectedness are formed and violence may be experienced in the nuclear family. Early childhood attachment styles strongly influence violent attachments in adult life (Fonagy, 1999; Fonagy & Target, 1995). I am proposing that DV can only be treated by moving from a symptom focus to a psychological science, based on identifying and treating its root causes.

The third tier of treatment introduces a group system to work on root causes of DV (Agarzarian, 2004; Hopper, 2003). It involves a relational (Mitchell, 1988) and psychodynamic component (Nicholas, 2013; Rutan et al., 2007; Shedler, 2010) to address root causes. This approach focuses on the findings of psychotherapy research that have identified common factors in all forms of therapy associated with positive outcomes, notably the patient's relation to the therapist (Norcross, 2002) and the curative factors of group therapy noted by Yalom and Leszcz (2005). As part of the root cause analysis, the step-wise progression of focusing on psychological process as described by Shedler (2010) is advocated.

The group treatment model for DV fulfills a basic need for security, attachment, and connectedness (Lieberman, 2013). This allows us to get to the root causes faster, as the group- as-a-whole approach provides a major protective factor for survival against violence, and instills methods of gaining security and safety through interpersonal interactions and alliances without succumbing to triggers of humiliation, shame, and loss, all of which can lead to DV.

Group therapy, not to be confused with group programming,[1] approximates the fundamental neurobiological need of humans for social connectedness and security (Lieberman, 2013). Strong family systems enable individuals to deal with frustration tolerance and delay of gratification. Kohut (1977) noted how in many families the failure to help family members delay gratification led to weakened ego structures vulnerable to narcissistic rage that is very damaging to self and others. Indeed, Kohut (1971, 1977), Mitchell (1988), and Morrison (1989) noted that humans are also most prone to rage when they experience intense shame and humiliation in their primary intimate relationships. These issues are more easily handled in group therapy because issues of shame are identified earlier in the process of treatment and shared by group members.

Nicholas (2013) describes how "deadly repetitions" may occur as a repetition compulsion that emerges from reflex violence, often accompanied by paranoia, self-righteousness, compulsive infidelity, and escalating violence, followed by contrition, a compulsive begging for forgiveness, intense shame, and self-reproach. Such extreme emotional fluctuations may also lead to sadomasochistic relationships around intimacy and sexuality (Schnarch, 2009) that are very damaging to systems such as the family. The entitled narcissistic rage that accompanies ego vulnerabilities to shame is not fully responsive to a symptom-focused approach and needs to be addressed dynamically with a root cause analysis.

Children raised in families that instill chaotic and confusing attachment systems (Scharff & Scharff, 2011) may view marriage as a system that is toxic. They become at risk for engaging in DV later in life (cf. De Zulueta 1993; Motz, 2014; Varki & Bower, 2013).

---

1. Group therapy (GT) is a method of treatment as outlined by the AGPA in which group therapy is defined and credentialing standards for training group therapists are recognized. Group programming (GP) is the assembly of patients into distinct groups or classes focusing on a psychoeducational topic and led by a leader who may not be trained in group psychotherapy and may not be able to make use of group dynamics and process in the course of providing psychoeducational classes (Lothstein, 2014).

Many of the children raised in DV families compulsively act out the violence they witness by bullying other children (Klein, Rice, & Schermer, 2009).

While thinking about the theoretical issues underlying DV, consider the following case vignette as illustrative of the kind of clinical work involved in a tier 3 approach to treating DV.

The Volcano and Chaos[2]

The group consisted of ten patients (six women and four men) who all suffered from some form of DV. Sarah opened the group and talked about the relational messes she left behind as a result of her temper outbursts. When asked to imagine what was inside her that led to such explosive outbursts, she said that it was like having a volcano inside her. The group identified with the volcano metaphor, and it became the theme of the group. The discussion was lively and animated, as other group members spoke about their own volcanic rages that they had to keep under control. I commented to the group that the exploding volcano can be a beautiful creative force (as in building islands) while also a destructive force.

Ashley talked about the role of alcohol in her domestically violent home life and how her father's alcoholism led to destructive rages. Lily talked about how afraid she was in her family of origin, as she feared her father's rage threatened to destroy "everyone." For two of the group members (Jack and Sarah), their mental illness and economic circumstances forced them to return to live with their parents, and they found themselves back in the family crucible, with an aging parent being very aggressive toward them (reenacting the childhood drama of being in the middle of the parents' DV).

The shared image of the exploding volcano allowed the group to talk openly about their internal rages and how emotionally, verbally, and physically violent they could be at home. Many of the group members had witnessed DV in their nuclear families and recalled how they had internalized their volcanic rage and sworn they would never be like their parents. Now they found themselves acting just like their parents, even though they had

---

2. cf. Grossmark (2007).

once been the targets. Only with the image of the volcano was the group able to own the defensive impasses they found themselves in and to work together and to understand what they brought into their marriages and partnerships that nurtured violence. The theme of violence became a point of bonding for the group members. Sharing these familial experiences lessens their shame, as they experience a sense of universality that they are not alone and not bad, thus making the work of therapy progress more efficient.

Through the image of the volcanic explosion, the group was able to concretize the internal rage into something outside the self (i.e., identification with the enraged parent or spouse). The issue of whether it was safe to be in the group, and whether they would be protected from the retaliatory rage of the father-leader, was also discussed. Additionally, with the emergence of the transference theme of the dangerous therapist, the group was able to talk openly about fears of how the leader might help them change, a thought that was both welcoming (co-regulation) and terrifying (fear of the loss of individuality and increased anxiety). The messes present in the group became a conduit for opening up new themes about the volcano as an internal creative force that can be harnessed positively.

The group was given permission by the therapist to take ownership of their rage without increasing their shame and humiliation about how out of control several of them were at home. For groups with very stern superegos, I am often reminded of Theodor Reik's statement, "A thought murder a day keeps the psychiatrist away." He used this clinically to lessen the effects of patients' superego resistance to admitting anger, an emotion that is messy and contrasts with a perfectionistic view of the self as all loving. In this group, I was struck by the ease with which the women talked about their rages at home in front of the other patients. The cohesiveness and trust in the group allowed for an open discussion of a forbidden topic. Over time, group therapy members developed connections and attachments with other group members and the leader, and they had opportunities to change their responses to frustration and criticism. Now they were able to acknowledge themselves as having a nuclear family defined by "volcanic rage." Their rage had always felt ugly and unmanageable, but talking about it in the group felt healing.

Their rage may not have been pretty, but it was *their* rage, and it was the first time that most had shared this with anyone. Universality, cohesion, and the nonjudgmental atmosphere enabled group members to talk from their hearts. Competent leadership prevents the group from becoming overstimulated, toxic, and dangerous. In the context of new challenges, patients typically resort to using old childhood defenses, such as the repetition compulsion and identification with the aggressor. It is often very difficult for patients to admit to feelings of rage coming from inside the self rather than from outside. When suppressed feelings of rage surface, they are often experienced as alien and are projected onto a feared object outside the self, often in identification with the aggressor.

Moving from the direct or vicarious experience of DV as a child to the acceptance of one's rage means allowing others to see a different side of oneself and to resist becoming immobilized by shame. As the group co-regulates the distressed individual's fear of her rage, the angry self is allowed to emerge without threat of censure and punishment. Under these conditions, change takes place. Porges (2011) notes that all group interactions involve communication between brains, what he calls "neuroception." Just being in the group allows for brain change to occur through the collectivity of group neuroception, as there is a hunger for social connectivity on the macro level and neuronal connectivity on the neurobiological level. These kinds of group interactions are what lead to the root causes of violence.

CONTRIBUTIONS OF COMMON FACTORS IN PSYCHOTHERAPY AND FINDINGS FROM THE NEURO- AND SOCIAL NEUROSCIENCES RELATED TO DV

Contemporary approaches to psychotherapy outcome research (Norcross, 2002) suggest that change occurs not necessarily as a result of interpretation, but rather because of the genuine caring and empathy of the therapist, and the relationship formed between the therapist and group. Patients often describe change differently than their therapists, focusing more on relational issues in the treatment.

While research in the social neurosciences suggests how the default neurocircuitry of the brain parallels that of the social circuitry we all need to thrive and stay healthy in our stressful worlds (Lieberman, 2013; Lothstein, 2012), a body of literature also focuses on possible causal relationships between abnormal brain neurocircuitry and violence. Such abnormalities in neurocircuitry can lead to disruptions in social connectivity and violent behavior directed toward the very people we need to relate to intimately (Fishbein, 2000; Glenn & Raine, 2014; Raine, 2013).

In this context, a new discipline of neurolaw (http://www.lawneuro.org/ cf. The Research Network on Law and Neuroscience) has been set up to respond to forensic issues around the human brain and violent behavior. Brain studies also show how some humans with identified neuroanatomical impairments of brain structures related to violence (Fallon, 2013; Kiehl, 2006; Miczek et al., 2007; Raine, 2013) may have impaired and insufficiently structured self-systems that prime their behavioral violence. Brain abnormalities leading to violence or sexual violence (Langevin et al., 1989) suggest how brain damage located deep within the brain (the amygdala, insula, and limbic system) may be exacerbated by alcohol and drugs, traumatic brain injury, and sports injuries associated with chronic traumatic encephalopathy. Without acknowledging the micro root causes of violence related to genetics and impaired brain mechanisms, our understanding of the roots of violence would be incomplete. Contemporary research from the neurosciences has expanded our awareness of the biological roots of DV, including the underlying neurochemistry, neurology, and the etiology of DV (Miczek et al., 2007).

Raine (2013) and Glenn & Raine (2014) have written extensively about which specific brain structures are viewed as contributory to, if not responsible for, violent behavior as measured by neuroimaging on fMRIs. The evolutionary brain structures responsive for adaptive aggression include the limbic system and deep brain structures, including the hypothalamic-pituitary-adrenal circuit (H-P-A axis) and the fight/flight response. Recently, the polyvagal theory (Porges, 2011) suggests a more primitive response system for survival, in which important social information from the "gut" informs a different type of survival response—dissociating and playing dead—in order to survive instrumentally directed violence and threat from others.

Fallon (2013), a neuroscientist, has also postulated the existence of a "warrior gene" present in certain personality styles (antisocial and psychopathic) that may be responsible for violent outbursts and triggered in some fighting couples. Though Fallon believes that women are less susceptible, the gene may be expressed differently for females in verbal fighting and provocation. Fallon argued that having such a gene may lead to antisocial and psychopathic behaviors in which violence may reach unexpected levels of aggression, especially if environmental factors cause significant stress. In this context, a person's DV in group may require different caring interventions that provide the capacity to understand how their unique neurobiology contributes to angry behaviors and disturbed relationships (Badenoch & Cox, 2010; Cozolino, 2006, 1010; Flores, 2010; Siegel, 2010). Findings in the social neurosciences (Badenoch & Cox, 2010; Iacoboni, 2008; Lieberman, 2013; Porges, 2011; Schore, 2003a, 2003b; Siegel, 2010) provide a unique way of understanding some of the underlying root causes of violence that are neurobiologically determined.

Patients in group therapy get better through engaging in neuroception, or relating empathically to other group members' brains, a process Iacoboni (2008) believes begins with mirror neurons and which can lead to brain repair (Porges, 2011). In the healing context of group, members act as co-regulators of affect for the violent-prone individual, thereby defusing potentially lethal situations. There is always the possibility that transferences and counter-transferences could lead to interference with healthy neural networks and the co-regulation of object relationships. In group therapy, the group's neural networks approximate that of the individual's brain, in terms of a social being seeking connectedness with others.

CLINICAL VIGNETTES: UTILIZING GROUP PROCESS IN THE TREATMENT OF DV

The following group vignettes suggest how some of the themes discussed above play out, and how the therapist makes use of concepts related to DV to identify the root causes of relational violence.

The Group Mess: Help!

In this group (six men and two women), all had a history of DV and childhood trauma marked by abandonment and separation-loss.

At the outset, there was a lot of emotional chaos and aggression surfacing in the group. At least one patient noted that her conflicting feelings about experiencing her rage were too shameful and frightening to express. Sandy talked about having a great mess that she was bringing to the group. She told the group that the mess that caused her to attempt suicide was related to having been "incested" by her brother and then rejected by her family when she disclosed it to them. The family treated her as an outcast for disclosing a family secret. She was called a liar, a selfish woman who was breaking up the family. After her disclosure, there was dead silence in the group. No one wanted to talk about it. The group was at an impasse. The tension was so thick you could feel it. She felt as though the group was treating her the same way her family did by giving her the silent treatment.

I wondered if the group members could put their mental images and daydreams into words to express what they were experiencing after Sandy's disclosure of her sibling rape. Karley started to express herself and said she imagined vomit in the group, an odorous mess that was smelly and awful. Chrissie said she saw broken glass, blood, sharp objects, stickiness, but also a beautiful thing. Ted said he saw a pile of shit in the room that was overpowering, at which the group members laughed nervously. Gary replied that he had an image of a GI Joe doll (the double meaning of GI as soldier and GI tract did not go unnoticed) in which the "Joey doll" was eating another doll and the Joey doll defecated it out of his butt and there was an arm sticking out that said "help me" (and he was not being humorous). Sam replied that he envisioned a monster roaming in a village and people running away from it. Andrew, stirred from his slumber, said he experienced chaos in the group and saw everything pouring out and just chaos. The total effect of the disturbing images paralleled the affective internal life of Sandy's family when she opened up the family mess to them. Sandy's shame and disgust were now present in all the group members. They were alive in the here and now of the group images.

The group was urged to think about their own messy and chaotic parent-child experiences. As small children, their messes (shit and vomit) were integral parts of their childhoods, and those moments were both scary and precious to them. During those disturbing moments of confusion, mess, and excitement, the child needs the parent (the group leaders) not to be enraged at the messes. The parallel processes in the group were that the members wanted the leaders to listen and stay in contact with the deeper meanings of the messes being conveyed, while also being disgusted by the mess. Indeed, there was a time when each of them was two years old and their shit was wonderful and their vomit was an important internal part of their bodies. I restated for the group Gary's image of the GI Joe doll whose hand was sticking out of the shit asking for help, and that each of the moments of mess reflected a moment of relatedness for the group, a reaching out and making contact with another person to soothe and comfort them but also a test to see if someone (the leader) would be comfortable enough with messes to not flee from the enormity of the task. Group members opined that the images reflected something in the self that had to come out and be held by the group as an important, precious gift, and no matter how big the mess, this was a safe place where they could be listened to and understood and the therapists could relate to the group without judgment, criticism, teasing, or rejection.

While the group members felt connected, listened to, and supported, they had entered a minefield of the heart, bringing out horrific images of their violent messes, in graphic bodily and regressive terms, which made them sick and ashamed. A prolonged silence culminated in the group identifying the danger of engaging in the therapy process and being overwhelmed by their primitive shame and disgust and being unable to heal it. The image of the GI Joe doll coming out of the rectum waving for help summarized the group's dilemma. It was a monumental image of Gary's existential situation, alluding to early childhood sadomasochistic dynamics and somatic distress. The metaphor of the odors of shit permeating the group suggested regressive, depressive, and sadomasochistic relational dynamics that were also present in their families of origin, a dynamic that had ruined many of the group members' intimacy in their love and work-related lives. How could these unresolved early childhood images be integrated into the current life situation and be reframed in a positive way?

In some ways, these images reflected a synesthesia of sensory images that were olfactory and rooted in temporal lobe memories of early childhood affective-somatic aggression. In the group, brains were sharing images with other brains and connecting with others on a regressive and primitive level. By voicing themes of sadism in the context of a nonjudgmental listening and holding environment, the group calmed down, as they felt understood and not judged by other group members and the therapist. Despite the gruesomeness of the images, they now had a name for the internal experiences that were kindling chaotic messes and violence in their lives. However, the images were now reframed by the leader into playful ones that could be restorative. The group members were working on root causes in terms of fantasies of violence that now had a voice and were listened to without fear and punishment. A new mood of hope suffused the group, as the GI Joe image became the sign of survival and hope, going through a long and dangerous journey, sullied but strong and surviving. Sharing private images left some group members feeling exposed, but it also allowed them to process difficult sadomasochistic and violent material.

As leader, I wondered how the group members felt leaving their messes behind for the therapist to contain until the next group meeting. Sandy's disclosure of how her rape was handled by her mother left me concerned about whether she thought I had handled the material correctly. The image of GI Joe covered in shit, his arm waving out of the anus of the person who ate him, symbolized a question about whether the group felt I would be able to identify, recognize, and contain their messes and work with them to help them change. Would I contain their secrets without harming them? Or would I criticize and attack them? All of these would return in different forms in the "working through" process. For the moment, the group now had lived through a potential crisis of shared self-revelation and, like the GI Joe, survived and asked for help. What was once a potentially disorganizing and violent prophecy was transformed into a relational dilemma.

Post-Thanksgiving and Pre-Christmas Group: Going Home and Facing the Unthinkable

The following group, focusing on relationships and intimacy, took place in an intensive outpatient program where the group meets twice weekly.

Bill says he is looking forward to going home this Thanksgiving. Lorraine says she is not looking forward to Thanksgiving; she is estranged from her family, and her brother Samuel has not spoken to her in two years. "I am the black sheep in the family," she says. Ben asks her if she is able to talk to the group about the reasons for being estranged from her family. Lorraine takes a deep breath and says, "There was long-term incest with my father." A silence sweeps over the group. Lara asks her where her father lives. Lorraine replies, "He is dead." This communication stifles inquiry, as the idea of not speaking ill of the dead emerges. "Try writing him a letter," Beth says, offering a way to still speak with the dead and work through her pain.

The emerging group material suggests that the group believes Lorraine is consumed with vengeance and rage (reflecting the group's projection). And that she wants to kill the father, or the representation of the father that lives inside her and that the group now contains. Lorraine tries to tell the group that she is troubled by all of her feelings, including her love for her father and missing him. The group resists. Initially, they do not want to hear anything positive about the father, Lorraine's love for her father, or her ambivalent feelings for him. They want Lorraine to hate even the dead father. They are at a level of black-and-white thinking where primitive superego concerns prevail. They cannot tolerate her ambivalence. They want her to write a hateful, vengeful letter to the dead father. At this point in the group, Lorraine is becoming the black sheep. All of this is acknowledged, clarified, and voiced by the group leader.

There is contagion in the group, and the anger toward Lorraine is taking a new form via identification. Stella reveals that two of her children were molested between the ages of 5 and 13. After the revelation, it was hard for her to think and feel, and she thought her mind was gone. Lara, glaring at the group, notes that as a young woman she was molested by a physician friend of the family. She now views all males as molesters, a view that was chilling to the men in the group. She looks enraged and sneers at the group. She is sitting next to the leader. She repeated her comments, beginning with, "I mentioned he is a doc, didn't I?," thus alluding to the danger of the father-leader and bringing the hated father to life in the group to be punished for his "transgression."

A parallel process emerged when Lara said that she did not think the group believed her. She was competing with Lorraine for the group's attention and was upset that the group was silent when she revealed her abuse. "You do not believe me," she said, adding, "As a group you are acting like my family," that is, being "non responsive." She was blind to the parallel between Lorraine's story and her own. As leader, I noted that Lara was treating the group as being Lorraine's rejecting family and the leader as the perpetrator. Melissa said, "There is so much suffering here, it is hard to know how to respond. What do you need from us?" May said, "I've been quiet. It is unlike me, as everyone knows. It's so hard to hear your issues. I was sexually assaulted as an adult, and I could not talk to my family about it and I'm not in the family now." The stories that emerged suggested that many group members had corrupt families. As a newly configured family, I wondered whether they felt that this family would also be corrupt and violate boundaries.

As leader I am concerned that so much attack on the body and mind is present in the group. I sense a potential for violence and a loss of group boundaries. I bring the group members back into the present and away from the transference, first by explaining what was happening and suggesting ways to understand and reframe what was being expressed in the group. I wondered if the group could stay with the messes and contradictions from the past that were originally perceived as attacks on their bodies and minds, and conceive of a different outcome? Could they eventually reframe it, now as adults, stay in the here and now, listen to each other's pain, and emerge with a different understanding of what happened and believe that change was possible? I encouraged the group to clear their minds of past solutions and move beyond old childhood realities involving passive acceptance and fear, and now, with group as the new family, engage in active listening, exploration, and understanding. At that point, the group fell into a long silence, and it felt as if the potential for healing was just beginning. As a group, they had choices, either to accept Lorraine and her genuine ambivalence toward her father, or to regress back to childhood solutions that life can be reduced to black-and-white issues. Could we as a group allow our violent selves to have a voice while also acknowledging ambivalence? Lorraine courageously brought her conflict into the group and was repelled by the group. The group's initial response was to repel the father and protect Lorraine. But this was not what she wanted or needed from the group, as their reaction was experienced as violent. In resisting the group's effort to deny her love for the abusing father, she opened the doors for the group's possibility of exploring their own ambivalence, an issue that was difficult for Lara who was clinically paranoid. Could hate and love exist in the same way among group members? Can we both hate and love the perpetrator-father and face our need for vengeance in a different way?

The content and themes that emerged in the vignettes relate to the here and now of group process and patients' needs to understand and accept their violent messes and use them as a conduit for change. The therapist's ability to listen and contain the attacks on the body and minds of the group members, without judging and keeping things open for discussion, allows the group members to feel safe and to one day acknowledge their own ambivalence. In social neuroscience terms, this allows for neuroconnectivity to begin and change in the brain to occur. This process is also stated in the group as part of the change process. And then comes the reframing of the messes (another code name for violent impulses). Using words, to acknowledge and accept the unbearable pain of the group, comforts the group members and allows for neurobiological changes in brain neurocircuitry to surface—brain changes that are necessary to inhibit violence and create a self-reflective state in which the group members can be both calm and curious about what this all means versus being focused only on one's own symptoms and how to deal with the depression, anxiety, emptiness, and numbness. They are faced with a paradox: In order to "get going" and change, they have to "be still," that is, be calm and use their minds differently, instead of panicking and being impulsive and fearful (Lew, 2005). By bringing this material to the group, we are presented with an opportunity for growth and reframing the messes in the language of neurobiology (cf. Doidge, 2007), allowing the group members to understand that change is taking place beneath the threshold of awareness. The power of the neurobiological symbolism is that it places the possibility for change in the *brain* and not only in the mind, allowing the group to feel as if their minds are now free to change as the brain heals. Change is happening now in the group and the group is surviving and growing.

GROUP THERAPY AS A NATURAL MODEL FOR DV

Because early patterns of violence were formed in the small family group, it is natural to think of a small group approach to therapy as also being the model within which to repair the self-deficits associated with violent behavior. The small group therapy treatment method approximates the original family and the neuroscience assumptions of how all brains are structured for social attachment and communication (Lieberman, 2013) and how social brains are formed and how they respond to change (Doige, 2007; Flores, 2010; Lieberman, 2013; Rutan et al., 2007), using group therapy to treat serious behavioral problems and possibly the root causes of violence (Buchele & Spitz, 2005; Burlingame, Fuhriman, & Mosier, 2003; Yalom, & Leszcz, 2005).

The blending of the efficacy studies on group psychotherapy (Burlingame, Strauss, & Joyce, 2013) with the findings of the social neurosciences (Cozolino, 2006, 2010; DeHaan & Gunnar,

2009; Eckhardt et al., 2013; Frith & Wolpert, 2003; Harmon-Jones & Winkielman, 2007; Iacoboni, 2008; Lieberman, 2013) suggests that relational problems of domestic violence can best be treated in a group psychotherapy setting where the connections and attachments necessary for healthy relationships can be established (Bowlby 1969, 1976, 1988; Flores, 2010; Lothstein, 2013, 2014; McGregor, Nunez, Cebula, & Gomez, 2007; and cf. issue no. 4 of the 2010 *International Journal of Group Psychotherapy*, especially the Denninger, Ferguson, Gantt & Cox, and Schermer articles).

Group therapy is a microcosm of the family group (Yalom & Leszcz, 2005), in which core conflicts and triggers learned in the original crucible of the DV family of origin can now be experienced differently in the safety of the group, and with competent group leadership (Cozolino, 2010; Flores, 2010).

Badenoch and Cox (2013) note that, "Because therapy group members often share some common implicit experiences—abandonment, shame, terror, grief—they can easily collaborate with one another in making meaning of the experiences that led to those painful states" (pp. 17-18). In this way, the group leader(s) can talk about relational structures (Mitchell, 1988) that create and describe the meaning of communications between group members, including the leader. Groups also have to deal with normative aggression across developmental phases, allowing for aggression to be experienced as a challenge but not a defeat (Hopper, 2003; Lothstein, 1978), thereby reducing some of the negative effects of DV on the evolving adult self.

In the course of group therapy, the developing relations between group members enhances brain development and increases neural connectivity, allowing for such change to occur (Holzel et al., 2011; Kirkpatrick et al., 2011). Under these conditions of group therapy, people who have been both victim and perpetrator, emotionally and physically harmed and harming, have the opportunity to be healed of their repetition compulsions and/or identification with the aggressor. In this way, a path is opened to reframe developmental relational failures and experience emotional change in the self and the group with the possibility of self-repair (Agazarian, 2004; Karr-Morse & Wiley, 2012; Karr-Morse, Wiley, & Brazelton, 2007; Kohut, 1971, 1977).

Siegel (2010) presents evidence that group therapy can facilitate the rewiring of the limbic system and the prefrontal cortex and lead to a more regulated self that exercises good judgment, demonstrates compassion, and engages in insight. In this way, there are quasi-causal relationships between the integration of brain mechanisms and outward calming behavior (Agazarian, 2004; Aronson & Schamess, 1989; Gantt & Cox, 2010; Twemlow et al., 1999). Porges (2011) has noted that when our nervous system perceives threat we are unable to use other people as a source of healthy soothing and regulation. Group therapy allows the self to reconnect to the soothing, regulating function of other people. Group therapy is effective in facilitating change in the lives of many people who were abused as children or adults, and the mechanisms of change can be identified, operationalized, and studied (American Group Psychotherapy Association, 2008; Burlingame et al., 2003; Burlingame et al., 2013; Johnson et al., 2005) as existing in DV.

CONCLUDING THOUGHTS

Current approaches to the public health crisis of DV have failed, and new models of intervention and treatment are needed. I am suggesting a tier 3 model that incorporates the earlier two tiers of psychoeducation and cognitive behavioral therapy but includes a third tier involving a psychodynamic group approach that searches for root causes of violence in the context of interpersonal neurobiological healing methods and the new brain science of violence. I also recommend that future research on tiers 1 and 2 not ignore the healing power of group systems interventions, and that these variables need to be included as part of any dependent measures in DV outcome studies that compare group programming with group therapy What we now need is research into this proposed model.

Because the root causes of early childhood patterns of attachment involve nonverbal, implicit, and procedural memory systems, they are governed by right-brained neurobiological processes (Schore, 2003a, 2003b), and it is not required that people entering into a tier 3 approach to DV be psychologically minded individuals. Indeed, there are new techniques related to motivational interviewing (Murphy & Baxter, 1997) that can help to build psychological-mindedness and increase the numbers of those who may potentially benefit from this approach.

Treatment with a group therapy approach (and engaging in research on the group therapy variables) is in keeping with our evolution as social creatures, living in social groups, and being dependent for survival by our inclusion in these social groups. The AGPA initiative on the efficacy of group therapy (2008) provides hope for those of us working with DV to develop psychological initiatives based on science, and not politics and ideology alone. We are at a crossroads, and must make intelligent decisions about where to apply our resources in an effort to treat DV and other forms of violence using multimodal treatments that get to the root of understanding and treating family and community violence.

REFERENCES

Agazarian, Y. (2004). *System-centered therapy for groups*. London: Karnac, London.

Alpert, E. J. (2002). Domestic violence and clinical medicine: Learning from our patients and from our fears. *Journal of General Internal Medicine, 17*(2), 112-116.

American Group Psychotherapy Association. (2008). Practice guidelines for group psychotherapy: Toward the integration of science and practice [Special issue]. *International Journal of Group Psychotherapy, 58*(4).

Anderson, K. (1997). Gender, status and domestic violence: An integration of feminist and family violence approaches. *Journal of Marriage and the Family, 59*(3), 655-669.

Aronson, S., & Schamess, G. (1989). *The role of group psychotherapeutic interventions in youth violence reduction and primary prevention–A white paper*. New York, NY: American Group Psychotherapy Association.

Babcock, J. C., Green, C. E., & Robie, C. (2004). Does batterers' treatment work? A meta-analytic review of domestic violence treatment. *Clinical Psychology Review, 23*, 1023-1053.

Badenoch, B., & Cox, P. (2010). Integrating interpersonal neurobiology with group psychotherapy. *International Journal of Group Psychotherapy, 60*(4), 462-481.

Badenoch, B., & Cox, P. (2013). Integrating interpersonal neurobiology with group psychotherapy. In S. Gantt & B. Badenoch (Eds.), *The interpersonal neurobiology of group psychotherapy and group process* (pp. 1-18). London: Karnac.

Black, M. C., Basile, K. C., Breiding, M. J., Smith, S. G., Walters, M. L., Merrick, M. T., et al. (2011). *The National Intimate Partner and Sexual Violence Survey (NISVS): 2010 Summary Report*. Atlanta, GA: National Center for Injury Prevention and Control, Centers for Disease Control and Prevention.

Bowen, E. (2009). *Domestic violence treatment for abusive women*. New York, NY: Routledge.

Bowlby, J. (1969). *Attachment and loss, Vol. 1, Attachment*. New York, NY: Basic Books.

Bowlby, J. (1976). *Attachment and loss, Vol. 2, Separation: Anxiety and anger*. New York, NY: Basic Books.

Bowlby, J. (1988). *A secure base: Parent-child attachment and healthy human development*. New York, NY: Basic Books.

Buchele, B., & Spitz, H. (Eds.). (2005). *Group interventions for psychological treatment of trauma*. New York, NY: American Group Psychotherapy Association.

Burlingame, G., Fuhriman, A., & Mosier, J. (2003). The differential effectiveness of group psychotherapy: A meta-analytic perspective. *Group Dynamics, 7*(1), 3-12.

Burlingame, G., Strauss, B., & Joyce, A. (2013). Change mechanisms and effectiveness of small group treatment. In, M. J. Lambert (Ed.), *Bergin & Garfield's handbook of psychotherapy and behavior change* (7th ed.; pp. 640-689). Hoboken, NJ: Wiley.

Caplan, A. (2006). Ethical issues surrounding forced, mandated or coerced treatment. *Journal of Substance Abuse Treatment, 31*, 117-120.

Corvo, D., & Dutton, D. (2008). Toward evidence-based practice with domestic violence perpetrators. *Journal of Aggression, Maltreatment & Trauma, 16*(2), 111-130.

Cozolino, L. (2006). *The neuroscience of human relationships: Attachment and the developing social brain*. New York, NY: Norton.

Cozolino, L. (2010). *The neuroscience of psychotherapy: Healing the social brain*. New York, NY: Norton.

Daly, K. (2003). Family theory versus the theories families live by. *Journal of Marriage and Family Therapy, 65*(4), 771-784.

DeHaan, M., & Gunnar, M. (2009). *Handbook of developmental social neuroscience*. New York, NY: Guilford.

Denninger, J. (2010). Commentary on the neurobiology of group psychotherapy: Group and the social brain: Speeding toward a neurobiological understanding of group psychotherapy. *International Journal of Group Psychotherapy, 60*(4), 595-604.

Department of Justice, Bureau of Justice Statistics. (2011). *Intimate partner violence. AVA summary report.* Available from http://bjs.ojp.usdoj.gov/index.cfm?ty=tp&tid=971#summary

De Zulueta, F. (1993). *From pain to violence: The traumatic roots of destructiveness.* Northvale, NJ: Aronson.

Doidge, N. (2007). *The brain that changes itself: Stories of personal triumph from the frontiers of brain science.* London: Penguin.

Dutton, D., & Corvo, K. (2006). Transforming a flawed policy: A call to revive psychology and science in domestic violence research and practice. *Aggression and Violent Behavior, 11*(5), 457-480.

Eckhardt, C., Murphy, C., Whitaker, D., Sprunger, J., Dykstra, R., & Woodard, K. (2013). The effectiveness of intervention programs for perpetrators and victims of intimate partner violence. *Partner Abuse, 4*(2), 196-231.

Fallon, J. (2013). *The psychopath inside: A neuroscientist's personal journey into the dark side of the brain.* New York, NY: Current.

Feder, L., & Dugan, L. (2002). A test of the efficacy of court-mandated counseling for domestic violent offenders: The Broward experience. *Justice Quarterly, 19*(2), 343-375.

Feder, L., & Wilson, D. (2005). A meta-analytic review of court-mandated batterer intervention programs: Can courts affect abusers' behavior? *Journal of Experimental Criminology, 1*, 239-262.

Ferguson, D. (2010). Introducing couples to group therapy: Pursuing passion through the neo-cortex. *International Journal of Group Psychotherapy, 60*(4), 572-594.

Fishbein, D. (Ed.). (2000). *The science, treatment, and prevention of antisocial behaviors: Applications to the criminal justice system.* Kingston, NJ: Civic Research Institute.

Flores, P. (2010). Group psychotherapy and neuro-plasticity: An attachment theory perspective. *International Journal of Group Psychotherapy, 60*(4), 546-570.

Fonagy, P. (1999). Male perpetrators of violence against women: An attachment theory perspective. *Journal of Applied Psychoanalytic Studies, 1*, 7-27.

Fonagy, P., & Target, M. (1995). Towards understanding violence: The use of the body and the role of the father. *International Journal of Psycho-Analysis, 76*, 487-502.

Frith, C. & Wolpert, D. (Eds.). (2003). *The neuroscience of social interaction.* Oxford: Oxford University Press.

Ganley, A. (2006). Court mandated treatment for domestic violent perpetrators. *Domestic violence manual for judges. Washington State Administrative Office of the Courts. Appendix A.*

Gantt, S., & Badenoch, S. (Eds.). (2013). *The interpersonal neurobiology of group psychotherapy process.* London: Karnac.

Gantt, S., & Cox, P. (2010). Introduction to the special issue: Neurobiology and building interpersonal systems: Groups, couples, and beyond. *International Journal of Group Psychotherapy, 60*(4), 455-460.

Gilligan, J. (1996). *Violence; Reflections on a national epidemic.* New York, NY: Vintage.

Glenn, A., & Raine, A. (2014). *Psychopathy: An introduction to biological findings and their implications.* New York, NY: New York University Press.

Gondolf, E. (1997). Batterer programs: What we know and need to know. *Journal of Interpersonal Violence, 12*(1), 83-98.

Grossmark, R. (2007). The edge of chaos: Enactment, disruption, and emergence in group psychotherapy. *Psychoanalytic Dialogues, 17*(4), 479-499.

Hamel, J. (Ed.). (2012). Partner abuse state of knowledge project facts and statistics on domestic violence at-a-glance. *Partner Abuse.* http://domesticviolenceresearch.org/pages/12_page_findings.htm - _ftn-1www.springerpub.com/pa.

Harmon-Jones, E., & Winkielman, P. (Eds). (2007). *Social neuroscience: Integrating biological and psychological explanations of social behavior.* New York, NY: Guilford.

Holzel, B., Carmody, J., Vangel, M., Congleton, C., Yerramsetti, S., Gar, T., & Lazar, S. (2011). Mindfulness practice leads to increases in regional brain gray matter density. *Psychiatry Research, 191*(1), 36-43

Hopper, E. (2003). *Traumatic experience in the unconscious life of groups: The fourth basic assumption: Incohesion: Aggregation/massification of (ba) I:A/M.* London: Jessica Kingsley.

Iacoboni, I. (2008). *Mirroring people: The new science of how we connect to others.* New York, NY: Fararr, Strauss & Giroux.

Johnson, J., Burlingame, G., Olsen, J., Davies, D., & Gleave, R. (2005). Group climate, cohesion, alliance, and empathy in group psychotherapy: Multilevel structural equation models. *Journal of Counseling Psychology, 52*(3), 310-321.

Karr-Morse, R., & Wiley, M. (2012). *Scared sick: The role of childhood trauma in adult disease.* New York, NY: Basic Books.

Karr-Morse, R., Wiley, M. S., & Brazelton, T. (2007). *Ghosts from the nursery: Tracing the roots of violence.* New York, NY: Atlantic Monthly Press.

Keihl, K. (2006). A cognitive neuroscience perspective on psychopathy: Evidence for paralimbic system dysfunction. *Psychiatry Research, 142*, 107-128.

Kirkpatrick, L., Suvenobu, B., Smith, S., Bueller, J., Goodman, T., Creswell, J., Tillisch, K., Mayer, E., & Naliboff, B. (2011). Impact of mindfulness-based stress reduction training on intrinsic brain connectivity. *Neuroimage, 56*(1), 290-298.

Klein, R., Rice, C., & Schermer, V. (Eds). (2009). *Leadership in a changing world: Dynamic perspectives on groups and their leaders.* Lanham, MD: Lexington.

Kohut, H. (1971). *The analysis of the self: A systematic approach to the psychoanalytic treatment of narcissistic personality disorders.* Chicago: University of Chicago Press.

Kohut, H. (1977). *The restoration of the self.* Chicago: University of Chicago Press.

Langevin, R., Reuben A., Lang, R., Wortzman, G., Frenzel, R., & Wright, P. (1989). An examination of brain damage and dysfunction in genital exhibitionists. *Annals of Sex Research, 2*(1), 77-87.

Lawson, J. (2012). Sociological theories of intimate partner violence. *Journal of Human Behavior in the Social Environment, 22*(5), 572-590.

Lew, A. (2005). *Be still and get going.* New York, NY: Little Brown.

Lieberman, M. D. (2013). *Social: Why our brains are wired to connect.* New York, NY: Crown.

Lothstein, L. M. (1978). The group psychotherapy dropout phenomenon revisited. *American Journal of Psychiatry, 135*, 1492-1495.

Lothstein, L. M. (2013). Group therapy for intimate partner violence (IPV). *International Journal of Group Psychotherapy, 63*(3), 499-452.

Lothstein, L. M. (2014). The science and art of brief inpatient group therapy in the 21st century. *International Journal of Group Psychotherapy, 64*(2), 228-244.

McGregor, E., Nunez, M., Cebula, K., & Gomez, J. C. (Eds.). (2007). *Autism: An integrated view from neurocognitive, clinical and intervention research.* Boston, MA: Wiley-Blackwell.

McWilliams, N. (2004). *Psychoanalytic psychotherapy: A practitioner's guide.* New York, NY: Guilford.

Meloy, R. (1997). *Violent attachments.* Northvale, NJ: Aronson.

Miczek, K. A., de Almeida, R. M. M., Kravitz, E. A., Rissman, E. F., de Boer, S. F., & Raine, A. (2007). Neurobiology of escalated aggression and violence. *Journal of Neuroscience, 27*(44), 11803-11806.

Mitchell, S. A. (1988). *Relational concepts in psychoanalysis: An integration.* Cambridge: MA: Harvard University Press.

Morrison, A. (1989). *Shame: The underside of narcissism.* New York, NY: Routledge.

Motz, A. (2008). *The psychology of female violence: Crimes against the body.* New York, NY: Routledge.

Motz, A. (2014). *Toxic couples and domestic violence.* London: Routledge.

Murphy, C., & Baxter, V. (1997). Motivating batterers to change in the treatment context. *Journal of Interpersonal Violence, 12,* 607-619.

National Center for Injury Prevention and Control, Centers for Disease Control and Prevention. (2003). *Costs of intimate partner violence against women in the United States.* Atlanta, GA: Author. Available from www.cdc.gov/ncipc/pub-res/ipv_cost/ipv.htm.

National Institutes of Health. (1997). *Substance abuse treatment and domestic violence. Treatment Improvement Protocol No. 25.* (SMA) 97-3163. Rockville, MD. Substance Abuse and Mental Health Services Administration. http://www.ncbi.nlm.nih.gov/books/NBK64437/

Nicholas, M. (2013). The compulsion to repeat relationships with abusive partners and how group therapy can help. *International Journal of Group Psychotherapy, 63*(3), 347-365.

Norcross, J. C. (Ed.). (2002). *Psychotherapy relationships that work: Therapist contributions and responsiveness to patients.* New York, NY: Oxford University Press.

Porges, S. W. (2014). *The polyvagal response: Neurophysiological foundations of emotions and self-regulation.* New York, NY: Norton.

Raine, A. (2013). *The anatomy of violence: The biological roots of crime.* New York, NY: Pantheon.

Roberts, A. (2002). *Handbook of domestic violence intervention strategies: Policy, programs and legal remedies.* New York, NY: Oxford University Press.

Rutan, J. S., Stone, W. N., & Shay, J. J. (2007). *Psychodynamic group psychotherapy* (4th ed.). New York, NY: Guilford.

Scharff, D. E., & Scharff, J. S. (2011). *The interpersonal unconscious.* Lanham, MD: Aronson.

Schermer, V. L. (2010). Mirror neurons: Their implications for group psychotherapy. *International Journal of Group Psychotherapy, 60*(4), 486-513.

Schnarch, D. (2009). *Intimacy and desire.* New York, NY: Beaufort.

Schore, A. (2003a). *Affect dysregulation and disorders of the self.* New York, NY: Norton.

Schore, A. (2003b). *Affect regulation and repair of the self.* New York, NY: Norton.

Shedler, J. (2010). The efficacy of psychodynamic psychotherapy. *American Psychologist, 65*(2), 98-109.

Siegel, D. (2010). Commentary on "Integrating interpersonal neurobiology with group psychotherapy: Reflections on mind, brain, and relationships in group psychotherapy." *International Journal of Group Psychotherapy, 60*(4), 483-485.

Twemlow, S. W., Fonagy, P., et al. (1999). *The role of group psychotherapeutic interventions in youth violence reduction and primary prevention – A white paper.*, New York, NY: American Group Psychotherapy Association.

van der Kolk, B. A. (2002). The assessment and treatment of complex PTSD. In R. Yehuda (Ed.), *Treating trauma survivors with PTSD* (pp. 127-156). Washington, DC: American Psychiatric Press.

Varki, A., & Bower, D. (2013). *Denial: Self-deception, false beliefs, and the origins of the human mind.* New York, NY: Twelve.

Webb, L. P., & Leehan, J. (1996). *Group treatment for adult survivors of abuse: A manual for practitioners.* Thousand Oaks, CA: Sage.

Welldon, E. (1997). Let the treatment fit the crime: Forensic group psychotherapy. *Group Analysis, 30*, 9-26.

Yakeley, J. (2010). *Working with violence. A contemporary psychoanalytic approach.* London: Palgrave Macmillan.

Yakeley, J., & Meloy, R. (2012). Understanding violence: Does psychoanalytic thinking matter? *Aggression and Violent Behavior, 17*(3), 229-239.

Yalom, I., & Leszcz, M. (2005). *The theory and practice of group psychotherapy.* New York, NY: Basic Books.

Yllo, K. A. (2005). Through a feminist lens: Gender, diversity, and violence: Extending the feminist framework. In D. R. Loseke, R. J. Gelles, & M. M. Cavanaugh (Eds.), *Current controversies on family violence* (pp. 19-34). Thousand Oaks, CA: Sage.

Terrorism and Right-Wing Extremism: The Changing Face of Terrorism and Political Violence in the 21st Century: The Virtual Community of Hatred

JERROLD M. POST, M.D.

ABSTRACT

There are no psychological characteristics or psychopathology that separates terrorists from the general population. Rather it is group dynamics, with a particular emphasis on collective identity that helps explain terrorist psychology. Just as there is a diverse spectrum of terrorisms, so too is there a spectrum of terrorist psychologies. Four waves of terrorism can be distinguished: the Anarchist wave, associated with labor violence in the United States in the late 19th century; the Anti-Colonial wave (nationalist-separatist), with minority groups seeking to be liberated from their colonial masters or from the majority in their country; the New Left wave (social revolutionary); and now the Religious wave. With the communications revolution, a new phenomenon is emerging which may presage a fifth wave: lone wolf terrorists who through the Internet are radicalized and feel they belong to the virtual community of hatred. A typology of lone wolf terrorism is proposed.

The group is the basic unit of political life. And this is particularly true of the world of political violence. A search to identify a unique individual terrorist profile has proved fruitless. Martha Crenshaw concluded that "the outstanding characteristic of ter-

---

Jerrold M. Post, M.D., is Professor of Psychiatry, Political Psychology, and International Affairs, and Director of the Political Psychology Program at the Elliott School of International Affairs at George Washington University in Washington, DC.

rorists is their normality" (Crenshaw, 1981). Similarly, a comprehensive review of the social psychology of terrorism concluded that "the best documented generalization is negative; terrorists do not show any striking psychopathology" (McCauley & Segal, 1987).

Post first introduced consideration of the importance of terrorist group dynamics at the World Congress of Psychiatry in 1983, and introduced this topic to the group psychotherapy literature in 1986 and to the terrorism literature in 1987 (Post, 1983, 1986, 1987a).[1] In reflecting on the implications of the basic assumption states delineated by Wilfred Bion (1961), the dependency group, the fight-flight, and the pairing group, one can make a case that all three of these states contribute to understanding terrorist group dynamics (Post, 1987b). The hate-mongering group leader, especially in charismatic groups and organizations, such as al-Qaeda under Osama bin Laden or the LTTE (Tamil Tigers) under Prabhakaran, are characterized by the followers subordinating their individual identity to the cause as articulated by the leader, and gaining a sense of belonging to something greater than themselves. What the leader says is moral and what he defines as evil is evil. They uncritically follow his leadership. It is the very essence of dependency psychology, especially with the underground group, with the group being idealized and the government being demonized. In terms of the "pairing" basic assumption group, there is often a sense that after the destruction of current society an idealized new society will emerge with the new messiah. This was particularly true with the followers of Shoko Asahara, the guru of Aum Shinrikyo, who, inspired by the book of Revelations, were attempting to precipitate the apocalypse, with true believers being resurrected to follow Asahara who had promoted himself as a version of Christ. A fourth basic assumption, which has been suggested by Earl Hopper in his book *The Social Unconscious* is that merger as an escape from annihilation or incohesion is particularly appropriate for minorities threatened with annihilation by the dominant state, which I have characterized as identicide. This is exemplified by Ocalan's

---

1. This drew on research that reviewed the group psychology of four models: religious cults, youth gangs, and organized crime, and resistance groups, supported by the Harry Frank Guggenheim Foundation.

forming the PKK, the Kurdish separatist terrorist group, in the face of Ataturk's attempts to deny the very existence of the Kurdish people and make it illegal to use the Kurdish language, or to even use the name of Kurds, instead using the derogatory term "mountain Turks." It was a defensive intensification of national identity. The same dynamic was at the root of the attraction of the Basque people threatened with "identicide" by Franco to form the nationalist-separatist terrorist group Euskadi ta Akatasuna (ETA) (Basque Homeland and Freedom).

Among the identified characteristics of terrorist group psychology were a tendency toward polarization and externalization, summed up in a substance-free version of terrorist ideology, justification, and motivation: "It's not us; it's them. They are responsible for our problems. And therefore striking out against them is not only not prohibited, it is morally justified, it is required." And this is particularly true, when there is religious justification, if it is "killing in the name of God."

It is important to emphasize the interaction between the political context and the ability of the hate-mongering leader to successfully emphasize the victim psychology of the minority and to mobilize defensive aggression against the majority. To externalize in a compelling manner requires not only political skills but a political context in which minority rights are ignored. When the system is indeed attempting to destroy the identity of the minority, it sets the conditions for development of a charismatic movement, in which the leader heightens the threat of annihilation by the dominant majority to destroy the identity of the minority group and mobilizes defensive aggression, associated with a heightened sense of identity. Three prominent examples of what I have called "identicide" concern the origins of the Kurdish separatist group, the Kurdistan Workers Party (PKK), the Tamil Tigers (the LTTE) and the Basque Homeland and Liberty (ETA) (Post, 2007).

In Turkey, seeking to consolidate a Turkic identity, the founding father of the Turkish nation, Mustafa Kemal Ataturk, sought to eliminate Kurdish identity and culture and denied their rights to a homeland. This set the stage for Abdullah Ocalan, founder of the PKK, to establish an organization devoted to Kurdish rights, heightening Kurdish national identity in the face of the campaign for "identicide" launched by Ataturk (Post, 2007). In his 1998 cease-fire declaration, Ocalan explained how Ataturk's denial of Kurdish identity prompted the violence:

> On the one hand, you say that the Kurds are as much owners of these lands as the Turks, that all their national and social rights will be recognized; on the other hand, even our name is denied. This is what led to the violence. We are surely the side that should be least responsible. We wanted our identity. We wanted our democracy. We wanted our culture. Can anybody live without culture? Can anybody live without democracy? What do you expect us to do after even our name has been denied? (Post, 2007, p. 67)

Similarly, in Spain, Franco's attempt to eliminate the Basque identity, including prohibition of the Basque vernacular language, Euskera, heightened the sense of Basque identity (Post, 2007). An ETA prisoner, recalling Franco's repression of the Basque people stated: "Franco made us nationalists by his persecution" (Woodworth, 2001, p. 5). Sabano Arana took up the banner of Basque nationalism and founded the Basque Nationalist Party. "My patriotism is founded in my love for God, and for which purpose I pursue to lead my brethren to God: my great family the Basque people" (History of Basque nationalism: Historical background, n.d.). Franco made it illegal to teach Basque history in schools. The aim of the Basque Nationalist Party (PV) was to teach Bizkainos "the history of their motherland" and to awaken his compatriots "who disgracefully ignored the language of their race" (Da Silva, 1975). Similarly, in Sri Lanka, the rights of the Tamil minority were ignored by the dominant Sinhala majority. Velupillai Prabhakaran, the charismatic founder of the Tamil Tigers, early on felt that:

> It is the plight of the Tamil people that compelled me to take up arms...I felt that armed struggle is the only way to protect and liberate our people from a totalitarian Fascist state bent on destroying an entire race of people. (Tamil National Leader Velupillai Prabhakaran's Interview, 1986)

Given that the group ideology is anti-authority, committed to striking out at the establishment, it is remarkable how conformist and authoritarian it is within the group. No doubt or questioning is permitted. As individuals with low self-esteem feel a sense of enhanced value in belonging to the group, anything which questions the group's justification is threatening. As individuals subordinate their individuality to the group, this creates an environment conducive to "groupthink," where a group can make riskier decisions than any individual in the group might make alone. Reflecting the "risky shift" phenomenon, individual doubts are suppressed because of the group ethos of bravery and courage in pursuit of the cause.

As reflected in the consensus document of the Committee on the Psychology of Terrorism at the International Summit on Democracy, Terrorism and Security in Madrid, Spain, 2005, there is a broad consensus among terrorism scholars that "explanations at the level of individual psychology are insufficient" (Post, 2005). Indeed, it was stressed that terrorist groups regularly screen out mentally unstable individuals; they would, after all, be a security risk. There was a general consensus that it is not individual psychopathology but rather group psychology, with a particular emphasis on collective identity, that is the most important lens through which to look at the psychology of terrorism (Post, 2005). Emphasizing the importance of group dynamics, Horgan, in his book *The Psychology of Terrorism* (2005), stresses that there are no psychological characteristics that distinguish terrorists from the general population. In *The Mind of the Terrorist*, Post singles out group dynamics as being of central significance in understanding terrorist psychology (Post, 2007).

In reviewing the history of terrorism, one is struck by the diversity of causes pursued. It would be unreasonable to suppose that such diversity is governed by a singular psychology. Rather, we should be talking of terrorisms, plural, and terrorist psychologies, plural. Each terrorism must be understood in its unique cultural, historical, and political context. But within this diversity, there are broad underlying themes in common. And the particularity of violence in America reflects the themes played out internationally in the area of terrorism and political violence.

VIOLENCE IN AMERICA

THE FOUR WAVES OF MODERN TERRORISM

In a seminal article summarizing the history of modern terrorism, Rapoport delineated four waves: the Anarchist wave, which began in Russia in the 1880s and spread to Europe, Asia, and the Americas and was associated with labor violence; the Anti-Colonial wave (nationalist-separatist), with minority groups seeking to be liberated from their colonial masters or from the majority in their country; the New Left wave (social revolutionary); and now the Religious wave, punctuated by the Iran hostage crisis and the 9/11 World Trade Center and Pentagon attack (Rapoport, 2004).

The First Wave: The Anarchist Wave

Setting the stage for the wave of anarchic violence, in 1847 Karl Marx and Friedrich Engels published the Communist Manifesto, which both stressed the international dimensions of oppression of the working men by the ruling classes and declared the requirement for "working men of all countries [to] unite":

> Let the ruling classes tremble at a Communist revolution. The proletarians have nothing to lose but their chains. They have a world to win. Working men of all countries, unite! (Marx & Engels, 1848)

The labor violence in America of the late 19th century was emboldened by the anarchic violence in Russia and Europe. While idealizing the plight of the working man, "the labor movement reveals... [a] mixture of glorious ends with inglorious means" (Gurr, 1989, p. 46), dramatically represented by the Haymarket riot of 1886. Labor militants were demonstrating for an eight-hour work day in Chicago's Haymarket Square. When police intervened, a bomb was thrown, leading to the deaths of seven police officers and four demonstrators in the explosion and riot that followed. The organizers were called anarchists, with eight convicted and four hanged, on the basis of tenuous evidence (Gurr, 1989). As the strike became a major tactic of unions attempting to organize, violence commonly accompanied the union efforts, leading Louis Adamic sardonically to characterize the period of the late 1800s to the early 1900s as "the dynamite era" in American labor relations (Adamic, 1934). This

	Parents' Relationship to the Regime	
Youths' Relationship to Parents	**L**oyal	**D**isloyal Damaged Dissident
Loyal	✕	National-Separatist Terrorism
Disloyal	Social Revolutionary Terrorism	

Figure 1. This generational pathways-to-terrorism matrix demonstrates the generational provenance of the second and third waves of terrorism. National-separatists constituting the second, or "anti-colonial," wave are loyal to parents and grandparents who are disloyal and dissidents to the regime. Social revolutionaries who characterize the third, or "new left," wave, were rebelling against the generation of their parents who were loyal to the regime

was well captured in the slogan of the anarchist newspaper, *Freiheit* (Freedom), which was published in New York. "*Freiheit*, five cents a copy, dynamite, fifty cents a pound. Read one. Use the other."

The Second Wave: The Anti-colonial Wave

The second wave, which Rapoport identified as the post-colonial wave, occurred in the wake of World War I, lasted through World War II, and saw the establishment of a number of independent nations as colonial empires of France, Great Britain, Netherlands, Belgium, Spain, and Portugal contracted and dissolved. Thus, as represented in Figure 1, these nationalist-separatist terrorists show the following characteristics:

- They are carrying on the mission of their parents;
- Their acts of terrorism are acts of retaliation for hurts done to their parents and grandparents by society; and

- They are loyal to parents damaged by, dissident to, the regime.

Be it in the pubs of Northern Ireland or the coffee houses on the West Bank and Jordan, they have heard their fathers talk about what "they" have done to them, depriving them of social and economic justice. And they are acting to redress their grievances.

The Third Wave: The New Left Wave

The revolution in information technology increasingly dissolved boundaries. While the island continent of North and South America was not as swept by revolutionary fervor as Europe, there was a broad awareness of, and influence by, the international environment. This was particularly so for the third wave, the social revolutionary wave. Through electronic media during the Vietnam War, students were simultaneously at the barricades in Paris, Berlin, Rome, San Francisco, and New York. The student protest movements were stimulated by each other, emulated each other, and felt a sense of common purpose. This can be considered large group psychology. Anti-fascist and anti-capitalist in their rhetoric, they shared an idealized version of Marxist-Leninism, and in their study groups justified striking out against the establishment. Just as the Red Army Faction in Germany and the Red Brigades in Italy split off from the largely peaceful student movement in Western Europe—becoming what Dennis Pluchinsky has called "fighting communist organizations" (Yonah and Pluchinsky, 1992)—in the United States, the Weather Underground split off from the Students for a Democratic Society. Impatient with the pace of change through peaceful protests, they came to believe that violence was necessary to sensitize the masses. In the words of the Bob Dylan song, "Subterranean Homesick Blues," which became emblematic for the group, "You don't need a weatherman to know which way the wind blows." The generational provenance of the social revolutionary groups can be identified as rebelling against the generation of their parents, identified with the regime, as reflected in Figure 1.

In their manifesto, which was couched in Marxist-Leninist terms, the Weather Underground declared their goal to be: The destruction of U.S. imperialism and the achievement of a classless world: world communism...Someone not for revolution is not actually for defeating imperialism either...Long live the Victory of People's War (Asbley et al., 1969).

Exulting in their underground guerilla identity, echoing the anarchist rhetoric of the Russian anarchists of the 1880s, in 1970, the Weather Underground published a 150-page creed, *Prairie Fire: The Politics of Revolutionary Anti-Imperialism*, defining their goals. Their spokeswoman and one of the principal leaders, Bernadine Dohrn, declared in 1970:

> We are a guerilla organization. We are communist women and men, underground in the United States for more than four years. We are deeply affected by the historic events of our time in the struggle against U.S. imperialism... . Our intention is to disrupt the empire, to incapacitate it, to put pressure on the cracks to make it hard to carry out its bloody functioning against the people of the world, to join the world struggle, to attack from the inside... . Our intention is to engage the enemy, to wear away at him, to isolate him to expose every weakness... .
>
> Without mass struggle, there can be no revolution. Without armed struggle, there can be no victory. (Weather Underground Organization, 1974, p. 30)

The fall of the Berlin Wall in 1989 and the subsequent implosion of the Soviet Union marked the end of the third wave, the social revolutionary wave.

The Fourth Wave: The Religious Extremist Wave

Overlapping with the end of the third wave, the event that marks the beginning of the fourth wave, the religious extremist wave, is the seizure of the U.S. embassy in Tehran, Iran, by Shiite Iranian mujahedeen in 1979. The religious terrorism wave continues to be the dominant form of terrorism.

Although Muslim fundamentalist terrorism played a major role, terrorism with religious motivations was found in the other Abrahamic religions as well. Thus, Yigal Amir, the assassin of Israeli Prime Minister Yitzhak Rabin, was a Jewish fundamentalist religious student inspired by the radical rabbinate in Israel that "the judgment of the pursuer" had been fastened to Rabin, drawing on the book of Leviticus, 19:16: "Thou shall not stand idly by the brother's innocent blood." Amir's stated motivation for his assassination of the Israeli Prime Minister in 1995 was that by entering the Oslo negotiations, Rabin was placing a group of murderous terrorists on the borders of Israel, endangering his innocent Israeli brethren. The violence in the United States toward abortion clinics and murders of health care providers in these clinics can be seen as a form of Christian fundamentalist terrorism. Former Roman Catholic priest David C. Trosch called such actions "justifiable homicide." He had likened doctors, nurses, and healthcare workers in clinics performing abortions to perpetrators of the Holocaust during World War II, for a holocaust was being committed against the unborn children of this nation:

> "Defending innocent human life is not murder... . You're comparing the lives of morally guilty persons against the lives of manifestly innocent persons... . That's like trying to compare the lives of the Jews in the incinerators in Nazi Germany or Poland...with the lives of the Gestapo." (Niebuhr, 1994, p. 12)

Aum Shinrikyo's 1995 sarin gas attack on the Tokyo subways was justified by the peculiar theology of Aum Supreme Truth and its guru Shoko Asahara. He was seeking to precipitate an apocalyptic struggle, from which he and his true believer followers would be resurrected as the Christ and his followers (Post, 2007).

Islamic Fundamentalism

The dominant form of religious terrorism in the fourth religious wave, however, is that perpetrated by Islamist extremists. The Koran specifically prohibits suicide. But radical interpretations of the Koran have led to employing suicide terrorism, justifying this as defensive aggression, rationalizing that this is not suicide but martyrdom, which is rewarded with a higher place in paradise (Ali & Post, 2008). Rapoport dates the beginning of this wave to 1979, when Shiite Muslim militants, screaming "Death to the Great Satan," seized the U.S. embassy in Tehran and held the occupants hostage for 444 days, not releasing them until the inauguration of President Ronald Regan in January 1981. A dramatic event in the early years of this wave was the truck bombing of the marine barracks in Beirut, Lebanon, in October 1983, in which 241 U.S. military personnel were killed. At the same time, a suicide bomber driving a pickup truck laden with explosives drove into a building housing French paratroopers, killing 58. The attacks, carried out by Hezbollah, the militant Shiite Lebanese Islamic terrorist group, and sponsored by Iran, were justified by their spiritual mentor, Sheikh Fadlallah, who indicated that the prohibition against suicide was overridden by the special times and justified the martyrdom action of the militants (Kramer, 1998). Thus the prohibited act of suicide was reframed as the revered act of martyrdom (Ali & Post, 2008). This act transformed the role of the United States in the Middle East as honest broker. Ayatollah Khomeini was impressed by the innovative tactic of the Hezbollah terrorists, and suicide terrorism was to become a staple of militant Islamist terrorists.

While Ayatollah Khomeini was a Shiite Muslim, Osama bin Laden, a Wahhabi Sunni Muslim, used the same justification for the terrorist violence of his group, al-Qaeda (the base). Despite the substantial aid the United States provided to the Muslim militants in their ultimately victorious struggle to expel the Soviet Union, which had invaded the Muslim state of Afghanistan, bin Laden was accorded near God-like status after his victory over the Soviet superpower. He next turned his attention to the remaining superpower, the United States, whose troops still remained on bases in Saudi Arabia, "the land of the two cities" (Mecca and Medina), after the first Gulf War that was precipitated by the invasion of Kuwait by Saddam Hussein in July 1990. Initial fatwas focused on the need to expel U.S. military from the bases in Saudi Arabia.

In February 1993, the first World Trade Center bombing occurred. A van with a 1,336-pound fertilizer bomb was detonated in the underground garage of the North Tower. Had the van been parked in a position in the underground garage some 100 yards from where it was placed, the plan to have the North Tower collapse against the South Tower, killing tens of thousands, would have succeeded.

While only six were killed, there were more than a thousand injured. A massive task force was able to identify the perpetrators.

Evidence established that the plot was carried out by a group of Islamist terrorists headed by Ramzi Yousef, an electrical engineer ultimately captured in Pakistan. A plan to explode 12 airliners bound for the United States from Asia was found in encrypted form on Yousef's computer. While al-Qaeda never claimed responsibility for the bombing, the attack was financed by Yousef's uncle, Khalid Sheik Mohammed, the architect of the 9/11 attacks on the World Trade Center and the Pentagon. Khalid Sheik Mohammed was to become the chief of operations of al-Qaeda. No longer was the United States immune from international terrorism; yet quickly Americans forgot and basked in their customary sense of invulnerability.

In 1996, in what was to be the second largest terrorist attack since the bombing of the U.S. Marine barracks in Beirut in 1983, a truck bomb was detonated in a U.S. military housing compound, Khobar Towers, in Saudi Arabia, killing 19. Hundreds of thousands of the U.S. military were now based in the holy land of Saudi Arabia, incensing Muslim extremists against this invasion of the holy land by infidels. In 1998, in a coordinated twin city attack, al-Qaeda–supported terrorists detonated massive truck bombs against U.S. embassies in Nairobi, Kenya, and Dar es Salaam, Tanzania, leading to hundreds of deaths and massive damage. This resulted in the FBI putting Osama bin Laden, identified as the mastermind behind this plot, on its ten most wanted list. In October 2000, the USS Cole, a Navy frigate, was attacked by a small craft laden with 300–700 pounds of explosives during a routine refueling stop in Aden, Yemen. The craft hit the port side of the frigate; the resulting explosion led to 19 deaths and 37 casualties. An al-Qaeda operation, this success and the success in the Khobar Towers attacks against U.S. military and against the U.S. embassies in Kenya and Tanzania only added to the luster of bin Laden's heroic reputation. He was on a roll.

In February 1998, confirming the United States as a potential target, an important fatwa, "The Jihad Against Jews and Crusaders," was issued that signaled a broader purpose and target than earlier religious declarations.

> The ruling to kill the Americans and their allies—civilians and military—is an individual duty for every Muslim who can do it in

any country in which it is possible to do it, in order to liberate the al-Aqsa Mosque and the holy mosque [Mecca] from their grip, and in order for their armies to move out of all the lands of Islam, defeated and unable to threaten any Muslim. This is in accordance with the words of Almighty God, "and fight the pagans all together as they fight you all together," and "fight them until there is no more tumult or oppression, and there prevail justice and faith in God."

We—with God's help—call on every Muslim who believes in God and wishes to be rewarded to comply with God's order to kill the Americans and plunder their money wherever and whenever they find it. (as cited in Post, 2004, p. 8)

Take note of the phrase: "The ruling [was] to kill the Americans...—civilians and military—...in any country in which it is possible to do it." No longer was the struggle to expel U.S. military from Saudi Arabia. Now the gloves were off, but when the attacks of 9/11 occurred, it was a devastating blow to the American psyche.

The coordinated twin city attack in which hijacked U.S. airliners crashed into the World Trade Center and the Pentagon with 3,000 casualties transformed the international landscape. In a television posting after the devastating attack, bin Laden warned pious Muslims not to live or work in high rise buildings or fly, because there were thousands of Muslims committed to martyrdom who would kill the weak Americans clinging to life. Betraying his narcissistic preoccupation with his heroic image, in a home video bin Laden wondered how the event had played in Jiddah and indicated that the results had exceeded his expectations.

The victory in Afghanistan against the Soviet superpower became the basis of bin Laden's charismatic leader-follower relationship with his followers. He had preached during the ten-year struggle that Allah favored the underdog, and when bin Laden and his Afghan Arabs succeeded in expelling the Soviet forces from Afghanistan, this confirmed that he was an all-knowing, all-powerful leader. But with success, bin Laden had lost his enemy. The presence of the U.S. military in Muslim lands provided him with the rationale to shift his attention to the United States, the last remaining superpower. Initially, attacks were targeted against the U.S. military in the Middle East. The magnitude of the 2001 attacks in New York and Washington, the most devastating terrorist attack in history, confirmed for bin Laden and his followers that they had a historic role to play in the struggle to liberate Islam from Western domination and its corrupt influences. The architect of the twin towers attacks was instantly promoted to international stardom, the greatest terrorist of all time, a hero to alienated Muslim youth who were empowered by his dramatic act and flocked to al-Qaeda recruitment offices.

This attack on the U.S. homeland led President George W. Bush to declare a war on terror and within a few weeks to begin mobilizing for a military strike against al-Qaeda central, which was based in Taliban-controlled Afghanistan. This was not state-supported terrorism, but rather wealthy al-Qaeda led by wealthy Osama bin Laden supporting the failed state of Afghanistan. For the first 20 years of the fourth wave, the religious extremist phase, the first wavelet concerned the growth and international expansion of religious extremist terrorism, especially Islamist extremism under his charismatic leadership of al-Qaeda. Concomitantly, Shiite terrorism, supported by Iran, with the growth of Hamas and Hezbollah, continued apace.

Pseudo-Christian Ideology

In the mid 1990s, reflecting a pseudo-Christian ideology, an act of domestic terrorism within the United States occurred when the right wing extremist Timothy McVeigh, consumed by hatred of the United States government, carried out a major attack on the Alfred P. Murah federal building in Oklahoma City on April 19, 1995, the largest domestic terrorism attack to date, until the later attacks of 9/11. One hundred sixty-eight people were killed in the massive explosion, timed to create "maximal body count," and more than 680 were injured. Within a 16-block radius, 324 buildings were destroyed or damaged, with an estimated property loss of $652 million. The date of the attack is significant as it was timed to coincide with the anniversary of the conflagration at Ranch Apocalypse, the Branch Davidian headquarters in Waco, Texas, in which David Koresh and 75 of his true believer followers perished during the FBI siege of their headquarters.

VIOLENCE IN AMERICA

The paranoid right in the United States had delegitimized the federal government, developed a pseudo-Christian ideology to provide a rationale for their fear and distrust of Washington, and formed the Church of Jesus Christ, Christian. Why "Jesus Christ, Christian"? Because for these intensely racist anti-Semitic individuals, it was unthinkable that Christ could have been a Jew. The outlines of their creative theology, the basis of the Christian Identity movement, can be summarized as follows:

> In the Garden of Eden, Eve mated with two: Adam, who was blond haired and blue eyed, from whom the true chosen people descended, the Adamic line, the Aryan nation. Abel was first of the Adamic line. She also mated with the serpent who was the devil in disguise, from whom the Jews, the spawn of the devil descended. Cain was the first of this line. The Garden of Eden was God's second attempt at creation. The first attempt failed, from which a group of sub-humans emerged, the "mud people," blacks and people of color. When Cain slew Abel, it was the prototype of the genocide of the whites, the true chosen people, by the spawn of the devil, the Jews, who controlled and manipulated the "mud people." The apocalypse is approaching, the final battle will be between the true chosen people, the Aryan nations, the forces of good, and the Jews, the forces of evil. It is the God-given task of the Aryans to warn of the dangers represented by the Jews in league with "the mud people," and to prepare for the final battle and destroy them. The Aryan Nation is the action arm of the Christian Identity movement.[2]

The creedal statement of the Aryan Nations and the Church of Jesus Christ, Christian, to which new members swear on joining, embodies this ideology:

> We believe that there are literal children of Satan in the world today. These children are the descendants of Cain, who was a result of Eve's original sin, her physical seduction by Satan...There is a battle and a natural enmity between the children of Satan and the children of the Most High God...We believe there is a battle being

---

2. For an extensive discussion of the origins of the Christian Identity movement and its justification of violence against Jews and people of color, see Robins and Post (1997, pp. 182-187).

fought this day between the children of darkness (known today as Jews) and the children of light (God), the Aryan race, the true Israel of the Bible. (as cited in Barkun, 1994, p. 131)

Thus, the extremists in the militia movement, which achieved great prominence in the 1990s, are not weekend warriors but are preparing for this final battle. While this extremist sentiment has not been the basis for violent actions in the United States in recent years, these sentiments are related to the radical right in Europe, which has carried out violent actions against Muslim émigrés. A recent example was Anders Breivik who killed 77 in a rampage in Norway in 2011, first killing 8 in a bombing of government buildings in Oslo, then killing 69, mostly teenagers, in a mass shooting at a labor youth camp on the island of Utoya. Breivik characterized himself as "the point of the spear," seeking to warn of the danger of Muslim "mongrelization" of Christian Europe. He has been convicted of mass murder and is now serving a life sentence in a Norwegian prison.

As noted earlier, the second phase of the wave of religious terrorism was precipitated by the al-Qaeda attacks of 9/11 on the World Trade Center and the Pentagon, with the subsequent declaration of a war on terror by President George W. Bush and the initiation of the war in Afghanistan in October 2001, as the first battle of that continuing war. That led to the destruction of al-Qaeda central in Afghanistan and the flight of al-Qaeda leadership. From a place of hiding in the mountainous region of Pakistan, bin Laden sent out a communiqué instructing his franchised groups that it was now up to them to plan and fund operations previously planned and funded by al-Qaeda central, under the leadership of bin Laden and his deputy Ayman al-Zawahiri. A decision to decentralize was an adaptive response now that al-Qaeda leadership was on the run. It was up to such organizations as al-Qaeda in the Arabian Peninsula, al-Qaeda in Iraq, and other affiliates to continue the struggle against the West, but the leaders would continue to provide guidance. The West mounted a strategy of decapitation of al-Qaeda, relying on sophisticated remotely piloted aircraft (drones). This program, while producing a major outcry of invasion of sovereignty by Pakistan, was quite successful in killing a significant number of senior al-Qaeda leaders and placing al-Qaeda on the defensive.

This phase of the wave of religious extremist terrorism was concluded with the successful raid on bin Laden's headquarters in Abbottabad, Pakistan, conducted from Afghanistan by a joint CIA/Navy Special Forces (U.S. SEALs) operation in which bin Laden was killed. The identification of bin Laden's refuge in Pakistan was the result of a massive intelligence effort.

With this punctuation mark, the third phase of the wave commenced. Now, however, the al-Qaeda elements, such as al-Qaeda in the Arabian Peninsula and al-Qaeda in the Islamic Maghreb, pursued nationalistic objectives, although still attacking the West in the name of radical Islam. A good example of this was the September 2013 attack which killed 72 people in an upscale shopping mall in Nairobi, Kenya, carried out by the Somali terrorist group, al-Shabaab, in revenge for Kenya's support for the Somali government.

A NEW PHASE: THE VIRTUAL COMMUNITY OF HATRED AND LONE WOLF TERRORISM[3]

Another phase is emerging, a reflection of the communication revolution, which is increasingly evident. Indeed, it would be demeaning to consider this just another "wavelet." Rather, it may prove to be a tsunami. While it is difficult in the midst of a historical process to have the perspective to identify this as the beginning of a fifth wave, the social media revolution may indeed prove to be the next one.

The wave of social protest that swept the Middle East, popularly known as the Arab Spring, began in December 2010, catalyzed by a cell phone photo of a vegetable peddler in Tunis who set himself on fire to protest the confiscation of his cart and the humiliation by public officials. The image went viral, leading to widespread protests, forcing then President Zine al-Abidine Ben Ali, who had ruled Tunisia for 23 years, to step down after 23 days of protest. The success of the social media–inspired revolution in Tunisia also inspired citizens throughout the Middle East, leading to the overthrow of the authoritarian leaders of Egypt, Libya, and Yemen and sparking the civilian rebellion in Syria. A

---

3. This section of the paper draws significantly on a paper on lone wolf psychology (McGinnis, Moody, & Post, 2013).

major slogan of the protesters throughout the Arab world was: "The people want to bring down the regime." Hosni Mubarak, who had ruled Egypt with an iron fist for 30 years, was forced to step down after only 18 days of protest, in what came to be called the cell phone revolution.

In fact, a year and a half earlier, it was the bloody image of a young Iranian woman, Neda Agha-Soltan—who was shot in the chest while speaking on her cell phone during a political protest in June 2009—that demonstrated the power of the new media. The image, captured on a bystander's cell phone, went viral and led to widespread protests in Iran against the election results. The image of Neda bleeding to death was posted on YouTube, Facebook, and Twitter and was widely shown on the Internet and television. It became the spark that precipitated the short-lived wave of political protests, until government security ruthlessly suppressed them. With every citizen potentially a photojournalist, no longer could dictatorial regimes control the media and suppress news of popular expressions of protest.

While the initial sentiment facilitated by the Internet and social media was that of the people of oppressed societies yearning to be free, the overthrow of these regimes did not produce a yield of budding democracies. It powerfully demonstrated, however, the power of the new media. And in the world of terrorism and political violence, it has been a power that has been exploited to create a virtual community of hatred.

The Psychology of the Lone Wolf and Wolf Packs

> No longer is the threat just from abroad, as was the case with the attacks of September 11, 2001; the threat is now increasingly from within, from homegrown terrorists who are inspired by violent Islamist ideology to plan and execute attacks where they live.
> —U.S. Senate Committee on
> Homeland Security and
> Governmental Affairs, 2008

During the past decade, there has been an increasing incidence of violent terrorist actions carried out by individuals unaffiliated with al-Qaeda central or its affiliates. This appears to be due to the fact that al-Qaeda's new strategy is "to empower and motivate individuals to commit acts of violence completely outside any terrorist chain of command" (Hoffman cited in Thompson, 2009). Homegrown terrorism, or for the purposes of this paper, lone wolf terrorism, has been defined as "radicalized groups and individuals that are not regularly affiliated with, but draw clear inspiration and occasional guidance from, al-Qaeda core or affiliated movements" (Nelson & Sanderson, 2011, p. vii). While new research continues to surface on this particular topic, there still remains a surprising lack of research on identifiable psychological commonalities and patterns of lone wolves that can help combat the threat of the lone, violent jihadist.

There has been some preliminary work on virtual group dynamics with reference to hacking groups. In research on the dangerous IT insider, consideration was given to how a seemingly mild introverted individual can become very aggressive online. Accordingly, the group dynamics of virtual groups in the hacking world tend to be unstable, with a shifting leadership. There is characteristically a competition for leadership, with the bolder hackers temporarily dominating. This puts a premium on bolder and more aggressive schemes, and cautionary criticism is rare. For the virtual radical group online, aggressive language and dangerous plans can be rewarded in this competitive information space, and ideas can lead to dangerous actions, pushing the isolated individual online to ever more aggressive plans, seeking the admiration of their fellow online radicals. For these isolated individuals, there is a premium on belonging, and that in turn can lead fantasy to become reality, as exemplified by several of the "wolf packs" to be discussed.

The lone wolf terrorist phenomenon is very diverse. In Europe, many extremists have come from impoverished and isolated communities (Leiken, 2005; Pregulman & Burke, 2012). However, in the United States, homegrown terrorists come from a diverse group of educational, socioeconomic, ethnic, and family backgrounds. Some have criminal backgrounds, while others are highly educated. They vary in levels of operational ability, training and access to financing. Their plots require varying degrees of planning, and the likelihood of success tends to be rather limited, with plots often thwarted prior to any real threat. But as is demonstrated by the case of the Tsarnaev brothers, the perpetrators of the Boston Marathon bombings, even the simplest of plots can create devastating consequences.

Osama bin Laden was acutely aware of the importance of strategic communication. Indeed, on an al-Qaeda website, a specific Internet strategy was spelled out.

> Due to the advances of modern technology, it is easy to spread news, information, articles and other information over the Internet. We strongly urge Muslim Internet professionals to spread and disseminate news and information about the Jihad through e-mail lists, discussion groups, and their own websites. If you fail to do this, and our site closes down before you have done this, we may hold you to account before Allah on the Day of Judgment…This way, even if our sites are closed down, the material will live on with the Grace of Allah. (Weimann, 2006, p. 66)

First in the United States and then internationally, the American-born cleric Anwar al-Awlaki, who became known as "the bin Laden of the Internet," played a lead role in advancing al-Qaeda's cause and perspective through the Internet. His eloquent sermons reflect three themes:

- Muslims are victims. Their economic and social difficulties are caused by their enemies.
- They, the enemy out to humiliate and defeat Muslims, are the West, especially the United States, Great Britain, and Israel.
- Therefore, jihad is required by all Muslims to defend Islam, which is under attack, against them. It is justified defensive jihad.

Three dramatic cases in recent years suggest the psychological qualities of individuals particularly attracted to this virtual community of hatred. And there are suggestions of a generational provenance as well. All three had contact with al-Awlaki. Major Nidal Hasan, the Army psychiatrist responsible for the massacre at Fort Hood, was impressed by al-Awlaki's sermons, which he heard in Northern Virginia. He contacted Imam al-Awlaki by e-mail when he was stationed in Fort Hood, indicating he was lonely and sought friends. They exchanged some 20 e-mails. In one, he asked al-Awlaki, "Is it OK for a Muslim to kill soldiers if their mission is to kill Muslims?" He was told, "Yes." Indeed, he was told it was an obligation. In effect, it was explained that this was consistent with defensive jihad. After the November 5, 2009, Fort Hood massacre, in which Major Hasan killed 13 and wounded 32, al-Awlaki praised Major Hasan as a hero. Hasan, who offered no defense, was sentenced to death by an Army court martial.

In considering the psychodynamics of the social revolutionary terrorists of the third wave, it has been suggested that they were rebelling against the generation of their parents, which was identified with the regime.

- The goal of the group is to destroy the world of their fathers.
- Their acts of terrorism are acts of retaliation for real and imagined hurts against the society of their parents.
- They are symbolically dissenting against parents loyal to the regime.

These are the generational dynamics of Osama bin Laden. When he criticized the Saudi ruling class from Yemen for hosting the U.S. military in the "land of the two cities," he was rebelling against the older generation of his family, which is strongly identified with the Saudi regime that enriched them. For his trouble, bin Laden was stripped of his Saudi passport, and his family turned against him. Thus, bin Laden was not merely a Muslim fundamentalist terrorist leader; he also displayed the psychological characteristics of a social revolutionary. And these are the dynamics of Anwar al-Awlaki. His father was cosmopolitan, had served as minister of agriculture and was chancellor at two Yemeni universities. He was not especially religious. From his youth onward, al-Awlaki was an ardent Muslim preacher, who increasingly blamed the West, and saw Muslims as victims.

Umar Farouk Abdulmatallab, "the underwear bomber," showed the same generational provenance. The son of a wealthy cosmopolitan Nigerian banker who was not particularly pious, Abdulmatallab became increasingly religious and intolerant in the several years preceding his attempted martyrdom attack on the Detroit-bound aircraft by trying to detonate explosives in his underwear. He complained that his father ate meat that was "haram" (forbidden); he would not eat with his family and became increasingly distant.

Faisal Shahzad, the "Times Square bomber," also displayed the same generational dynamics. He was the son of a prominent cosmopolitan senior Pakistani military officer who was not particularly pious. Shahzad became increasingly religious and intolerant in the several years preceding his attempted car bomb attack in Times Square. He stopped drinking and tried to get his father and friends to stop drinking. He also tried to force his wife to wear the hijab. He broke contact with his family.

To be sure, the pattern of pious sons of prominent secular fathers associated with the regime rebelling against their fathers' world as they became increasingly pious and consumed by the world of radical Islam is merely suggestive. But this is not just self-radicalization. Rather, there is trolling of social networking sites by *radicalizers* like al-Awlaki, seeking lonely, alienated individuals to whom they give a sense of belonging and significance. Major Hasan, Abdulmatallab, and Shahzad were lonely and isolated, found in the language on the radical Islamist web sites that they were not alone, and received comfort in feeling they belonged to the virtual community of hatred. Their difficulties were not of their making; rather, they were victims of oppression by the West. Therefore, striking out violently at their oppressors was not only justified, it was required. Gabi Weimann, author of *Terror on the Internet*, estimates there are more than 7,000 radical Islamist web sites at the present time (2006). Although there may be only a handful of radicalizers, like al-Awlaki, who was killed by a drone strike in Yemen in December 2011, the radical sermons and messages spread rapidly from site to site, as emphasized in the al-Qaeda Internet strategy quoted above.

To summarize, it is suggested that the lone wolves are isolated loners and "losers," with fractured relations with family. In search of belonging, they found the virtual community of hatred an attractive environment, with its repetitive messages of oppression which reinforced their view of themselves as victims. Some showed compensatory grandiosity, as demonstrated by this message from Hosam Maher Husein Smadi: "'We shall attack them in their very own homes,' he wrote on March 29, speaking about Americans. 'Brother, by God, we shall attack them in a manner that hurts, an attack that shakes the world'" (McKinley, 2009, p. A12).

Seeking recognition, some sought to go out in a "blaze of glory." Not all were immediately consumed by the quest for martyrdom but were persuaded to strike in such a manner that they could survive. This was the case with Antonio Martinez, who was persuaded that by using a car bomb he could avoid a shootout and live to fight another day. In reviewing the demographics of U.S. lone wolves, there was a wide spectrum of countries of origin. Many of the U.S.–born lone wolves were prison converts. They demonstrated a wide age range from teenage to late 60s.

On the basis of a review of 28 U.S. lone wolves, McGinnis, Moody, and Post (2013) developed a typology with four types of lone wolves. These types overlap extensively, but they reflect some of the variance within the lone wolf population. The four types are: *glory seekers, hero worshippers, naïve romantics*, and *radical altruists*).

The *glory seekers* were "losers" who demonstrated a pattern of personal failure. Through an act of terrorism, they were seeking fame and a sense of significance in their otherwise empty lives. Examples of glory seekers are: Abu Khalid Abdul-Latif (aka Joseph Anthony Davis) and Walli Mujahidh (aka Frederick Domingue, Jr.). Latif and Mujahidh plotted to attack a Seattle military entrance processing station using machine guns and grenades they had purchased from undercover law enforcement officers. Demonstrating the magnitude of their quest for glory, Latif stated: "We're trying to send a message. We're trying to get something that's gonna be on CNN and all over the world" (Esposito & Ryan, 2011).

The *hero worshippers* feel empty, and they seek to emulate an idealized other seen as embodying all they would like to be. They fall under the charismatic influence of others like Osama bin Laden, Abu Musab al-Zarqawi, and Anwar al-Awlaki. Major Nidal Hasan, who has already been discussed, and Naser Jason Abdo are both examples. Nidal Hasan was inspired by al-Awlaki. Hasan had been impressed by the sermons of the charismatic al-Awlaki he had heard in northern Virginia, and sought his guidance online. Naser Jason Abdo in turn was inspired by Nidal Hasan. Abdo was a U.S. Army soldier who went AWOL and traveled to a town near Fort Hood, where he planned to carry out an attack on a crowded restaurant using bombs made from pressure cookers. The restaurant was popular with soldiers from the nearby base. At his trial, Abdo referred to Nidal Hasan as "my brother," and he stated that he lived in Hasan's shadow despite "efforts to outdo him."

The *naïve romantics* are notable for their psychological immaturity. As "wannabe" terrorists, they struggle with self-identity. They have a romanticized notion of "revolution." They are so naïve as individuals that they might not have been able to plot effectively without the assistance of the undercover agents carrying out the sting. Antonio Martinez is an example of the naïve romantic. He emigrated from Nicaragua with his mother and siblings, did not graduate from high school, and was arrested at age 16 for armed robbery. He then decided to become a Christian and was baptized but converted to Islam a year later. Martinez posted radical messages on a jihad social networking site about joining the mujahedeen, which drew the attention of the FBI. He was arrested in an undercover FBI operation after attempting to detonate a fake car bomb outside a military recruiting center. He chose the recruiting center because he had considered enlisting in the Army before converting to Islam. He stated that his dream was to join the ranks of the mujahedeen, but admitted to the FBI informant that he did not know how to build a bomb and had suggested stuffing socks up exhaust pipes to kill soldiers.

The *radical altruists* subordinate their individuality to the group cause. They act "for the sake of my people." They have been persuaded that martyrdom is necessary for the greater good of besieged Muslims everywhere and will win them a higher place in paradise. The psychology of the radical altruist is well conveyed by these words of Leila Khaled, an early example of the radical altruist:

> I knew that I had a role to play. I realized that my historic mission was as a warrior in the inevitable battle between oppressors and oppressed, exploiters and exploited. I decided to become a revolutionary in order to liberate my people and myself. (Post, 2007, p. 24)

Faisal Shahzad, the "Times Square bomber" discussed earlier, is an example of a contemporary radical altruist. He had come to believe it was his duty to carry out an act of violent jihad. Referring to himself as a "Muslim soldier," he believed he was acting for the greater good of all Muslims, to ease their suffering and to fight back against the oppressor. "'It's a war. I am part of the answer to the U.S. terrorizing the Muslim nations and the Muslim people,' he said. 'On behalf of that, I'm revenging the attack.'" (Shifrel & Martinez, 2010).

Lone Wolf Packs

Examples of lone wolf packs include the Lackawanna Six, Fort Dix Six, and the northern Virginia Five. They show powerful group dynamics, demonstrating that groups can make more dangerous decisions than individuals acting on their own. Reflecting "groupthink," they both reinforce their sense of superiority and suppress dissent.

The Fort Dix Six is an interesting example. The three Duka brothers from former Yugoslavia and their friends plotted to attack Fort Dix with firearms and grenade launchers. The members were not well-adjusted in their roles in American life and displayed signs of antisocial traits. They had a "gangster attitude." The group became more extreme in religious beliefs as time went on, and their evolving radicalization provided a deeper sense of belonging. They continually fed off each other, marshaling their resolve but not giving voice to their doubts.

Another prominent example of a quite large wolf pack, a romanticized brotherhood of alienated diasporans, is well represented by more than forty youths in the Somali diaspora in the Minneapolis area. They came to the United States seeking refuge from the political violence in Somalia but were rebuffed by the host society. Defensively, they sought "brotherhood," and formed a wolf pack of what was initially a fantasized organization. Failing to assimilate in the United States, they were sold a romanticized version of al-Shabaab and came to idealize this Somali terrorist group. They sought altruistically to join the struggle in Somalia, traveling there to become fighters.

With the rapid technological changes of the communications revolution, we have moved into dangerous and uncharted waters. Reflecting the communication revolution, frustrated, alienated individuals and small groups can be stimulated through the Internet and social media to become radicalized and to feel they belong to the virtual community of hatred. This is not merely "homegrown" terrorism but represents a deliberate strategy of radical Islamic terrorist organizations. Countering this online strategy is a daunting counter-terrorist challenge, requiring great care that in the name of security, privacy and civil liberties not be abused. How to inject countering arguments into this multicentric information space is extremely challenging; for individuals exposed to radicalizing messages will be resistant and ready to reject Western-sponsored web sites as propaganda. A healthy democracy must be able to tolerate dissent. One cannot eliminate terrorism without eliminating democracy. What is technologically possible, as witnessed by the degree of electronic surveillance conducted within the United States by the National Security Agency, and as revealed by the Snowden leaks, does not mean it can be done without violating the sense of privacy and civil liberties that are at the heart of robust democracy. And that would mean becoming a terror state.

REFERENCES

Adamic, L. (1934). *Dynamite: The story of class violence in America*. New York, NY: Viking.

Ali, F., & Post, J. (2008). The history and evolution of martyrdom in the service of defensive jihad: An analysis of suicide bombers in current conflicts. *Social Research, 75*(2), 615-654.

Asbley, K., Ayers, B., Dohrn, B., Jacobs, J., Jones, J., Long, G., et al. (1969). You don't need a weatherman to know which way the wind blows. *New Left Notes*. Retrieved from http://archive.org/stream/YouDontNeedAWeathermanToKnowWhichWayTheWindBlows/weather_djvu.txt

Barkun, M. (1994). *Religion and the racist right*. Chapel Hill, NC: University of North Carolina Press.

Bion, W. R. (1961). *Experiences in groups: and other papers*. New York, NY: Routledge.

Crenshaw, M. (1981). The causes of terrorism. *Comparative Politics*, *13*(4), 379-399.

Da Silva, M. (1975). Modernization and ethnic conflict: The case of the Basques. *Comparative Politics*, *7*(2), 227-251.

Dylan, R. (1965). Subterranean homesick blues. On *Bringing it all back home* [Record]. New York, NY: Columbia Records.

Esposito, R., & Ryan, J. (2011, June 23). Feds: Converts to Islam planned Ft. Hood-style assault in Seattle. *ABC News*. Retrieved from http://abcnews.go.com/Blotter/prison-converts-extremist-islam-planned-ft-hood-style/story?id=13915159

Gurr, T. R. (Ed.). (1989). *Violence in America*, Volume 2, *Protest, rebellion, reform*. Newbury Park, CA: Sage.

History of Basque nationalism: Historical background. (n.d.). *Euskal Herria Journal*. Retrieved from www.ehjnavarre.org/navarre/na_history_pnv.html

Hopper, E. (2003). *The social unconscious*. London: Jessica Kingsley.

Horgan, J. (2005). *The psychology of terrorism*. New York, NY: Routledge.

Kramer, M. (1998). The moral logic of Hizballah. In W. Reich (Ed.), *Origins of terrorism: Psychologies, ideologies, theologies, states of mind*. (pp. 131-157). Washington, DC: Woodrow Wilson Center Press.

Leiken, R. S. (2005). Europe's angry Muslims. *Foreign Affairs*, *84*(4). Retrieved from http://www.foreignaffairs.com

Marx, K., & Engels, F. (1848). *The Communist manifesto*. London: The Communist League.

McCauley, C., & Segal, M. (1987). Social psychology of terrorist groups. In C. Hendrick (Ed.), *Review of personality and social psychology* (pp. 231-256). Beverly Hills, CA: Sage.

McGinnis, C., Moody, K., & Post, J. (2013, July). *The psychology of lone wolf and lone wolf pack terrorists: Joining the virtual community of hatred*. Paper presented at the annual scientific meeting of the International Society of Political Psychology, Herzliya, Israel.

McKinley, J. C. (2009, September 27). Friends' portrait of Texas bomb plot suspect at odds with F.B.I. *New York Times*. Retrieved from http://www.nytimes.com/2009/09/28/us/28texas.html?pagewanted=all&_r=0

Neibuhr, G. (1994, August 24). To church's dismay, priest talks of "justifiable homicide" of abortion doctors. *New York Times*. Retrieved from http://www.nytimes.com/1994/08/24/us/to-church-sdismay-priest-talks-of-justifiable-homicide-of-abortion-doctors.html

Nelson, R., & Sanderson, T. (2011). A growing terrorist threat? Assessing "homegrown" extremism in the United States. *Center for Strategic and International Studies*, 3. Retrieved from http://csis.org/files/publication/110203_Nelson_AThreatTransformed_web.pdf

Post, J. M. (1983, July). *Individual and group dynamics of terrorist behavior*. Paper presented at the 7th World Congress of Psychiatry, Vienna, Austria. In P. Pichot, P. Berner, & K. Thau (Eds.), (1985), *Drug dependence and alcoholism, forensic psychiatry, military psychiatry* (pp. 381-386). New York, NY: Plenum Press.

Post, J. (1986). *Individual, group, and organizational psychology of political terrorism*. Paper presented at the 9th annual meeting of the International Society of Political Psychology, Amsterdam.

Post, J. M. (1987a). *Terrorist psycho-logic: Terrorist behavior as a product of psychological forces*. Paper presented at the international conference on Psychological Dimensions of Terrorism, sponsored by the Woodrow Wilson Center for International Scholars, The Smithsonian Institution. In W. Reich, (Ed.), (1990), *Origins of terrorism: Psychologies, ideologies, theologies, states of mind* (pp. 25-40). New York, NY: Cambridge University Press; Washington, DC: Woodrow Wilson International Center for Scholars.

Post, J. M. (1987b). "It's us against them": The basic assumptions of political terrorists. In J. Kranz (Ed.), *Irrationality in social and organizational life* (pp. 68–75). Washington, DC: A.K. Rice Institute Press.

Post, J. M. (2004). *Leaders and their followers in a dangerous world: The psychology of political behavior*. Ithaca, NY: Cornell University Press.

Post, J. M. (2005). Psychology. In the *Club de Madrid Series on Democracy and Terrorism*, Volume 1, *Addressing the causes of terrorism* (pp. 7-12). Madrid, Spain: Club de Madrid. http://safe-democracy.org/docs/CdM-Series-on-Terrorism-Vol-1.pdf

Post, J. M. (2007). *The mind of the terrorist: The psychology of terrorism from the IRA to Al Qaeda*. New York, NY: Palgrave Macmillan.

Pregulman, A., & Burke, E. (2012). *Homegrown terrorism*. AQAM Futures Project Case Study Series Case Study Number 7. Washington, DC: Center for Strategic and International Studies. http://csis.org/files/publication/120425_Pregulman_AQAMCaseStudy7_web.pdf

Rapoport, D. C. (2004). The four waves of modern terrorism. In A. K. Cronin & J. Ludes (Eds.), *Attacking terrorism: Elements of a grand strategy* (pp. 46–73). Washington, DC: Georgetown University Press.

Robins, R. S., & Post, J. M. (1997). *Political paranoia: The psychopolitics of hatred*. New Haven, CT: Yale University Press.

Shifrel, S., & Martinez, J. (2010, June 21). Times Square terror suspect Faisal Shahzad admits plot to use weapon of mass destruction. *New York Daily News*. Retrieved from http://www.nydailynews.com/news/crime/times-square-terror-suspect-faisal-shahzad admits-plot-weapon-mass-destruction-article-1.181711

Tamil National Leader Velupillai Pirapaharan's Interview. (1986, March). *The Week*. Retrieved from www.eelam.com/interviews/leader_march_86.html

Thompson, M. (2009, November 11). Fort Hood highlights a threat of homegrown jihad. *Time*. Retrieved from http://www.time.com/time/nation/article/0,8599,1937912,00.html.

Weather Underground Organization. (1974). *Prairie fire: The politics of revolutionary anti-imperialism: Political statement of the Weather Underground.* n.p.: Weather Underground.

Weimann, G. (2006). *Terror on the Internet: The new arena, the new challenges.* Washington, DC: United States Institute of Peace.

Woodworth, P. (2001). Why do they kill? The Basque conflict in Spain. *World Policy Journal, 18*(1), 1-12.

Yonah, A., & Pluchinsky, D. (Eds.). (1992). *Europe's last Red terrorists: The fighting Communist organizations.* Washington, DC: Frank Cass.

Commentary on "Toward Understanding and Treating Violence in America: Some Contributions From Group Dynamic and Group Therapy Perspectives"

BONNIE J. BUCHELE, PH.D.

We abhor violence—so we say. But we do not, as a nation or as individuals in the United States,[1] always act that way. The articulate authors in the collection of articles in the special issues "Toward Understanding and Treating Violence in America: Some Contributions From Group Dynamic and Group Therapy Perspectives," Parts I and II, of the *International Journal of Group Psychotherapy* (volume 65, numbers 1 and 2) on the subject give the reader a broad perspective from which to view this paradox and the dilemma in which it leaves us. I will organize my commentary into three sections: an overview of the commonality of themes in the articles in both issues, the video review, and the interview; suggestions of ways to address an implicit and, at times, explicit set of questions raised about the problem; and questions that remain unaddressed or unanswered.

---

1. When I use the concept "violence in America" or the modifier "American," I refer specifically to the United States of America. America includes South America, Central America, and North America (besides the U.S.), so I utilize the referent U.S. whenever grammatically possible.

Bonnie J. Buchele is a group psychotherapist and psychoanalyst in private practice in Kansas City, Missouri, and President-Elect, International Association for Group Psychotherapy and Group Processes.

VIOLENCE IN AMERICA

THEMES

First, we are reminded that the capacity to behave violently is inherently human. Rice (2015) reminds us that violent behavior is sometimes necessary to ensure survival. Lothstein (2015) adds that research from neuroscience tells us that the evolutionary brain structures such as the limbic system and other deep brain structures hardwire human beings to respond adaptively with aggression, especially when necessary for survival. So, truthfully, the impulse to act violently is part of human nature. Keeping this in mind is crucial because our tendency to decry our violent behavior while participating in its destructive expression may reflect our difficulty integrating the violent side of our individual and national selves into the whole.

A second common theme (or assumption) is that the U.S. is a violent nation. I will focus on the psychological aspects of our struggles with violence, especially those related to group life, but before I do, I want to note some facts stated by Klein and Schermer in their introductions (2015a, 2015b), as well as by Rice (2015), that are startling and support the characterization of us as violent: the focus on violence in American culture has recently intensified because of a number of mass tragedies, but actually these events only account for 0.13% of all homicides in the U.S.! Another astounding fact is that it is estimated that there are more firearms in the U.S. than people, excluding those owned by the military! We are the most violent nation of all the Western industrialized countries. Our country's birth was fueled by energy derived from fight/flight and pairing behaviors (Bion, 1959) in response to violence undergone by our founding fathers in their countries of origin; violence is very much part of us and always has been.

That violence begets violence is a third theme addressed in some way in every article in these two issues. Most authors agree that the infliction of narcissistic injury (damage to the sense of self) plays a crucial role at the individual and societal levels. The experiences of trauma, victimization, empathic failures, losses, failures in life, and humiliation (public or private), all may be experienced as painful narcissistic injuries, which, in turn, can lead to rage and violent retaliation, enhanced by a sense of powerlessness. The survival of the self is in one way or another threatened, thus activating the need to respond. Less emphasized but suggested by those writing about violent offenders, e.g., Roller (2015) and Lothstein (2015), and terrorists (Post, 2015) is the role of insecure and/or disorganized attachment histories and styles that leave such persons more vulnerable to painful narcissistic injury than those with secure attachments.

In the U.S. by far the most prominent defense mechanism, individually and collectively, utilized to manage the psychological pain of narcissistic injury is to split off our rage and violent responses and then to project them into other vulnerable people. We see terrorists as violent, sick people when, according to Post (2015), the outstanding characteristic of terrorists is their normality. We see violent offenders as bad people, when, in fact, they are often carrying projections related to the dark side of masculinity. In our schools and in various societal groups we scapegoat those more vulnerable, a contribution to bullying and cyber-bullying. We feel justified in taking violent military action because of our "chosen trauma" (Volkan, 2009), the events of 9/11. (A chosen trauma is the shared mental representation of an event in the history of a large group wherein the group suffered a catastrophic loss, humiliation, and sense of helplessness at the hands of its enemies.). Less obvious, but perhaps even more disturbing, are the ways that destructive expression of violence is woven into the fabric of our culture with approval and enthusiasm as a defense against narcissistic injury at the societal level. Examples include the violence inherent in daily metaphors used by all of us such as "the war on drugs" or "illegal aliens," so eloquently described by Thomas (2015). And then there are our entertainment preferences. Klein and Schermer (2015a) draw attention to our national fascination with football, video games, and stories featuring "special operatives." Another instance (Klein, personal communication, 2014) relates to how we view the military in the U.S. This example is from the movie *A Few Good Men*. The main character, an Army colonel played by Jack Nicholson, screams, "The truth! The truth? You can't handle the truth," referring to what soldiers must do at times while defending their country. This sentiment throws light on the collusion of the society, knowing that we rely on violence projected into members of the military but choose not to know what those soldiers are required to do.

This tendency to manage our narcissistic injuries by splitting and then retaliating not only perpetuates a cycle of violent actions from group to group and generation to generation, but also impedes integration of the capacity for violence into our sense of ourselves. Dealing with aggression by splitting off and projecting by definition means it is disavowed, unassimilated, unacknowledged, and poorly integrated. The lack of integration leads to an impaired capacity for empathy (Phillips, 2015) or failure of intersubjectivity (Thomas, 2015). Additionally, Rice and Phillips point out that the fragmentation complicates mourning, a process necessary for healing. Phillips underscores the role of silence in impeding the working through of trauma and its accompanying wounds to the sense of self. She talks about two kinds: willful silence by conscious choice, and dissociation, an unconscious freezing response to trauma that can be adaptive but can also contribute to the silence of victims of violence and block integration.

A fourth theme involves the role of reflection and talking. Rice as well as Klein and Schermer speak of how reflection is valued less and less. Reflection is central to containment of aggressive impulses if they are to be managed in other ways. The role of technology may interact with the scarcity of places in our world to reflect, talk, and see the response of the Other. Post tells us that the community of virtual hatred provides a group home for the lone wolf terrorist. The growth of Internet communication leaves us with less time to "look each other in the eye" (Gottlieb, as quoted in Shermer, 2015) or have neuro-connectivity. This reliance on technology enhances dehumanizing the Other and further disables the ability to empathize.

Another theme addressed by all the authors is the role of group life in the management of violence. In the U.S., group life is emphasized less than that of the individual. Our highly valued sense of "rugged individualism" runs counter to a sense of collectivity. As a society we may delude ourselves into thinking that we really do not need to belong to any group and certainly do not need to value the group above the individual, a fact underscored by a preference for individual therapy over group therapy in this country. However, these authors point out that the need for connection and belonging is crucial for all, including Americans. As every group therapist learns in "Group Dynamics 101," nonparticipation in any group of which one is a member is not a choice. Silence is a form of participation, most often indicating tacit support for the dominant party: silence equals being a bystander and within the victim/perpetrator/bystander paradigm of violent situations; assuming the role of bystander facilitates the violence. Everyone counts! You can choose how to participate, but nonparticipation is not an option. Passivity increases our vulnerability to engage in destructive basic assumption life by fight/flight responses, pairing behaviors, and participation in what Hopper labels "incohesion," a regressive state wherein individuals, fearful of annihilation, become increasingly disconnected from one another or fuse together to survive threats to identity. Rice (2105) cogently observes that incohesion facilitates scapegoating as well. The devaluing of collectivism also reduces the number of potential containers available because, as many of the authors emphasize, healthy groups can serve as safe containers where angry, aggressive feelings can be reflected upon and worked through.

QUESTIONS AND ANSWERS: WAYS TO ADDRESS THE PROBLEM

These authors unanimously believe that understanding life in groups can help to address the psychological causes of violence in the U.S. Of special significance is providing opportunities to repair the wounds of narcissistic injury. An alternative coping mechanism is repair, a process including reflection, verbalization, taking ownership of the disowned parts of ourselves, and mourning the accompanying losses. Rice (2015) suggests that we build memorials rather than continue wars. So what do these authors have to say about addressing the role of narcissistic injury and finding alternative ways of coping?

At the societal level Thomas (2015) suggests that we replace our justice system, based on achieving retribution, with a restorative justice system; she cites several countries where this has occurred. Restorative justice includes establishing culpability for the injury sustained, promoting mutual understanding of its causes and effects, and developing a process for making amends. She believes that use of a restorative justice approach would work to eliminate the failure of intersubjectivity and decrease the need for revenge.

Rice (2015), as well as Klein and Schermer (2015a, 2015b), address the problem with their conviction that group therapy itself holds much unrealized potential for addressing the problem of violence in the U.S. They cite the concept of isomorphy, emanating from systems theory, which holds that structures and functions existing at one level of a complex system also exist at every other level within that system. They suggest that changing how we manage our violent tendencies at the lower level of our therapy groups will have an impact on higher levels of the society. Schermer has formulated a concept he has named the "penumbra group," a designation meant to include all those whose lives interact with, and are impacted by, the psychotherapy group members. Rice (2015) emphasizes how well psychotherapy groups can provide safe containers where words rather than actions can be encouraged and reflection promoted. One is reminded of a statement by Volkan (2009) that if people talk, they do not kill. Phillips (2015) also advocates the use of groups to provide safe containment following violence, as an antidote to willful and chosen silence, as differentiated from dissociation. Like Thomas, she emphasizes how the capacity for empathy can be increased when silence is broken, talking with others who are accepting and the working through of feelings in the group.

Lothstein (2015) and Gerhart, Holman, Seymour, Dinges, and Ronan (2015) also address the problem of managing narcissistic injury in their descriptions of treatment programs for male perpetrators of domestic violence, as does Roller (2015) in his review of the video series *The Voices of Violence*. The video describes two treatment programs for incarcerated violent offenders, both advocating group therapy for treatment of these men. Importance is placed on establishing the secure attachments and neuro-connectivity that is possible within therapy groups. Groups are useful in providing an antidote to the absence of a societal collective for this population, so that scapegoating can be countered and narcissistic injury healed. Emphasis is also placed on growing the capacity for reflection. Lothstein quotes Theodor Reik, "A thought murder a day keeps the psychiatrist away."

Gottlieb, in his interview with Shermer (2015), also addresses the role of narcissistic injury when he states that we are an undernourished society. He believes that as a culture we would do well to provide more acknowledgement and positive recognition so that we could come together at times other than when there is a crisis. "If you look someone in the eye long enough, you'll see their soul" (p. 34). This is a philosophical statement in support of the importance of neuro-connectivity in our brains. However, when we are surrounded by people who experience themselves as impoverished and powerless with the attached anxiety, we will absorb that anxiety because the mirror neuron response is activated. Thus, it is important to have access to empowered individuals and groups in one's life.

The most distressing way to address the problem of violence in the U.S., at least as it relates to terrorism, is implicit in the conclusion of Post's article (2015): "One cannot eliminate terrorism without eliminating democracy" (p. 266). The statement is likely to send chills down the spines of most Americans. Perhaps the way to cope with this disturbing idea is to counter it with another idea advanced in the introduction by Klein and Schermer (2015a) that as group therapists with a wealth of knowledge about the role of group life in human existence, we must stay in the dialogue and contribute what we know to the discussion.

QUESTIONS UNANSWERED

Several questions are unanswered or unaddressed. The most prominent one is how we as a community of group therapists and experts in group life implement the solutions proposed by these authors on a scale large enough to make a significant difference. The consciousness of all who read these pieces is raised and that in itself is important, but it is an upstream swim (I almost said "battle" but remembered Thomas's words about violent metaphors) against the flow of huge cultural forces, such as the growth of technology. Even though it may be overwhelming when approached in that way, it remains an important question.

Perhaps the identity of U.S. citizens includes denial of the importance of the collective. This could be conceived as a continuum with individualism at one end and collectivism on the other, which is more flexible than singling out "rugged individualism" as a value standing alone. Might it be easier to effect change if we thought about it in this way? And, in a related matter, do we have a collective need to deny our need for the collective that leads to dichotomous thinking, as if collectivism and the need for connection simultaneously were invisible?

No specific mention is made in these articles of the role of financial superiority as a part of national identity for the citizens of the U.S. In American culture money equals power. In a changing world where the financial superiority of the U.S. can be challenged, do we become financially violent as a result? What role does the need to be financially superior, sometimes to the point of embracing ruthlessness, play in our dilemmas around violence within this country and in our international relationships? In other words, how do our proclivities for violence interact with our need to be superior economically?

Post (2015) says in his superb history of four phases of terrorism in the world that the Religious Extremist Wave of terrorism is coming to a close with the rise of a new phase: the Virtual Community of Hatred and Lone Wolf Terrorism. This may be true of terrorism internationally, but the situation might be different in the U.S. Since the events of 9/11, the religious right has been gaining power and momentum. Is it possible that as our economic identity in its superiority is threatened worldwide, we are vulnerable to coping with the fear of annihilation and despair by engaging in pairing basic assumption behavior so that religious fundamentalism has new appeal as its leaders emerge paired with the ideology to rescue us from our despair? Is incohesion more likely during this time in our history? If so, how do we counter the effects of incohesion and pairing on the violence in our culture?

Finally, we might benefit from examining the role of the unconscious more explicitly in the problem of violence in America. There is an implicit thread running throughout the articles that unconscious functioning has importance, one of them being Thomas's (2015) discussion of violent metaphors and another the significance of defense mechanisms in general functioning and in psychotherapy. However, the unconscious may be important at a level not raised in these writings and that is the role of the unconscious in culture itself. Ogden (1990) and Winnicott (1971) speak about how cultural experience occurs within potential space, that intermediate area of unconscious experience that lies between a person's inner world and the actual external world. Potential space is the experiencing of the world of paradox where it is unclear whether we create it or it creates us—where everything, in part, is defined by its opposite. Play, creativity, transitional phenomena, cultural experience, and therapy all take place in potential space. The internal potential space of paradox and creativity collapses when we are fearful, stressed, or anxious or our survival is threatened. Volkan (2009) says that we have an unconscious need for enemies, perhaps a manifestation of a tool waiting in the wings available at all times to manage threat and narcissistic injury and resulting in the ebb and flow of potential space.

Gutmann and Millat (2013) state that there is inevitably some trauma, real or mythical, in the history of any institution. Without the process of working through, the institution unconsciously creates conditions for repetition. How does this principle apply to the role of unconscious, historical dynamics in the existence of excessive amounts of violence in the U.S. and its culture? Looking at violence in America through this lens might be helpful in preventing us from taking the position that we can "do away with" our violent capacities, but, rather, aid in finding new ways of self-regulating, thereby adding depth to the discussion.

CONCLUSION

The articles in this collection address the problem of violence in the U.S. in a way that opens new avenues for us as we think about the causes. Sometimes it seems daunting. However, in the end we are left with one basic truth that we as group people know: We cannot choose not to participate. Silence exercises influence; withdrawal from the situation is not an option.

So we owe it to ourselves, our patients, and our country to learn what we can about this vexing problem, to increase our awareness as well as the awareness of others, and to apply what we know about the role of group life in the problem. This collection of articles moves us farther down that path than ever before.

REFERENCES

Bion, W. (1959). *Experiences in groups.* New York, NY: Basic Books.

Gerhart, J., Holman, K., Seymour, B., Dinges, B., & Ronan, G. F. (2015). Group process as a mechanism of change in the group treatment of anger and aggression. *International Journal of Group Psychotherapy,* 65(2), 181-208.

Gutmann, D., & Millat, J.-F. (2013, July). The nuclear accident of Fukushima (March 2011): A revealed work area for group psychotherapy and group processes. *Forum, Journal of the International Association for Group Psychotherapy and Group Processes,* (6), 101-110.

Klein, R., & Schermer, V. L. (2015a). Introduction to Part I. Toward understanding and treating violence in America: Some contributions from group dynamic and group therapy perspectives. *International Journal of Group Psychotherapy,* 65(1), 1-28.

Klein, R., & Schermer, V. L. (2015b). Introduction to Part II. Toward understanding and treating violence in America: Some contributions from group dynamic and group therapy perspectives. *International Journal of Group Psychotherapy,* 65(2), 163-179.

Lothstein, L. M. (2015). A multi-tiered group therapy model to identify and treat the root causes of domestic violence: A proposal integrating current social neuroscience findings. *International Journal of Group Psychotherapy,* 65(2), 211-240.

Ogden, T. H. (1990). *Matrix of the mind: Object relations and the psychoanalytic dialogue.* Northvale, NJ: Jason Aronson 1990.

Phillips, S. B. (2015). The dangerous role of silence in the relationship between trauma and violence: A group response. *International Journal of Group Psychotherapy,* 65(1), 65-87.

Post, J. M. (2015). Terrorism and right-wing extremism: The changing face of terrorism and political violence in the 21st century: The virtual community of hatred. *International Journal of Group Psychotherapy,* 65(2), 243-271.

Rice, C. A. (2015). A group therapist reflects on violence in America. *International Journal of Group Psychotherapy,* 65(1), 41-62.

Roller, B. (2015). The Voices of Violence Series. *International Journal of Group Psychotherapy,* 65(1), 109-114.

Schermer, V. L. (2015). Violence, threat, and emotional "malnourishment": An interview with Dr. Dan Gottlieb. *International Journal of Group Psychotherapy*, *65*(1), 31-39.

Thomas, N. K. (2015). There's always a villain to punish: Violence in America. *International Journal of Group Psychotherapy*, *65*(1), 89-107.

Volkan, V. D. (2009). Large-group identity, international relations and psychoanalysis. *International Forum of Psychoanalysis*, *18*(4), 206–213.

Winnicott, D. (1971). *Playing and reality*. New York, NY: Basic Books.

Commentary on "Toward Understanding and Treating Violence in America: Some Contributions From Group Dynamic and Group Therapy Perspectives"

ZACHARY GABRIEL GREEN, PH.D.

It is an ambitious task to address the issue of violence in America. There is a degree of courage implied in exploring the role that group psychotherapists play as active agents in this complex and textured condition that pervades the life of this country. We share in the shock of what it means for a massacre of the innocents to be a part of the fiber of our collective psyche. We continue to experience the residual collective trauma associated with being the witness to the fiery, smoldering collapse of those two once mighty towers. We grow weary of seemingly endless wars aimed at silencing shadowy threats but leave us no more secure. Perhaps most troubling, in our cities, towns, and homes we see a trend where some of our citizenry walk into our schools, restaurants, shops, and places of worship openly armed, ever vigilant and trigger-ready to act preemptively to fight off that feared, inevitable next attack from anyone and anywhere. Klein and Schermer, the convenors and co-editors of these special sections "Toward Understanding and Treating Violence in America: Some Contributions From Group Dynamic and Group Therapy

---

Zachary Gabriel Green is a professor of practice in Leadership Studies, University of San Diego, and cofounder of Group Relations International.

Perspectives," Parts I and II, of the *International Journal of Group Psychotherapy* (volume 65, numbers 1 and 2), document and explore the prevalence of such incidents and anxieties, which provided the impetus for these special sections.

These patterns speak to how we have entered a collective time and space of paranoid-schizoid adaptation. What has become normative is a narrative that suggests that the danger "out there" is real and ever present. The dominant discourse calls on people to be prepared to meet these threats with a show of violent and lethal force that will thwart the aggression and somehow make us safe. So entrenched is this fantasy that the reality of our own collective everyday violence, evidenced by the fact that we kill ourselves and are killed by those we know in disproportionate numbers when compared to deaths from war and terrorism, does nothing to stem our orientation to violence.

DIAGNOSING AND TREATING VIOLENCE IN THE SMALL GROUP CONTEXT

What makes these particular articles on violence in America so powerful is the unflinching way the authors make visible the pervasive and malignant state of where we are as a nation. Through offering perspectives from classic and prevailing theory, chronicling the history, providing case examples, and venturing hypotheses about root causes, the authors make readers conscious of the complexity and challenges of addressing violence. Each article is its own treatise yet a part of an interwoven whole. In the face of convention where facile fixes could be presented to offer more patchwork to the problem, guest editors Klein and Schermer are asking us to remain engaged with the issue of violence in a new and more nuanced light. Implicitly there is an invitation to move beyond the familiar responses of depression, discomfort, and despair so that group psychotherapists may discover the unique role they are poised to play in helping to heal this epidemic of violence.

In particular, we learn, especially from Phillips (2015) in her article on groups as a response to the silences that surround trauma, how a collective collusion towards silence contributes to unspoken shame, serving to perpetuate the impact of trauma on the lives of those affected by it. Whether they are the victims of violence or the perpetrators, the silence quiets the quest for healing and places hopes for wholeness on hold. Similarly, we are given the opportunity to explore the ways that cultural trends sanction vicarious violence. Thomas (2015) presents us with the premise that the language of "illegal immigrants" and a "war on terrorism" creates a convenient *other* at whom projections can hurled. The abdication in creating the conditions for violence is made all but palpable. Repeatedly the authors yield evidence of how violence is displaced and denied, leaving trauma and death as its marks. Even our entertainment, most notably in the popularity of football, blockbuster "action" movies, and graphically intense video games, reveals the unconscious extension and unexamined expression of an orientation towards pervasive violence.

The arguments and research in this collection of articles are compelling without being pedantic and proselytizing. Importantly, most group psychotherapists will see reflections of their own practices in these pages. Many will also hear the subtle yet persistent call to action. Each contributor helps us to see how our groups serve as mirrors and microcosms of the larger national dynamic. Among our patients are survivors of abuse, perpetrators of domestic violence, alienated persons with suicidal ideation, witnesses to horrors and traumas, and those who suffer in silence without knowing the source of their ceaseless anxieties. As group psychotherapists our capacity to meet these issues in a way that offers empathy, compassion, and care goes beyond known and familiar norms of therapeutic intervention. In addition to empathy and compassion for our patients, these writings also challenge us to become deeply acquainted with the ways that violence has touched our own lives. If group psychotherapists are to be a part of shifting the prevailing discourse from where violence is seen as external to ourselves, where carrying a lethal weapon is seen as a cure to our fears, and where silence is preferred to shared inquiry into pathways for peace of heart, we must be prepared to do the work of exploring our own inner conditions. As group therapists, our own inner work will be central to addressing the symbolic and substantive nature of violence in this nation.

VIOLENCE IN AMERICA

EXTENDING THE INSIGHTS TO THE SOCIETAL LEVEL

These articles also eloquently open a portal for the next level of exploration, one that engages the conditions that promote peace. We are essentially asked to consider how giving attention to violence may be at the expense of learning about what promotes peace. In particular, the interview with Dan Gottlieb (Schermer, 2015) offers emotional "malnourishment" as a metaphor for how violence gains sway in our lives, thereby inviting the reader to think about achieving peace with others in different terms. We see in Gottlieb's thinking an embrace of our common humanity. We are also confronted with how often we fail to recognize the value and dignity of others. Accordingly, violence becomes a maladaptive consequence rooted in the failure to see ourselves in the Other. The cumulative impact of such emotional micro-aggressions becomes the source and substance of very real attacks on others (Sue et al., 2007). We know this to be consistently true in the troubled youth who have terrorized school after school. We hear it in the cyclical debates about gun violence and the role of mental illness in its execution. What makes Gottlieb's perspective unique is that he invites us to consider how this pattern is also present in our neighborhoods and in our families—and in our groups. Both Gottlieb and Phillips leave us with the question of how we all may be contributing to nurturing violence through numbness as a normative response, overwhelmed by the magnitude of hurt, woundedness, and alienation that violence leaves in its wake.

When this thinking is taken to the societal level, there has been a rightful tendency to elevate the figures of nonviolence as models of an alternative way to bring change. We all think of Martin Luther King, Jr., and Mahatma Gandhi as exemplars of the practice and promise of nonviolence, and the authors go beyond this to articulate how group psychotherapists broaden the conversation about both violence and its alternatives in terms of the dynamics of groups as such.

In our society, the one potentially unfortunate consequence of attending primarily to the role of Gandhi and King is that it perpetuates a particular narrative, that of the heroic individual leader. It is a more facile cognitive and psychological exercise to think about the One Leader than about the interactive impact and influence of an emergent group dynamic. As a consequence, the group dynamic gets left out of the story as little more than a footnote. An exception in recent years, though not sustained, was the heavy emphasis placed on the will of the group in the Occupy Movement. Organizers insisted on collective leadership, empowering the group over individuals. The encampments were, at core, an effort to challenge a discourse that perpetuated social and economic inequity, obliquely naming it as the same sort of violence that brought previous generations to march for racial justice and against an unpopular war. While these articles do not address the Occupy Movement as such, the authors consistently close their contributions with a suggestion that the true work on alleviating violence at this kind of collective level has just begun.

ADVANCED TECHNOLOGY, CYBERSPACE, AND THE DISTANCE BETWEEN PERPETRATORS AND VICTIMS

A possible subsequent special issue might address the emergent dilemmas of the coming decades of the 21st century. There is an opportunity for the next phase of this work to explore the faceless, boundless, and increasingly invisible nature of violence. What may become increasingly the norm is a violence that is more subtle and pervasive. At the interpersonal and virtual level there are those young people who have taken their own lives when their private moments were made public and became viral videos through social networking. The distance and disembodiment of anonymous aggression behind keyboards, coupled with the permanence of postings on the Internet, mean that the boundaries of self, space, and time have radically shifted. Nonetheless, the feelings that are generated when one is a victim of cyberbullying or scores a kill in "Call of Duty" (a popular video game series that engages the viewer in active simulations of war) become internalized as real embodied consequences. Those who come to group bring this context of cyber-violence with them as part of their psyche.

This boundless cyberspace also extends to the societal level. Cyberattacks are waged against individuals, large-scale corporate entities, and nation states by invisible forces of indistinct identity. With the prevalence of drone attacks, the conduct of warfare comes from a physical distance that yields an illusion of psychological distance from the death and destruction that is wrought. The increased distance between agency and the impact on the lives of others allows the violence to be disowned. As such, these forms of violence can be thought of more classically as grand forms of collective dissociation. The underlying dynamics of these trends in violence may well be on the edge of what our current theories and practices prepare us to address as group psychotherapists. Yet we cannot ignore the fact that the nature of such technological distancing will frequently, directly and indirectly, influence the lives of those who join our groups.

Thus, new theory is needed that attends to unconscious systemic representations of violence made evident through these emerging and more amorphous trends. While concepts such as "incohesion," cited by Rice (2015), help us better understand what we are currently facing, what group psychotherapists may be called to consider is a greater degree of complexity in how we approach our work. Probably the rapidly evolving nature of global convergence means that we can no longer operate from a stance entirely within our national boundaries. As Post suggests, we have generations of Digital Natives who live in a world where communication with different corners of the world is routine. While violence may be taking faceless and boundless forms, the potential for new pathways to peace are seen in the seeds of an Arab Spring and increased consciousness about the impact of climate change. These situations extend the boundary of group consciousness to a boundless international space where there is an effort to find coherence, compassion, and common language. Group psychotherapists are charged with attending not only to the individual needs of a particular member and the group as a system of therapeutic action, but also to the ways in which their groups may be a dynamic microcosm of a global process where the alleviation of violence is an aim.

VIOLENCE IN AMERICA

A CHANGE IN COLLECTIVE CONSCIOUSNESS TOWARDS PEACE-MAKING AND A BETTER WORLD

These articles begin to address a direct challenge to those who conduct groups to engage the inner work that model practices of peace. We need to see our groups as microcosms of society within their own implicit nested social network. It is relatively easy to point to a Newtown, a Columbine, a 9/11, the murder rate, and the mayhem that the media chooses to present us about violence. What is far more challenging is learning as therapists to be aware of the subtle ways we may be complicit in attending to these projections while leaving obscure and unexamined the more subtle substance of the self in peril—which includes all of us. In other words, if we step back long enough to look at it, we will see how we are embedded in the same context as those who come to our groups. As Thomas suggests, we largely share elements of language and culture that influence how we see and value life. For example, the economic inequities that pervade the planet and the consequences of climate change are not "out there" beyond the boundaries of our groups; they are also in our groups. As Klein and Schermer suggest in their introductions to both issues, therapy groups are "isomorphic" (Agazarian, 1997) to real life groups and the society at large, so that each of us—leaders and members—cannot help but bring into our groups prevailing social attitudes, myths, and values as well as our own feelings and belief systems that we need to be aware of and examine.

At deeper levels of consciousness, we will need to recognize that our individualistic and aggressive American way of life has an immense impact on the planet and its inhabitants. In this respect, the central question that emerges for group practitioners is how are we preparing those in our groups and ourselves to cope with the rapidly approaching impact of global shifts in power, opportunity, and allocation of resources. Perhaps we can see the rampant presence of suicides, the soldiering of arms, and the abuses of sex trafficking as early symptoms of a larger dynamic that we do not yet dare name. What we call an absence of cohesion could also be related to the rapid reconstitution needed in resilience. I speculate that collective inattention to these dynamics reflects a collusion of epic narcissistic proportion that leads us to remain in an empathy gap with the rest of humanity. If we are agents of a paranoid-schizoid distancing that is dissociated from the shared reality of billions in the world, we are healers who do not heal because we participate in an illusory therapeutic milieu that promotes a normative reality with little resemblance to the new world that is rapidly emerging.

As an antidote to such anachronism, group psychotherapy has the opportunity to be at the nexus of societal transformation of violence—the pervasive face of it in this nation and the faceless, boundless nature of what is becoming present in the larger world. When Wilfred Bion (1961) postulated the original basic assumption groups of pairing, fight-flight, and dependency, it was the result in no small part of his attempt to give meaning to group experience after the violent period of World War II. We operate as if these formulations are sufficient to account for what we now see. Yet we already know that the notion of the nation state is shifting, and hierarchical ways of leadership are flattening. Marriage equality, as cogently advocated by Lothstein (2015) in the context of treatment of domestic violence, while representing a major step towards human justice, also means the metaphor of pairing needs to be rethought and expanded. While there is much made, for example, by Rice, of fight, flight, and freeze responses, there is little attention to emergent work in the consciousness literature about its healing alternative: flow states that invite stillness and reflective action in the face of conflict and confrontation (Csikszentmihalyi, 1990; Jackson, Thomas, Marsh, & Smethurst, 2001; Privette, 1983).

Peace writers may have something to offer group psychotherapists. These scholars and practitioners are increasingly attending to the interface between self and system, seeing one as reflective of the other (Chappell, 2013; Hanh, 1991). While group-as-a-whole models offer a way of thinking of individual contributions as a function of the group, peace practitioners see these processes as one and the same. They extend this thinking by holding in consciousness how each community of practice reflects the larger society and informs both our individual understanding and collective opportunity to move forward with deliberative action.

The contribution that group psychotherapists can make to this discourse is to examine their own group practices and preferred theoretical orientations to see where innovation in thinking and practice converge. Much as in what these articles provide, this process is a conversation that is foundational and firmly grounded in prevailing thought. It also requires that group psychotherapists increasingly engage in their own processes of self-reflection, inner work, and innovative exploration. Such practices will serve to better prepare our profession to meet the challenges that we face in the United States and in the world, holding in consciousness the transformative idea that the microcosms of our groups may well form the makings of the world of tomorrow…

REFERENCES

Agazarian, Y. M. (1997). *Systems-centered therapy for groups*. New York, NY: Guilford Press.

Bion, W. (1961). *Experiences in groups*. London: Tavistock.

Chappell, P. K. (2013). *The art of waging peace*. Wesport, CT: Prospecta Press.

Csikszentmihalyi, M. (1990). *Flow: The psychology of optimal experience*. New York, NY: Harper & Row.

Hanh, T. N. (1991). *Peace in every step: The path of mindfulness*. New York, NY: Bantam Books.

Jackson, S. A., Thomas, P. R., Marsh, H. W., & Smethurst, C. J. (2001). Relationships between flow, self-concept, psychological skills, and performance. *Journal of Applied Sport Psychology, 13*, 129–153.

Lothstein, L. M. (2015). A multi-tiered group therapy model to identify and treat the root causes of domestic violence: A proposal integrating current social neuroscience findings. *International Journal of Group Psychotherapy, 65*(2), 211-240.

Phillips, S. B. (2015). The dangerous role of silence in the relationship between trauma and violence: A group response. *International Journal of Group Psychotherapy, 65*(1), 65-87.

Post, J. M. (2015). Terrorism and right-wing extremism: The changing face of terrorism and political violence in the 21st century: The virtual community of hatred. *International Journal of Group Psychotherapy, 65*(2), 243-271.

Privette, G. (1983). Peak experience, peak performance, and flow: A comparative analysis of positive human experiences. *Journal of Personality and Social Psychology, 45*, 1361-1368.

Rice, C. A. (2015). A group therapist reflects on violence in America. *International Journal of Group Psychotherapy, 65*(1), 41-62.

Schermer, V. L. (2015). Violence, threat, and emotional "malnourishment": An interview with Dr. Dan Gottlieb. *International Journal of Group Psychotherapy, 65*(1), 31-39

Sue, D. W., Capodilupo, C. M., Torino, G. C., Bucceri, J. M., Holder, A. M., ... Esquilin, M. (2007). Racial microaggressions in everyday life: Implications for clinical practice. *American Psychologist, 62*(4), 271-286.

Thomas, N. K. (2015). There's always a villain to punish: Group processes contributing to violence and its remediation. *International Journal of Group Psychotherapy, 65*(1), 89-1007.

Index

Abbottabad raid (2011) 199
Abdo, Jason 205–6
Abdulmatallab, Umar Farouk 203–4
abortion clinics 192
abuse of power 50; *see also* child abuse
Adamic, Louis 188
Adams, L. 48
adult-onset trauma 66
affect 109
Afghanistan 9, 11, 90, 195–8
African Americans 47, 51–5, 84–5, 92
Agazarian, Y.M. 4
agency 66
aggression: boundary setting for 111–13, 120; healthy outlets for 111; as an inherent aspect of human neurobiology 158; potential for 111–18
Agha-Soltan, Neda 200
al-Qaeda 184, 193–204; affiliates of 198–9
altruism 73–4
American Civil War 16
American Revolution 15
Amir, Yigal 191–2
anarchist wave of terrorism 188–9
Anderson, Cornealius ("Mike") 95–7
anger: forms of 126; regulation of 127–32, 137, 146
anger management 114–17, 121, 128, 131
annual uniform crime reports 8
"apocalyptic despair" 87
Arab Spring 199, 228
Arana, Sabano 186

Asahara, Shoko 184, 192
assertive communication 135
Ataturk, Mustafa Kemal 184–6
attachment theory 103–4, 109, 119, 161, 214
Aum Shinrikyo 184, 192
Aurora movie theater shooting 33–5
autism 34
al-Awlaki, Anwar 202–5

Badenoch, B. 174
Bass, A. 112
Beale, S.S. 97
Beirut truck bombing (1983) 193
Ben Ali, Zine al-Abidine 199
Benjamin, J. 85, 93
Benson, J. 51
Bertalanffy, L. von 4
bin Laden, Osama 184, 193–6, 199, 202–5
Bion, Wilfred R. 15, 38, 46, 117, 122, 184, 230
"black on black" violence 88, 91
Blair, Tony 54
Bloom, S.L. 67–8
border fences 91
Boston Marathon bombing (2015) 8, 19, 39, 120, 201–2
Boulanger, Gloria 66
brain function 65–6, 165, 175, 213
Branch Davidian sect 196
Brandt, Willy 53–4
Breivik, Anders 198
Brison, Susan J. 61, 65, 67
Buber, M. 32

INDEX

Buchele, Bonnie J. 122, 212
bullying 10, 47–8, 64, 162
Burns, J.W. 128, 145
Bush, George W. 196, 198
bystanders to violence 68

California Corrections 105
Camus, Albert 104
Caruth, Cathy 61
child abuse 67
childhood experiences 103
children as victims of suicide 70
"chosen trauma" 4, 22–3, 51, 85, 90, 114, 119, 214
Church of Jesus Christ, Christian 197–8
civil rights movement 16
climate change 228–9
clinicians' responses to clients 136–7
cognitive-behavioral therapy 121, 127
Cold War 17
collective interests and needs 20
collectivism 219
Columbine shootings (1999) 87, 229
Columbus, Christopher 15, 50, 55
combat exposure 63
common factors across theories of psychotherapy 158
communication, impeding of 6
Communist Manifesto (1847) 188
community interventions 113
community meetings 49
community service 36
conflict-management strategies 142, 144
consciousness-raising 19
"containing" the potential for violence 72, 111–15
countertransference 21
covert actions 11
Cox, P. 174
Crenshaw, Martha 183
crime rates 8–9
crimes of violence 8–9
cultural identity 49
cyber-violence 227–8

Da Silva, M. 186
DeMare, P.B. 52
dependency psychology 184
"digital natives" 228

Dinges, B. 121, 125, 217
dissociation 67
distal stimulus 118
distancing, technological 228
"do no harm" code 20
Dohrn, Bernadine 191
domestic violence (DV) 64, 115, 119, 121, 153–76; alternative names used for 154; historical models of treatment for 158; new approaches to 155, 157–8; research foundations for treatment of 159; root causes of 160, 164–6; as a social disease and an intergenerational problem 159; "tier3" model for treatment of 160, 162, 175; triggers for 159
Dowd, Maureen 18–19
drone attacks 198, 228
drugs, war against 17
Duka brothers 207
"Duluth model" for treating domestic violence 121, 153–5
Dylan, Bob 190
Dyregrov, K. and A. 72–3
Dzur, A.W. 97

emotional expression 66
empathy and empathetic understanding 111–14, 164, 166, 217
Engels, Friedrich 188
ETA (Basque separatists) 185–6
eye contact with oneself 35

Fallon, J. 166
family violence 23
Feigelman, Bill and Beverly 68
Fein, Robert 64
A Few Good Men (film) 214
fight/flight response 15, 66, 118, 120, 127, 138, 165, 216, 230
financial superiority of the US 219
firearms *see* gun control laws; gun-related violence; guns, availability of
football and football hooliganism 17–18, 46
Forming-Storming-Norming-Performing-Adjourning process 52
Fort Dix Six 207
Fort Hood massacre (2009) 120, 202–6

INDEX

Franco, Francisco 185–6
Freud, Sigmund 70
Friedman, R.A. 12
Fromm, Erich 104
frustration-aggression hypothesis 131–2, 146

Gandhi, Mahatma 37, 40, 226–7
gang violence 46, 89
gay bashing 17
genocide 53–4
Gerhart, James 114–15, 121, 125, 217
Germany 53–4, 89
Gilligan, J. 159
"giving voice" 72–3
Glencree Sustainable Peace Network 92–3, 95
Glenn, A. 165
"glory seeker" terrorists 205
Gobodo-Madikizela, Pumla 60–1, 69, 78
Gottlieb, Daniel 21–2, 29–30, 35, 114, 118, 218, 226
Gottlieb, Sam 30, 34
Gourevitch, Phillip 10
Green, Zachary Gabriel 122, 223
Grendon Therapeutic Prison 102–6
group dynamics 41, 50, 52, 118, 120, 122, 183–4, 187, 201, 207, 227
group leaders 48–9
group life's role in the management of violence 215
group process 22; conflict as part of 136; connected to violence 89; contributing to restorative justice 95–8
group psychology 89–90
group therapy 4, 6–7, 22, 35, 38–45, 48–9, 52, 55–6, 74, 77–8, 102, 105–6, 110, 114, 117–21, 125–30, 133, 138, 153–4, 216–18, 228–31; as a microcosm of the family 174; for treating domestic violence 153–4, 159–61, 166, 173–6
groups, power of 21–2
groups of belonging, *primary* and *secondary* 49–51, 54–6
"groupthink" 187, 207
Grundy, Dominick 1
gun control laws 87
gun-related violence 8–9, 12, 226

guns, availability of 9–10
Gurr, T.R. 188
Gutmann, D. 220

Hankey, Bette 48
Hasan, Nidal 202–6
hate crimes 8, 10, 17
Haymarket Square riot, Chicago (1886) 188
"hero worshipper" terrorists 205–6
Hezbollah 193, 196
Historical-Clinical Risk Management-20 (HCR-20) 133
historical perspective on violence 14–18
Hitchens, C. 53
"holding" the potential for violence 111–15
Holman, Krista 121, 125
Holocaust, the 53–5
Holocaust Memorial Museum, Washington DC 55
Homeland Security Committee, US Senate 200
Hopper, Earl 6, 41, 46, 184, 216
Horgan, J. 187
"hot thoughts" 141
humiliation 51, 86–90, 98, 161
Hurricane Sandy 32
Hussein, Saddam 193

Iacoboni, I. 166
"identicide" 184–6
identification with the aggressor 103–4, 164, 174
if–then rules 137–8
illegal immigrants 85, 91, 225
impulsive reactions 132
"incohesion" (Hopper) 6, 216, 228
individualism 219
intake evaluation 132–3
International Survivors of Suicide Day 70–1, 74, 77
interparental violence (IPV) 64
interpersonal violence 62
The Invisible War (film) 69
Iran 11
Iraq 4, 9, 11, 62–3, 90
Irish Famine 51, 54
Irish Republic 53–4
irritability of clients 128

INDEX

Isabella, Queen of Spain 15
Islamic fundamentalism 191–6
isomorphy 4, 7, 217, 229
Israel, ancient 44
Iverson, K.M. 62

Jensen, M.A.C. 41, 52
Johnson, Lyndon 16
Johnson, Mark 83–4, 90–2, 98
Judaism 32
justice *see* restorative justice; retributive justice

Kazdin, A.E. 145
Khaled, Leila 206
Khalid Sheik Mohammed 194
Khobar Towers truck bomb (1996) 194
Khomeini, Ayatollah 193
Killgore, W.D.S. 63
King, Martin Luther Jr 16, 40, 55, 226–7
King, Rodney 50–4
Klein, M. 85, 88–9, 98
Klein, Robert H. 1, 12, 39, 52, 108–9, 213–18, 223–4, 229
Kohlenberg, R.J. 139
Kohut, H. 88, 161
Koran, the 192
Koresh, David 196
Ku Klux Klan (KKK) 47
Kupers, Terry 105

Lakoff, George 83–4, 90–2, 98
language: use of 23, 51; of violence 84
Lanza, Adam 3, 20, 113
Latif, Abu Khalid Abdul- 205
Leary, M.R. 86
Lee Daniel's The Butler (film) 55
Leszcz, M. 160
Lincoln, Abraham 38
"lone wolf" terrorism 122, 183, 204, 215; definition of 201; packs in 207; types of 205
Lothstein, Leslie M. 14, 114–15, 119, 121, 153, 213, 217–18, 230
Lotto, D. 86

McCarthyism 17
McCaule, C. 184
McGinnis, C. 205

McVeigh, Timothy 196
Madoff, Bernie 11
male role belief system 105
"malnourishment", emotional 31, 226
Marinoni, Rosa Zagnoni 30
marriage equality 230
Martin, Trayvon 32, 51, 54
Martinez, Antonio 205–6
Marx, Karl 188
masculinity, iconic 16
mass violence 8, 13
massification 46–7
media coverage of violence 3, 13, 72, 229
Meloy, J.R. 40
mental illness 12, 19, 226
metaphor 83, 85, 98; as a way to shape thinking 90–2
Middleman, Dori 33
military sexual trauma (MST) 62, 69, 75–6
military women 74–5
Millat, J.-F. 220
minority groups 17
mirror neurons 35, 166
Mitchell, S.A. 161
Moody, K. 205
"moral accounting" 91–2
Morrison, A. 161
motivational interviewing 134, 175–6
Motz, A. 159
Mubarak, Hosni 200
Muenster, B. 86
Mujahidh, Walli 205
murder 104

Nairobi attack (2013) 199
"naïve romantic" terrorists 206
"narcissistic injury" 213–18
"narcissistic rage" 88, 161
National (US) Centre for Post Traumatic Stress 62
National (US) Comorbidity Survey Replication Study 62
Native Americans 15, 50, 53–5, 85
nature/nurture controversy 117
neural networks 166
"neuroception" (Porges) 164, 166
neuropsychology 65
neuroscience 115, 121–2, 158, 165–6, 173–4, 213

INDEX

Newtown (Connecticut) school massacre (2012) 2–3, 39–40, 229
Nicholas, M. 161
9/11 attacks 2, 4, 19, 23, 32, 90, 113, 194–8, 214, 219, 223, 229
Norcross, J.C. 158
Northern Ireland 36–7, 51, 92–3

Obama, Barack 2, 54
Ocalan, Abdullah 184–6
Occupy Movement 227
Ogden, T.H. 220
Oklahoma City attack (1995) 196
Olson, S.M. 97
Orlowski, Janis 18–19
"otherness" 225

paranoid-schizoid position 52, 88, 224, 230
Paymar, Michael 64
peace, promotion of 226, 230
"penumbra group" concept 20, 217
perpetrators of violence 116–20; who were formerly victims 13
Phelps, Fred 44
Phillips, Suzanne B. 22, 60, 114, 119, 215, 217, 224–6
PKK (Kurdish separatists) 184–5
Pluchinsky, Dennis 190
"polite" crimes 11–12
polyvagal theories 165–6
Porges, S.W. 164, 175
Post, Jerrold M. 21, 116, 120, 122, 183–4, 187, 205, 213, 215, 218–19, 228
post-traumatic stress disorder (PTSD) 13, 19, 62–3, 91
"potential space" concept 220
Poulson, B. 94–5
power struggles 34
Prince, Phoebe 48
prisoners, treatment of 64, 103–4, 119
"privatized" violence 14
probation officers' receipt of reports on attendance of and participation by trainees 139
process interpretations and *process interventions* 138
projective identification 89, 98, 112
proximal stimulus 118
psychodynamic therapy 102, 106, 175

psychologically-minded individuals 175–6
psychopaths 56
Psychotherapy Checklist 133

Quinlivan, E. 86

Rabin, Yitzhak 191–2
"radical altruists" as terrorists 206–7
radicalization 208
Raine, A. 165
Raine, Nancy 66–7
rape victims 66, 75
Rapoport, D.C. 188–9
readiness to change 134
recidivism 95, 98, 115
Red Army Faction 190
Red Brigades 190
redecision therapy 104
reflection 215–18
Reichert, M. 67–8
Reik, Theodore 111, 218
religious fundamentalism 219; *see also* Islamic fundamentalism
"religious right" groups 219
religious terrorism 191–2, 196–9
reparation 55–6
Resolve to Stop Violence Project (RSVP) 102–7
restorative justice 23, 83, 85, 92–8, 114, 119, 216–17; group contributions to 95–8
retributive justice 23, 85, 216
Rice, Cecil A. 14, 22, 38, 51, 114, 118, 213–17, 228, 230
risk factors for use of violence 13
"risky shift" phenomenon 187
"robber barons" 16–17
role models 112
Roller, Bill 13, 23, 102, 119, 217
Ronan, George F. 121, 125, 217
Rouchy, J.C. 41, 49–51
Roussakoff, D. 48
"rugged individualism" 15, 215, 219
Rutan, J.S. 41

Sandy Hook massacre (2012) 87, 33–5, 113
scapegoating 19, 21–2, 38, 44–8, 83, 89, 105, 107, 114, 118–19, 214–17
Scheidlinger, S. 89

237

INDEX

Schermer, Victor L. 1, 12, 20, 29, 39, 85, 108–9, 213–18, 223–4, 229
Schwab, Gabrille 69
Segal, M. 184
self-disclosure by practitioners 137
self-regulation 114
Seymour, Bailey 121, 125, 217
shadowing experienced practitioners 138–9
Shahzad, Faisal 204, 207
shame, experience of 161
Shay, J.J. 41
Shedler, J. 158, 160
Shepard, Matthew 43–4
Shneidman, Edwin 70
sibling relationships 72–3
Siegel, D. 175
silence: centrality to the impact of violent trauma 65–6; different kinds of 215; group responses to 69; influence of 220; military code of 68–9, 74–7; role of 22, 60, 64–9, 77–8
slavery 16, 50, 55, 85
Smadi, Hosam Maher Husein 204–5
Snowden, Edward 208
social health 33
social media 199–200, 208
social problem-solving theory 131–4, 137, 145–6
social revolutionary terrorism 203
sociocultural context of violence 11–12
South Africa 69, 93, 95
Speck, R.V. 113
splitting 84, 88
spouse relationships 73–4
Stannard, D.E. 50
stereotyping 110–11, 119
stimulus, "proximal" and "distal" 118
Stolorow, R. 67, 69, 73
Stone, W. 41
Stopford, A. 83, 88, 98
"storming" in a group 52–3
Strain (film) 65
Strozier, C.B. 87–8
student protest movements 190
suicide 62–5, 94–5, 104, 192–3; of children and young people 70, 227; survivors and survivor groups 68–70, 72

suicide bombers 193
"surds" 65
survival behaviors 65–6
survival mechanism, violence as 39–40
Syria 11
systemic support for violence 13

Tamil Tigers 184–6
Tehran embassy hostages (1979–81) 192
terrorism 9, 116–17, 120, 122, 183–208, 214; waves of 183, 188–92, 219; *see also* "war on terror"
therapeutic alliance 128
therapists' "inner work" 225
therapy and the promotion of healthy change 18–21; *see also* group therapy
Thomas, Nina K. 11, 22–3, 83, 113, 119, 214–19, 225, 229
threats, perceived 31
training videos 102–3, 106–7
transgenerational phenomena 51, 55–6
trauma, psychological 36, 60–9, 74, 77–8; adult-onset type 66; difficulty in telling stories about 69; *primary* and *secondary* impact of 74; *relational* or *developmental* 67; resulting in violence to self 62–3; resulting in violence toward others 63–9; role of violence in causation of 61–2; *see also* "chosen trauma"; violent trauma
trauma groups 72
trauma theory 19
"trolling" 204
Trosch, David C. 192
trust 95
Tsai, M. 139
Tsarnaev brothers 201–2
Tuckman, B.W. 41, 52
Twenge, J.M. 86

unconscious, the, role of 219
under-reporting of violent crime 14
United States compared with other countries 9–10
USS Cole, attack on (2000) 194

van der Merwe, Chris N.-M. 60–1, 69, 78

INDEX

Vermont 97
Versailles Treaty (1919) 89
veterans 63–4, 75–6
victims who later become perpetrators 13
video games 17–18
violence: awareness of 21; callous and dehumanizing view of 18; causes of 3, 12–13, 85–6; cycle of 64, 93, 95; definition of 3, 61–2; early history of 15–16; effects of 35, 62; forms of 3, 8–11, 14, 17, 227–8; glorification of 17; justifications for 18; occasional need for 213; orientation towards 225; as part of US culture 84–5; perpetuation of 111, 119; potential for 19; predatory 104; prediction of 13–14, 19, 86, 116; prevention of 33–4, 110–16; as a problem for American society 1–2; prohibition of 110; proneness to 56; protective 40; psychological precursors of 86–9; reactive 104; recent history of 16; relevance of clinical experience to 5–8; responses to 19; to self 62–3; sources of 55; toward others 63–9; treatment of 110–16
"violence prevention" groups 20
Violence Reduction Training Program (VRTP) 115, 121, 125, 130–46; conceptual foundations of 131–2; mechanisms of change in 144–6; research from 143–4
violent trauma 65–6
"virtual communities of hatred" 202, 204, 208

virtual groups 201
Voices in the Family (radio program) 29
Voices of Violence (video series) 102, 217
Volkan, V. 41, 47, 51, 85, 88, 90, 98, 217, 220

"war on terror" 4, 11, 196, 198, 225
warfare 11, 17, 91, 223
"warrior gene" 117, 166
Washington DC Navy Yard shootings (2013) 18
Wayne, John 16
Weather Underground 190–1
Weil, Simone 89
Weimann, Gabi 204
Westboro Baptist Church, Topeka 44
"White Wolf" 53–4
"Wild West" 15
Williams, Betty 36
Winnicott, D. 220
women, treatment of 16; *see also* military women
women's movement 16
World Health Organization (WHO) 61–2
World Trade Center bombing (1993) 193
World War I 89
World War II 89, 230

Yalom, Irving D. 125, 136, 160
Yousef, Ramzi 194

al-Zarqawi, Abu Musab 205
al-Zawahiri, Ayman 198
Ziering, A. 75
Zimmerman, George 32, 54